T0374809

Beyond Jefferson

Beyond Jefferson

The Hemingses,
the Randolphs, and the Making of
Nineteenth-Century America

Christa Dierksheide

Yale
UNIVERSITY PRESS
New Haven and London

Published with assistance from the Louis Stern Memorial Fund.

Copyright © 2024 by Christa Dierksheide.
All rights reserved.
This book may not be reproduced, in whole or in part, including illustrations,
in any form (beyond that copying permitted by Sections 107 and 108 of the U.S.
Copyright Law and except by reviewers for the public press), without written
permission from the publishers.

Yale University Press books may be purchased in quantity for educational, business,
or promotional use. For information, please e-mail sales.press@yale.edu (U.S. office)
or sales@yaleup.co.uk (U.K. office).

Set in Bulmer type by Integrated Publishing Solutions.
Printed in the United States of America.

Library of Congress Control Number: 2023952230
ISBN 978-0-300-22652-2 (hardcover : alk. paper)

A catalogue record for this book is available from the British Library.

This paper meets the requirements of ANSI/NISO Z39.48-1992
(Permanence of Paper).

10 9 8 7 6 5 4 3 2 1

For Andrew, and for Susan

Contents

Genealogy

Sarah (Sally) Hemings -
(1773–1835)

Beverly Hemings   Harriet Hemings   Eston [Hemings] Jefferson   =   Julia Ann Isaacs
(1798–after 1822)   (1801–after 1822)   (1808–1856)   (1814–1889)

John Wayles [Hemings] Jefferson
(1835–1892)

Anna [Hemings] Jefferson
(1837–1866)

Beverly [Hemings] Jefferson
(1839–1908)

Madison Hemings   =   Mary Hughes McCoy
(1805–1877)   (1810–1876)

Sarah E. Hemings
(1835–1884)

Thomas Eston Hemings
(1838–1863)

Harriet Hemings
(1839–1925)

Mary Ann Hemings
(1843–1921)

Catherine J. Hemings
(1844–1880)

William Beverly Hemings
(1847–1910)

James Madison Hemings
(1849–1900)

Julia Ann Hemings
(1851–1866)

Ellen Wayles Hemings
(1856–1940)

Thomas Jefferson   =   Martha Wayles Skelton
-    (1743–1826)   (1748–1782)

John Wayles Eppes   =   Maria Jefferson   Martha Jefferson   =   Thomas Mann Randolph, Jr.
(1773–1823)   (1778–1804)   (1772–1836)   (1768–1828)

Francis Wayles Eppes   Ann Cary Randolph
(1801–1881)   (1791–1826)

Thomas Jefferson Randolph
(1792–1875)

Ellen Wayles Randolph
(1796–1876)

Cornelia Jefferson Randolph
(1799–1871)

Virginia Jefferson Randolph
(1801–1882)

Mary Jefferson Randolph
(1803–1876)

James Madison Randolph
(1806–1834)

Benjamin Franklin Randolph
(1808–1871)

Meriwether Lewis Randolph
(1810–1837)

Septimia Anne Randolph
(1814–1887)

George Wythe Randolph
(1818–1867)

Introduction

DURING THE LONG, HOT SUMMER OF 1776, Thomas Jefferson put pen to paper, drafting the now iconic words of the Declaration of Independence. In a working draft, Jefferson repeated an important phrase in both the first and second paragraphs of his transformational treatise. No longer dependent colonies of the British Empire, he asserted, America was now an "equal & independent" nation in the world. And within that new nation, "all men"—by which Jefferson meant *white males,* a deliberate exclusion of women and people of color—were "equal & independent." Though this phrase was edited out of the final version by Congress, its repetition in the earlier draft suggests that Jefferson viewed these two entangled concepts, separated only by an ampersand in the original text, as the defining principles of the American Revolution and the basis for human freedom.[1]

The Declaration made the case for the legitimacy of American independence—and nationhood—to a "candid world" and sought to mobilize support for the patriot cause at home. Yet upward of a fifth of former British American colonists doubted the viability of a sovereign American state, choosing instead to reaffirm their loyalty to King George III in their "Declaration of Dependence" of 1776. And while a handful of nations (most of them enemies of Britain) recognized and signed treaties with the United States between 1776 and the end of the Revolutionary War, American autonomy was not legally secured until the enemy nation (Britain) recognized the thirteen former colonies as "free and independent states" in the Treaty of Paris of 1783.[2]

The war itself underscored how contingent American claims to independence and equality "among the powers of the earth" remained. Waging yet another imperial war for the American interior against one of the world's most powerful nations only highlighted the profound weakness and incapacity of the new United States. In a conflict that quickly metastasized from a colonial tax revolt into a global war for empire, America found itself sorely outmatched, depending heavily on military resources and financial support from Spain, France, and the Dutch Republic to prosecute a war fought on multiple continents: the last battle transpired not at Yorktown in 1781 but in Cuddalore, India, in 1783. Even with substantial support from allies, the prospect of victory remained slim for most of the war's duration; British military occupation or a return to the pre-1776 status quo—"reconciliation"—loomed as very real potential outcomes of the conflict.[3]

At home, few Americans met the threshold for "independence" after 1776, for in the late eighteenth century, only whiteness and property ownership connoted independence. And as contemporaries noted, independence undergirded "disinterestedness"—the foundation of public virtue in a republic. In America, a gendered and racialized society was divided into two main groups: propertyless dependents, which included the poor, women, children, and enslaved people, and independents, often known as "free men." In perpetuating this master-servant framework in the new American society, elite patriot leaders created a highly exclusionary republic through new state constitutions: only a minority of the entire population (perhaps 20 percent) could vote or hold public office. And critically, a further 20 percent of the population remained enslaved—according to the first federal census of 1790, enslaved people were held in bondage in every state.[4]

Jefferson admitted that the American Revolution was an unfinished project; claims to sovereign nationhood, whether at home or on the world stage, remained tenuous at best. Anxious that new Americans should relinquish British power and abolish all vestiges of the colonial regime, Jefferson prescribed the eradication of race-based chattel slavery, the "removal" of all people of African descent (whether free or enslaved) to another country, and an end to British imperial power—the three greatest threats, as he saw it, to America's survival in the world after 1783. To underscore the importance and urgency of this task, Jefferson invoked a series of binaries—freedom and slavery, African and American, Anglophile and Anglophobe. These highly artificial fault lines, he imagined, would help white Americans better separate their colonial past from a national future. They would enable former British American provincials to become a truly postcolonial "people."[5]

The most important undertaking of the postrevolutionary era was to permanently jettison these dangerous holdovers of the British imperial state, since they threatened to sustain inequality and jeopardize independence. This fear, always at the forefront of Jefferson's mind, heightened his anxiety that these systems of inequality and dependence, which the British government had foisted upon the colonies "in their infant state," would *not* be eradicated, leaving the American Revolution incomplete—and unfulfilled—in his generation, and in others.[6]

Jefferson fervently hoped that his own generation would either end slavery or make enormous inroads toward its abolition. As he told Edward Rutledge of South Carolina (the youngest signer of the Declaration) in 1787, "This abomination must have an end." Yet slavery was problematic not just because it was unjust; it also imposed a dangerous system of artificial hierarchy, enabling "one half of citizens thus to trample on the rights of another," and forging a profoundly unequal society perpetuated across the generations. Continued dependence on the labor of "another" jeopardized the independent status of white people at home and abroad, destroying their morals and "industry." Only with slavery's abolition, Jefferson believed, could white Americans embrace "settler republicanism": non-slaveholding yeoman farmers who owned their property and labor, all while sustaining a fervent "amor patriae"—the bedrock of a highly decentralized imperial republic.[7]

But even if white enslavers consented to free their human property, few people—outside of Black activists and a small number of white religious leaders—envisioned a future U.S. society that included Black people as free and equal citizens. In his rough draft of the Declaration, in wording that was later deleted by Congress, Jefferson cleaved what had been a multiracial colonial society into two separate nations. Just as Americans constituted "one people," as Jefferson asserted in the opening line, so too did individuals of African descent form a supposedly different and "distant people." According to this logic, a separate African nation could only be "free and independant" elsewhere, beyond the borders of the United States.[8]

Jefferson and other white members of the Revolutionary generation did not believe that white people could "retain and incorporate blacks into the state." The reasons, he explained, were many. "Deep rooted prejudices entertained by the whites" and "ten thousand recollections" of the Middle Passage and the horrors of enslavement acted as a "powerful obstacle" to the inclusion of formerly enslaved people. Moreover, Jefferson argued, people of African descent were "inferior to the whites in the endowments both of body and mind"—a condition that was either "natural" or created through centuries of "degrading" enslavement. Allowing manumitted African Americans to remain on U.S. soil only perpetuated inequality. "They are pests in society by their idleness," Jefferson decreed of free Black Americans, suggesting that their status was perpetually dependent and inferior.[9]

The other source of inequality and threat to U.S. independence was Britain's global power. Though Jefferson had been a loyal subject of the British crown for more than three decades, 1776 was the breaking point—Jefferson traded his Anglophilia for Anglophobia. Anything that appeared to resemble continued dependence on Great Britain threatened the legitimacy and staying power of the new nation's independence. But while Jefferson tried to limit British influence for most of his political career, he developed a new strategy after the Napoleonic Wars, primarily because British hegemony could only be controlled, not removed. An alliance with Britain could better assure U.S. sovereignty, he suggested in the 1820s. Rather than British power being used to further subjugate the United States, it could be channeled—through a diplomatic and military alliance—to strengthen and preserve America's standing in the world.[10]

Jefferson acknowledged that his strategies to secure independence and equality, both for individuals and for the United States on the world stage, were tied to a specific historical moment: the decades immediately following the American Revolution. As times changed, he knew that the means to safeguard and secure those principles would also change. Indeed, it was only European monarchs who "clung to old abuses, entrenched themselves behind steady habits," a "preposterous idea which has lately deluged Europe in blood," Jefferson observed. To force nineteenth-century Americans to look backward, to be beholden to the ideas of an earlier generation, was to forge a new kind of hierarchy, enabling the "dead hand of the past" to rule over the present. Equality and independence remained entwined and definitive principles that would influence and direct successive generations of U.S. citizens as they sought to perfect their republic. But each new generation would have to look to its own "reason and experience"—not that of the Founders in the Revolutionary era—to interpret and apply those principles in new and more progressive ways.[11]

This critical idea—enduring principles harnessed to changing circumstances—defined the United States in the long nineteenth century. And it allowed the rising generation of Jefferson's own family members to redefine equality and independence within a historical context that was at least a half-century removed from the American Revolution. The question of how to better secure or preserve the founding-era principles remained pressing questions for all these individuals, yet their answers varied widely, reflecting the "experience of the present" rather than the "wisdom" of the past. Their ideas about how to secure independence and equal rights were not Jefferson's. They moved beyond him, correcting the "crude" endeavors of "our first and unexperienced" Revolutionary generation, often in surprising and troubling ways.[12]

A rising generation of Hemingses and Randolphs—respectively, Jefferson's African American and white descendants—encountered a world that could not have been more different from the mid-eighteenth-century one that Jefferson knew, first as a British subject and then as a Revolutionary patriot. The union that knit together the American states, long considered a fraught and fragile experiment, had held for a half a century. And in an effort to extricate itself from Anglo-French imperial rivalries and commercial dominance and prove its viability on the world stage, the United States waged and won an array of military conflicts, including the Barbary Wars off the coast of North Africa and the War of 1812, fought both at sea and in the American interior. Loosed from British metropolitan control, white settlers wholeheartedly embraced colonization, displacing and killing Native Americans, trafficking enslaved people, and carving out farms and plantations from a country that, thanks to the Louisiana Purchase of 1803, was more than double the size of the one founded in 1776.[13]

Cotton was fast becoming king of the South and West; planters and farmers cultivated the lucrative crop from the Carolinas to the Gulf South. And as cotton became central not just to a national but also to a global economy, so too did the transportation infrastructure and the labor system that underpinned it. With the abolition of the transatlantic slave trade in

1807, enterprising traders turned their attention to a domestic trade, which forced nearly a million human beings from Upper South cities like Alexandria and Richmond, Virginia, to Lower South markets. Skyrocketing demand for cotton also drove up the price of enslaved people, leading to their increased commodification through buying and selling, leasing, insuring, and mortgaging. While abolitionists and women leveled challenges to the Founders' idea of the United States as a white male democracy and to the continued existence of chattel slavery, state lawmakers thwarted these efforts, introducing legislation that disenfranchised free people of color in the "free states." And Britain continued to exert a powerful influence over its former colonies, consuming the lion's share of southern cotton, injecting huge amounts of capital into northern industries and western land speculation schemes, and facilitating U.S. trade outside the Atlantic world. These were the circumstances that surrounded Jefferson's family members in the 1820s—this was the context that forced them to rethink and redefine Revolutionary-era principles.[14]

In part because of the differences that a nineteenth-century world presented, the Hemingses and Randolphs confronted—and interpreted—the persistence of inequality and dependence in the United States in new ways. In a nation transformed by slavery's capitalism, two of Jefferson's white grandsons abandoned "settler republicanism"—non-slaveholding yeoman farmers expanding across a continent—as the means to secure independence and equality as white men in the United States. Instead, the rapid commodification of African Americans and their labor presented the Randolphs with an enormous opportunity for exploitation and profit when a massive inherited debt of nearly $4 million in today's dollars threatened to destroy their family's wealth and status. Yet the opportunities for generating capital through slavery varied across the South. In the Upper South, where cotton would not grow, white investors and enslavers sought profits primarily through the internal slave trade, slave leasing, and emergent industries, including coal and salt mining and "internal improvements"—all of which relied on the rising value of enslaved people and their labor. But in the burgeoning cotton empire of the Southwest, speculators bet big on land that would, they predicted, soon be transformed into slave plantations. Buying stolen Native American land at U.S. land offices or clearing the "wilderness" and planting crops with enslaved labor in federal territories promised steep profits for white men on the make. For the Randolphs, it was slavery, not its absence, that enabled them to be independent and equal members of a democracy predicated on whiteness and masculinity.[15]

In the "free states" of the Northwest, formerly enslaved people, including members of the Hemings family, believed that they could claim independent and equal status as African Americans outside the oppression of the slave states. Instead, state officials borrowed from the Poor Law tradition to develop legal technologies to exclude or control the migration of runaway slaves and free Black people in states north of the Ohio River, including Ohio, Indiana, Illinois, and Michigan. Just as in slave states, African Americans were forced to register with county clerks—and often pay an enormous indemnity—to be considered legal residents. And while African Americans could own property, they could not vote, testify in court, serve on juries, send their children to public school, or claim state resources. Men and women who chose not to comply with immigration restrictions, including the Hemings family, were legally defined as "aliens" who could be "removed" from these states at any moment. The settler colonialism deployed in "free states" in the nineteenth century, from Ohio to California, was not predicated on slavery, but rather on the creation of legal categories that classed African Americans as dependent and unequal, and therefore as non-settlers and noncitizens.[16]

And outside the United States, U.S. merchants and diplomats, including Jefferson's white grandsons-in-law, encountered an unequal international system dominated by British imperial influence. Without a strong U.S. state to back them, consuls and traders remained dependent on British merchant banks, consignment houses, and military protection to conduct business in far-flung ports and territories. America's cultural and commercial weakness was often all too apparent—U.S. merchants found themselves shut out of preferential trading in the Atlantic world, and non-European traders often could not distinguish between Americans and their British counterparts. Yet the impact of this outsize influence on U.S. economic interests varied widely, sometimes acting as a facilitator and other times as a hindrance. In extra-European regions, Britain's commercial and military prowess accelerated the expansion of U.S. trade. But in some parts of the Americas, allowing Britain to consolidate political control threatened U.S. empire building and exacerbated the sectional crisis. What became clear to Americans operating outside the United States, including Jefferson's white family members, was that Britain's power could be used for opposing ends: to compromise a nation's sovereignty or to protect it.[17]

Though previous historians have examined Jefferson's white and African American family members, most of these investigations have culminated in biographical or genealogical treatments of the Randolphs and Hemingses. These studies have been valuable contributions, particularly with regard to the Hemings family, whose members were marginalized for some two hundred years.[18] But in this book I take a different tack: I use the lives and experiences of Jefferson's family members on both sides of the color line to chart the rise of the postcolonial United States in the nineteenth century. Recently historians have begun to use extended, multigenerational families to tell a larger story about the making of the nineteenth-century United States and Britain, explicitly connecting white settler, African American, and Native American families to national and global questions of race, law, capitalism, and empire. As I shall demonstrate, the Hemings and Randolph family members' narratives reveal that the American Revolution did not end in 1783—it remained a contested and protracted struggle that lasted well into the nineteenth century.[19]

Between 1772 and 1808, Thomas Jefferson fathered twelve children with two half-sisters. The women shared a father, the wealthy slave trader John Wayles. Both were born and reared in the Virginia Tidewater, on the periphery of the British Empire. Both women bore their children at Monticello, Jefferson's five-thousand-acre plantation in the Virginia Piedmont. And both women were reportedly beautiful, although paintings, drawings, or lithographs of neither person survive. But there their similarities ended. Martha Wayles Skelton was white and free. Sally Hemings was Black and enslaved for nearly the entirety of her life.[20]

Born in 1748, Martha Wayles wed Jefferson when she was a young widow of twenty-four, in 1772. For a decade, she presided over the inchoate plantation enterprise that was Monticello—only one small outbuilding, the South Pavilion, was extant when she first arrived at the mountaintop. When she married Jefferson, he was a subject of King George III; when she died, in 1782, her husband was a leading American patriot and the author of the Declaration of Independence. Of her early death, Jefferson wrote, "A single event wiped away all my plans and left me a blank which

I had not the spirits to fill up." Though she was pregnant for most of her married life, only two of her six children survived to adulthood: Martha and Maria Jefferson.[21]

Observers noted that Martha Jefferson resembled her father, while Isaac Granger, formerly enslaved at Monticello, recalled that Maria Jefferson, known as Polly, was small and a "pretty lady just like her mother." In 1790, Martha married the planter-politician Thomas Mann Randolph, Jr., and bore him twelve children between 1791 and 1818: Ann, Thomas, Ellen, Cornelia, Virginia, Mary, James, Benjamin, Meriwether, Septimia, and George (one child died as a toddler). In 1797, Maria married a cousin, John Wayles Eppes, gave birth to a son, and died soon after giving birth to a daughter. Only the son, Francis Wayles Eppes, survived to adulthood.[22]

Twenty-five years younger than her half-sister, Sally Hemings was born just before the outbreak of the American Revolution, in 1773. Jefferson eventually inherited her as one of 135 human beings—including John Wayles's other enslaved children—deeded to him when he married Martha Wayles. Her mother was Elizabeth Hemings, who was "taken by the widower Wales as his concubine, by whom she had six children," all of whom would later live at Monticello. Sally Hemings first encountered the forty-four-year-old Jefferson in Paris, where he was serving as minister plenipotentiary, when she was only fourteen years old. Two years later, in 1789, she was "enceinte by him," and only agreed to return to Virginia after Jefferson "promised her extraordinary privileges, and made a solemn pledge that her children should be freed at the age of twenty-one years." Between 1795 and 1808, Sally Hemings gave birth to six children, four of whom survived to adulthood: Beverly, Harriet, Madison, and Eston. Jefferson "was the father of all of them."[23]

Jefferson's children were born over the course of nearly four decades—his first child, with Martha Wayles, in the 1770s, and his last, Sally Hemings's son Eston, while he was U.S. president (1801–1809). His white children and his African American children were thus of two different generations, Maria and Martha born in the era of the American Revolution, and the Hemings children at the turn of the century. It was therefore Jefferson's white *grandchildren*—particularly the boys and girls born to Martha Jefferson Randolph—who were contemporaries of Jefferson's four African American children on the Monticello mountaintop.[24]

Madison Hemings pointed out this fact in his memoir, demonstrating at least as much knowledge of Jefferson's white grandchildren as of his own father. He implied that the white grandchildren and African American children grew up together at Monticello. But whereas the children of Martha Randolph lived in the main house, playing with their grandfather as his acknowledged and legitimate progeny on the West Lawn, the four children of Sally Hemings were his chattel and his "mechanics," relegated to living quarters in the house cellar or along Mulberry Row, the main plantation street. Jefferson openly acknowledged Beverly, Harriet, Madison, and Eston as his property, but never as his family.[25]

In this book I follow several of these Hemings and Randolph family members as they leave Monticello in the 1820s and make their way in the wider world—moving to places as proximate as Edgehill, a plantation just a few miles from Monticello, or as far away as new states in the U.S. West, Cuba, Mexico, Britain, and China. Between the Missouri Crisis (1819–1821) and the Civil War era, seven of these individuals—Ellen Wayles Randolph Coolidge, Joseph Coolidge, Jr., Thomas Jefferson Randolph, Meriwether Lewis Randolph, Madison Hemings, and John Wayles Jefferson—grappled with slavery, race, and British influence as they revised and reinterpreted the legacy of the American Revolution in the context of the nineteenth century. Focusing on the Hemingses and Randolphs allows for a compelling internal and external portrait of the development of an imperial United States, illuminating individual experiences of citizenship and belonging, as well as larger questions of war, slavery, international law, and the forging of world orders.

As we shall see, Jefferson's white and African American family members articulated very different solutions to the persistence of inequality and dependence in nineteenth-century America and the world—all of them shaped and legitimized by circumstance. Still, Revolutionary era challenges persisted. The "problem" of slavery remained unresolved until the 1860s, following the destruction of the federal union and a bloody civil war that claimed approximately seven hundred thousand lives. African Americans' inequality and exclusion were more fully addressed only in the postbellum era; the passage of the Reconstruction Amendments ended slavery and rendered African American men (at least in theory) equal citizens under the law. Even so, removing the "institutionalized" legacies of colonial slavery and racism remain an unfinished task—one taken up by Civil

Rights activists in the twentieth century and by social justice advocates in the twenty-first.[26]

And finally, British imperial dominance remained an issue until the Civil War, a conflict that would have an enormous global impact. A war over slavery precipitated a geopolitical shift in international relations, laying the framework for more collaborative Anglo-American imperial exploits and the beginning of a "proto special relationship" that would coalesce and culminate in World War II.[27]

PART ONE
Britain

Joseph and Ellen Coolidge

The Opium War and Anglo-Americans in China, 1838–1844

IT WAS 1838 WHEN THOMAS JEFFERSON'S granddaughter first set eyes on "beautiful England." After enduring "incessant" seasickness across the Atlantic, Ellen Wayles Randolph Coolidge was relieved when the packet ship *Wellington* finally made landfall. At Portsmouth, Ellen and her husband, the Boston merchant Joseph Coolidge, clambered aboard a fast coach for London. Though seasoned travelers might have called the route "dull," to Ellen's "unpracticed eyes" the trip traversed "a country of surpassing loveliness." Whirling by picturesque thatched cottages, green village commons dotted with sheep, and poppy-filled fields, Ellen found herself enchanted by the scene that unfurled before her. That she was so drawn to England was perhaps unsurprising. She was, after all, an "Anglo-American."[1]

In the wake of the American Revolution, Britain's commercial dominance appeared to threaten U.S. independence, rendering it nearly impossible for American merchants to trade as equals on the world stage. But a rising generation of U.S.-based China traders—including Ellen and Joseph Coolidge—had different views about Pax Britannia's global reach. In their eyes, a close collaboration with British merchants in London, India, and China offered Americans what they sorely lacked: knowledge of commercial networks, access to capital and markets, and military protection. In the early nineteenth century, the Coolidges and other traders reasoned that an unequal relationship with British merchants in the East gave the United States a seat at the table, ensuring commercial access, particularly in South and East Asia. But beginning with the abolition of the East India Company's monopoly in 1833 and culminating in the First Opium War (1839–1842), U.S. traders found themselves confronted with an unprecedented opportunity: independence from *and* commercial parity with the world's most powerful empire.[2]

The Anglo-American commercial equality achieved after the war for opium came at a steep cost—both the Treaty of Nanking (Nanjing) (1842) and the Treaty of Wanghia (Wangxia) (1844) made China a semi-sovereign state. U.S.–China merchants like Joseph Coolidge heralded the use of British imperial power and military might to force Chinese officials to accept the law of nations. He and other traders believed that British power should be deployed to *create* inequality—and establish a clear hierarchy of nations—in the international system. This was precisely what happened when Anglo-Americans imposed extraterritorial jurisdiction in China. Between the 1830s and the 1880s, Britain and the United States emerged as trading equals and co-imperialists jointly committed to imposing Anglo-American law on, and extracting wealth from, the East.[3]

That an unequal commercial relationship could benefit U.S. merchants was not something that Revolutionary patriots had foreseen in the 1770s and 1780s. Yet it was the close link between British merchants and U.S.–China traders that formed the basis for the Coolidges' effusive praise of the British world in 1838. Born in 1798, Joseph Coolidge was first introduced to Thomas Jefferson as "a young gentleman of Education & Fortune," and later married Ellen Wayles Randolph in the Monticello parlor in 1824. After settling in Boston's Bowdoin Square, Coolidge became a merchant like his father, first cutting his teeth in Asia in 1833, where he forged alliances with "country traders" in Calcutta (Kolkata) and Bombay (Mumbai), all to facilitate the increased traffic of Indian opium to China.[4]

To the Anglophilic Coolidges, the British Empire was far from the enemy—instead, it claimed the same history, culture, and racial identity as the United States. As the couple thundered toward London in their carriage in 1838, Ellen craned her neck to see the landscape of "a people not only in the highest state of civilization now, but who have been civilized for ages." This sentiment was confirmed in future weeks, when she saw Queen Victoria in Hyde Park, and when she visited Westminster Abbey. As Ellen walked through the abbey, she saw the "whole history of a nation advancing steadily from comparative barbarism & feebleness" to that "climax of power and civilization." Indeed, Ellen gushed, "hers is the great

Jean Baptiste Joseph Duchesne, *Portrait of Joseph Coolidge, Jr.*, 1820. (Harvard Art Museums/Fogg Museum, Gift of Catherine Coolidge Lastavica in honor of John Coolidge. Photo © President and Fellows of Harvard College.)

name among nations." But Ellen's admiration also implied something else—that the United States might also become "great."[5]

Ellen Coolidge read much of the Anglo-American "special relationship" back in time. When she visited the "raree shew" at the Tower of

London, forking over six shillings for admittance and a guided tour, she deemed "no place in England better worth seeing when we remember all that it's old grey walls have seen." Standing in front of the brutal tower, Coolidge could not help but be struck by the "common origin that connects us as nearly with the English of the times preceding the settlement of America, as the English of the present day can themselves be." Indeed, Americans "claim as ours all who lived before the time when our immediate ancestors sought a home in the new world." Ellen Coolidge asserted her own ancestral link to Britain. At the Herald's office in Guildhall, she pored over the "musty volumes which contain the names of so many families," finding "my own name & arms, and the arms belonging to my grandfather." She looked up the origins of the Coolidge family, noting that they originally hailed from Buckinghamshire and Lincolnshire. And her own English ancestor, the first Randolph to settle in Virginia, had married the daughter of a baronet.[6]

Coolidge also considered Americans' link to England through the lens of race. To her, the "Anglo-Saxon race"—to which both white Americans and the English belonged—were the "guardians & constituted defenders of liberty upon earth and of the best hopes and sights of man." England may have been a little "insolent and overbearing" during the American Revolution, she conceded, but nonetheless, "we cannot but feel that the fact of having sprung from such a stock has made us what we are, and will make us what we are going to be." America's fate—that it was destined for national greatness—lay not just in its historic or ancestral ties to Britain. The two peoples constituted the same "superior" white race.[7]

But blood ties were not always enough to ensure an amicable relationship between Britons and Americans. During her London trip, the two countries became embroiled in a dispute over the Maine boundary line. "Talk of war," Coolidge wrote critically, for a "few acres more or less of land, when both parties have millions of acres," seemed ludicrous. So "wicked an absurdity," as she described the bloodless Aroostock War of 1838–1839, amounted to little more than a few local militias being trotted out along the U.S.–Canadian border, with no casualties save two Canadian militiamen who were mauled by bears. Anglo-American enmity also occasionally flared in the drawing rooms of London townhouses. While at a dinner party thrown by an "old Indian"—a former merchant in the East India Company—Coolidge bristled when some of the company addressed

Francis Alexander, *Portrait of Ellen Wayles Randolph Coolidge*, 1830–1845. (© Thomas Jefferson Foundation at Monticello.)

her as if "speaking of some newly discovered tribe of barbarians" peram-
bulating on "all fours, or at least dressed in skins." In Coolidge's eyes, the
English looked down on Americans as inferior, and "dislike us as having
successfully resisted themselves." It was not a "union of affection," she
admitted. Instead, power and profit drew the countries together and offered some Americans—Boston-based China merchants in particular—a

toehold in English society and an insider's view of London as the engine of global capital.[8]

This hand-in-glove relationship was on full display as Coolidge toured London. It dictated what she saw and how she saw it. Her husband was in town to curry favor with Baring Brothers, the largest merchant bank in London, after having bungled a trade deal in Canton (Guangzhou) and attracting the ire of his partners in the Boston-based commission house Russell and Company. Fearing that he would be ousted from the firm once he set foot in Canton—where he intended to go after his extended stop in London—Joseph canvassed the city for new allies among Britain's merchant elite, hoping to leverage his position. In fact, he tried to convince Joshua Bates, a senior partner at Baring Brothers, that he could stay out of China altogether, and serve as Russell and Company's London agent. It had largely been due to Bates, a native of Massachusetts, that Baring Brothers had recently scaled up its business in America, India, and China and was enjoying enormous profits. As a gesture of goodwill, Bates and his partners rolled out the red carpet for the Coolidges during their visit.[9]

Deepening ties to Bates and his partners gave the Coolidges access to the commercial heart of London. Ellen and her husband visited the construction site of the Thames Tunnel, which would soon connect the ports of Rotherhithe and Wapping. A nervous Ellen stepped inside the partially built tunnel, marveling at the Thames "with all it's shipping . . . rolling far overhead," and speculating that perhaps "at that very moment, men-of-war, merchant vessels, and steamers were floating above." But there may have been no better place to view London as the "centre of the world's commerce" than from the London and West India docks. There Ellen saw bales of raw silk from Italy and Bengal, bags of spices from the East Indies, casks of fortified wines from the Madeira archipelago, packed tobacco that "reminded me of home, my old home of Virginia," boxes of Havana cigars from Cuba, hogsheads of sugar and rum from the West Indies, and stacks of enormous mahogany logs from the interior of the tropics. It was the docks, sprawling along the Thames, that gave Ellen the "best idea I have yet had of the immense trade & wealth of London." The city "is the heart of the civilized world," she declared, and "receives & propels the 'vital fluid' which circulates through the whole body."[10]

Baring Brothers also facilitated the Coolidges' visits to private art collections and exclusive clubs. But Ellen remained keenly aware of the gulf that separated the British merchant class and the aristocracy. "A merchant in the U.S. ranks with the best," she noted, but in Britain, financiers were "not gentlemen nor are their wives ladies." London merchants sometimes gained "painful admittance into fashionable society," Ellen observed, "but they are made to pay for it by a thousand vexations & mortifications." The peerage was an exclusive crowd, she found. Without introductions to society, the aristocracy held her at arm's length. Then Sally Stevenson, the popular wife of an unpopular American diplomat, took Ellen under her wing. Ellen occasionally looked down on Stevenson, noting that she "lived in the country in Virginia"—though she resided just a few miles from Ellen's birthplace at Monticello—and was not a woman of "much early education," but it was Stevenson who procured Ellen's invitations to dinner parties, balls, and even the queen's opening of Parliament in 1838. Pressed to the back of the room, Ellen praised Queen Victoria's "correct and exact" speech, but decided that she was "too short for Royalty."[11]

Even bankers had trouble breaking into high society in London. One of the few who succeeded was a Baring Brothers partner, Alexander Baring, first Baron Ashburton. After marrying the daughter of a wealthy U.S. senator, negotiating the financing of the Louisiana Purchase of 1803, and serving in the House of Commons for decades, he became a peer and thus a member of the House of Lords in 1835. To draw attention to his position, the new Lord Ashburton became a collector of sorts, buying land, country houses, and expensive art. When he purchased Bath House in Piccadilly, he razed the original structure and constructed a Georgian residence in its stead, filling the house with Dutch and Flemish masterworks. Lord Ashburton's nephew Thomas Baring enabled the Coolidges to visit the private art collection of Thomas Hope, the son of a wealthy Dutch banker. There Ellen saw Etruscan vases, paintings by Italian and Flemish masters, and rooms of Indian, Egyptian, and Chinese "relics." Though beautiful, the house had the "air of a magazine, a storehouse, a fancy Bazaar, rather than a dwelling house, a home where a family live." What bothered Ellen most about these exclusive homes and clubs was that they "weaned the husband from his home" and diminished the "inducements to marriage." By contrast, even among the elite merchant class of Boston, family remained paramount.[12]

Still, it was merchants, not the aristocracy, who revealed London as a gateway to empire. Ellen visited the British Museum with J. J. Dixwell, a

New England merchant and banker who was busy drumming up business in Paris, Geneva, and London for his new office and import warehouse on Boston's India Wharf. Dixwell and his younger brother George would later serve as Boston contacts for Joseph's commercial ventures in China. At the museum, Ellen and Dixwell saw the famed first-century Roman Portland Vase as well as Etruscan vases and Roman lamps that were "graceful forms but primitive construction." Later, Ellen visited the Adelaide Gallery and many other London sights in the company of another China trader, Augustine Heard. Heard was Joseph's avuncular mentor, a close friend of Ellen's, who often oversaw the education and well-being of the couple's far-flung children. Ellen thought so highly of Heard that she tried in vain to persuade him to marry one of her unwed sisters. At the Adelaide, Ellen and Heard saw an "electric eel of great size" from South America and a marble head of Lord Brougham that "looks like a Butcher's dog with a wig."[13]

With her husband, Ellen visited the East India Museum, housed in the headquarters of the East India Company. There she saw Sanskrit manuscripts, marveled at the jewels and pearls of Indian princes, and encountered Sultan Fateh Ali Tipu's tiger, a barrel organ "in the form of a Tiger standing on the prostrate figure of a man in European dress." With a turn of the handle, the Tiger grunted in satisfaction while clawing at the man's throat, his victim crying out "piteously." The sultan, who had been killed in 1799 by East India Company forces during the Fourth Anglo-Mysore War, was, in Ellen's opinion, "entertained at once by the exhibition of ingenious machinery and the pleasant idea of revenge on his enemies." That Joseph would bring his wife to the museum to see the East India Company's plunder reflected his close ties to India. Outside the partners at Baring Brothers and their network, Joseph spent most of his time in the company of men like Mountstuart Elphinstone, a civil servant in the East India Company, the first British envoy to the court of Kabul, and later a governor of Bombay.[14]

The Anglophone world that Ellen glimpsed in London afforded her husband access to enormous wealth and commercial opportunity, advantages that the weaker United States could not proffer him. Participating in the British imperial world that linked Russell and Company to Baring Brothers and which connected Boston, London, Bombay, Calcutta, and

Canton allowed Joseph to generate enough capital to sustain his family's wealth and power for generations, assuring their place among the Boston elite. The British imperial world was also a place where Jefferson and his white descendants retained influence. The warm reception that Ellen received at the balls and dinners she attended with Sally Stevenson was due in large part to her connection to Jefferson. "The desire to see Mr. Jefferson's Granddaughter extends to all classes," Stevenson reported, including "torys & radicals & I whisper around, very like him—educated by him &c, &c." Ralph Wormeley, rear admiral of the British navy, told Ellen that Thomas Jefferson was the "most remarkable man of his age." And when Queen Victoria opened Parliament, Ellen met Lord Palmerston, who "spoke to me courteously of my grandfather." At a dinner party, Lord Landsdowne, the lord president of the council, also talked of Jefferson "in high terms."[15]

By April 1839, the Coolidges were ready to sail east. Joseph presumed that he was journeying to Canton to resume his post as a partner in Russell and Company, where he would continue to nurture his close ties to Baring Brothers in London. But war was brewing. The First Opium War would soon change the nature of Anglo-American commerce in China forever. During a conflict fought to curb so-called Chinese arrogance and resistance to international law, Joseph and other U.S. merchants saw an opportunity. With all British trade suspended—and illegal—in Canton, Joseph became an agent for sidelined British traders, shipping opium, tea, and silk on their behalf. The successful wartime trading of Joseph Coolidge and other Canton-based U.S. merchants proved that enterprising Americans were no longer junior partners; they had become equal to their British counterparts.[16]

Neither Ellen nor Joseph Coolidge knew what awaited them in China in the late autumn of 1839. Sailing aboard the *Ellen Preble*, the Coolidges suffered through a five-month journey that took them first to Java, then to Batavia, and finally to the epicenter of the opium trade. Leaving the "sapphire blue" of the South China Sea behind, Ellen found herself far from her idea of paradise. Anchored at the mouth of a muddy river, among islands "quite as desolate as yesterday," she despaired, the "insignificant town of Macao [Macau]" came into view. Since the Chinese barred for-

eign women from Canton, Ellen would have to settle for the Portuguese-
controlled island instead, where she would live in a rented house with her
dog, her birds, and her French maid, Josephine.[17]

Meanwhile, Joseph sailed to the mouth of the Pearl River, known as
the Boca Tigris. From there he traveled upriver to Whampoa (Pazhou), an
island that served as the loading point for Chinese teas onto waiting East
Indiamen and clipper ships. He then proceeded about a dozen miles farther, along "green stripes of paddy-land" and against a backdrop of "distant yellow hills" to Canton, the only port city in China in which foreigners were allowed to trade. Canton was a "floating world," where a "crowd
of boats of all sizes, shapes, and colours, passing in every direction" combined with the "hubbub and clamour of ten thousand different sounds
coming from every quarter and with every variety of intonation." It was its
own cosmopolitan commercial hub, attracting merchants from the United
States, Europe, India, and East Asia.[18]

Ellen's banishment to Macao was only one feature of the restrictive
"Canton System," long criticized by ambitious foreign traders. In an effort
to curtail outside trade and influence, the Qing government had implemented a strictly regulated commercial system between Chinese and European merchants beginning in 1757. On the outskirts of the teeming port
city of Canton, European traders conducted business in more than a
dozen "factories"—long, narrow buildings set back from the edge of the
Pearl River which functioned as warehouses, offices, and living spaces.
One British observer noted how unimportant the factories appeared
within the context of the city. "Instead of seeing the foreign ensigns waving
far above the others and showing a superiority" over their Chinese neighbors, he wrote, "they look insignificant, and you then truly feel that you are
in a land where Europeans are obliged to play a second part." Merchants
were prohibited from residing in these factories outside the four-month
trading season. They also had to buy tea, porcelain, and silk exclusively
through the Cohong, an association of Chinese merchants licensed by
Qing authorities.[19]

These measures were designed to maintain the balance of trade in
China's favor and to prevent the empire's colonization by foreign powers,
all of whom sought to expand their commercial influence. Two British
imperial officials, Lord McCartney in 1793 and Lord Amherst in 1816, had
petitioned the Qing emperor to open new ports in northern China, but to

no avail. When Joseph Coolidge arrived in Canton in 1839, his world was framed—and restricted—by this system. He lived and worked in the same building—the American "factory"—along with U.S. traders from firms that included Russell and Company, Wetmore and Company, and Olyphant and Company. He traded tea, porcelain, silk, and opium through Cohong merchants, including Houqua (Wu Binjiang), as he was known to Anglo-American traders, an exorbitantly wealthy entrepreneur who maintained particularly close ties to Russell and Company, the British firm Jardine and Matheson, and Baring Brothers merchant bank. In fact, part of the reason Joseph Coolidge was on thin ice was because the trade deal that he had botched included a heavy loss of Houqua's investments. Russell and Company partners were keen to drop him before the Cohong merchant dropped them. Even Houqua agreed. "Coolidge will not be aware till he arrives that Houqua insisted on Mr. C being left out" of a restructured Russell and Company, firm partner Robert Bennet Forbes revealed to his colleague Samuel Russell in late 1839.[20]

But more pressing than Coolidge's job prospects was the threat of war—and the impending collapse of the Canton System. The Coolidges heard news of violence even before Joseph left Macao. Not only had Chinese authorities just destroyed twenty-three thousand chests of opium, but British merchants had all fled Canton. Several Americans followed suit, including Forbes, whom Ellen sized up as "vain, empty, &, at present, a little swollen and pompous." Skirmishes had broken out in Canton, causing a "strange state of things to exist at the present moment," Ellen noted anxiously, and the "English and Chinamen are fairly at logger-heads." Hearing reports that "there has been some action between some Chinese junks and British frigates," Ellen estimated that twenty-nine Chinese ships were "beaten off and destroyed, and one of them blown up." The reported casualties were five hundred Chinese and thirteen Englishmen. But these were no isolated entanglements. "It is said that the troubles are only beginning," Ellen wrote to Augustine Heard, who was living in Boston. Indeed, what the Coolidges glimpsed at Macao was the outbreak of the First Opium War.[21]

Opium had long been a critical commodity in trade with China. After the American Revolution, both U.S. and British traders imported a much higher volume of goods from China than they exported there, leading to a hefty trade deficit. To remedy this imbalance, enterprising U.S.

merchants began exporting Spanish dollars, otter pelts from the Pacific Northwest, sandalwood from Hawaii, ginseng collected from the Appalachian mountains, and seals hunted off the coast of South America. In 1808, on his way to China, the American sailor George Little recounted the "dire work" of clubbing the seals to death—a bloody prelude to harvesting their valuable pelts.[22]

But the British sought to extend a different commodity to Chinese buyers. In 1793, when the British East India Company gained control of the Mughal poppy fields after expelling French forces there, they began transporting Indian opium to China. By the turn of the century, the company had reaped enormous profits from the sale of Bengal-produced opium to Chinese customers, who paid for the drug in silver. The Qing emperor responded decisively to this new illicit traffic: he banned the drug's importation. But rather than complying with the law, East India Company officials simply changed course. They contracted "country traders" to transport the drug from India to China, thereby eliminating the company's responsibility for the drug traffic without shortchanging its profits. And U.S. merchants, who had begun their own commerce in Turkish opium after 1805, became increasingly enmeshed in the Indian opium trade, especially after the British Parliament ended the East India Company's trading monopoly between India and China in 1813. The outright dissolution of the East India Company's monopoly in 1833 presented another new opening for U.S. traders in the East. But Joseph Coolidge worried about whether Americans could compete with their British peers in the open market. The "charter having expired, will be of great Injury to the American trade with Canton" since the British could easily "supply the market." As it turned out, there was plenty of business to go around. Drug traffic increased from four thousand chests in 1790 to forty thousand chests in 1839, later reaching eighty thousand chests by 1880. Big profits followed suit—Coolidge's firm raked in $88,000 in 1834 and $240,000 in 1839.[23]

But the volume of the illicit drug trade—and the size of its returns— soon led to a crisis. The standoff began while the Coolidges were still in London. Chinese imperial officials, led by Commissioner Lin Tse-hsu (Lin Zexu), squared off against foreign merchants over the opium trade in March 1839. The Qing emperor concluded that drastic action was necessary to avoid permanent damage to the empire. Not only was silver, the currency used to purchase opium, flowing out of China, but addiction was rampant. Anglo-American opium merchants were not unaware of the baneful effects of the drug. During a visit to several Singapore opium dens, one Russell and Company trader (and an ancestor of Franklin Delano Roosevelt), Edward Delano, "found smokers in all of them," with one man prostrate under its effects: "pale, cadaverous, death-like." John Murray Forbes, another Russell and Company merchant, reported that Chinese addicts were "creatures who seemed half-way between the animal and the human race." For the Qing emperor, the rapid depletion of specie and widespread opium use spelled a grim future for the Chinese state. It was with these high stakes in mind that Commissioner Lin stormed into Canton, putting Qing imperial power on full display.[24]

Scores of Chinese troops and several war junks hoped to intimidate the foreign traders. To that end, Lin wanted to make examples of those who violated Chinese law—including Chinese citizens. He placed the Cohong merchants—many of whom, like Houqua, used bribes to facilitate the drug trade—in chains, ordered all foreign merchants to be confined to their factories in Canton, and demanded that merchants surrender their opium stores. Violators, Lin warned, would be put to death. British traders balked at having to turn over millions of dollars in merchandise, which they deemed private property. The British trade superintendent, Charles Elliot, hemmed and hawed over a response. Elliot, who forbade British ships to carry opium within a hundred miles of Canton, had failed to curry favor among British merchants. Joseph Coolidge confided that Elliot was a "man of impulse, and the last person" to "negotiate a caution with his cool and obstinate opponents." Though Elliot believed that opium was "injurious" to imperial commerce and stained the "British character," he refused to let personal opinion guide his decision.[25]

By the end of the month, Elliot had decided to hedge his bets. He agreed to Lin's terms, ordering British merchants to surrender 20,283 chests of opium. But he refused to comply with Lin's other requirement— that British merchants sign an affidavit declaring that they would discontinue any future involvement in the trade. Elliot and the British traders left Canton for Macao and Hong Kong, hoping to call Lin's bluff. Knowing full well that Chinese forces lacked Britain's military might and that most of the Cohong merchants were deeply complicit in the opium traffic, merchants like James Matheson predicted that the "obnoxious" opium "vessels will disappear for a time, and none will be more ready to welcome them back than the Mandarins themselves, on account of the fertile source of emolument derived to them from conniving at the prohibited trade." U.S. merchants, however, lacking a deep-pocketed treasury to reimburse them for lost property or a strong navy to come to their defense, broke from their British colleagues and signed Lin's bond.[26]

Over the course of several weeks, Chinese workers opened thousands of wooden chests, crushed balls of opium underfoot, slaked them with salt and lime, and drained the noxious liquid into the bay at Canton. It was this destruction of British "property," without any offer of compensation from Chinese officials, that ultimately created the grounds for a "just war" against China. In the view of British merchants, this act encapsulated the so-called arrogance of China. A war was necessary, they asserted, if only to force China to accept a European vision of international law, although a year earlier, Foreign Secretary Palmerston had not ascribed to this view. "With respect to the smuggling of opium," he warned Elliot, the British government could not "interfere for the purpose of enabling British subjects to violate the laws of the country to which they trade."[27]

But with Lin's very public destruction of British opium, Palmerston abruptly changed his mind. When arguing for making war on the Chinese in 1840, Palmerston charged that Lin had put down the opium trade by acts of arbitrary authority against British merchants—"a course totally at variance with British law" and "totally at variance with international law." Moreover, Palmerston suggested that Commissioner Lin's actions were "unjust and no better than robbery." This, he asserted, authorized the use of British force in China in 1840 and legitimized strongarming China into opening its ports and abolishing the much-maligned Canton System.[28]

British opium merchants had long complained about restrictive trade in China. The influential trader William Jardine observed that "Great Britain can never derive any important advantage from opening the trade to China, while the present mode of levying duties, extorting money from the Hong merchants etc. exists." Instead, "we must have a Commercial Code with these Celestial Barbarians, before we can extend advantageously our now limited commercial operations." And on the eve of war, Robert Bennet Forbes told his wife, "I hope the day is not far distant when they will be drubbed into the list of civilized nations & were it not for you I would volunteer under *any* flag to help do it." But Commissioner Lin, in an open letter addressed to Queen Victoria in 1839, asserted that it was the British who had violated Chinese law by selling opium—the buying and smoking of which were punishable by death—to Chinese consumers. Still, Britain's perception of China's disregard for international law tipped the scales in Parliament. By only a handful of votes, Britain opted for a war over opium.[29]

Of course, there *was* law in China—and had been for centuries. But Anglo-American traders' construction of the trope of Chinese "lawlessness" was new. As recently as the beginning of the nineteenth century, China's resistance to signing treaties had not seemed to be an insurmountable impediment to trade, particularly to marginalized Americans. As a result of commercial exclusion from preferential trading in the Atlantic world after the American Revolution and the outbreak of the Napoleonic Wars, some U.S. political elites advocated a turn away from Europe, rather than toward it. China, which boasted all the hallmarks of an ancient civilization that was "not inferior to, if not greatly surpassing" the "most refined nations of Europe," seemed a likely trading partner. As the eccentric and erratic Augustus Woodward, chief justice of the Michigan Territory, suggested to President James Madison, America "may be received in china on a footing more favorable" than in warmongering European nations and might gain direct access to sought-after goods like ginseng, rice, tea, porcelain, and silk. The only potential problem was forging a formal diplomatic relationship with the Qing Empire, which was "secluded from the rest of mankind" and "unacquainted with the European law of nations." But that obstacle, Woodward suggested, could be overcome through soft diplomacy; a Sino-American alliance was possible, even outside a more formal legal framework.[30]

The outbreak of the First Opium War crystallized the perception of Chinese violence and lawlessness among foreign merchants and provided grounds for war. Looking backward in time from Commissioner Lin's destruction of British property in the spring of 1839, Anglo-Americans synthesized a long train of "abuses" by Chinese officials. In 1784, in what was later termed the "*Lady Hughes* affair," a British sailor fired his gun in a salute, accidentally killing one Chinese sailor on a nearby boat, and mortally wounding another. The gunner, turned over to Chinese authorities, was tried and found guilty of murder and later sentenced to death by strangulation. This procedure was completely in accordance with Qing law.

Nonetheless, British merchants protested the verdict, arguing that the same act would probably have been judged a negligent homicide in a British court.[31]

Decades later, the incident would resurface during the notorious case of the *Emily*. On a September afternoon in 1821, Francis Terranova, an Italian sailor on board the U.S. vessel, bought fruit from a local vendor, Ko Leang-she, who was hawking produce from her boat at Whampoa. Terranova lowered a terracotta pot filled with money from the *Emily*'s deck. As Terranova reeled the pot back aboard ship, his face dropped in disappointment at the small amount of fruit inside. A quarrel soon erupted. Later the fruit seller was found dead in the water, her head bloodied by a gaping wound. A furor enveloped the port, and all trade was suspended, with fingers pointed at Terranova. The sailor went on trial, first on board the *Emily*, and then in a Chinese court. After being found guilty of murder by Chinese officials, Terranova was strangled to death. Outraged, Anglo-American merchants protested his punishment, believing that execution was an unjust punishment for the crime.[32]

And in an incident that sparked the first skirmish of the Opium War—at Kowloon in September 1839—several British sailors, drunk on rice liquor, beat a local villager to death. Fearing that the sailors would be handed over to Chinese authorities and sentenced to death for the murder, Superintendent Elliot acted quickly. He swiftly held a trial on board a British warship, with himself as judge and several merchant captains as jurors. He even invited Chinese officials to watch the proceedings, though they declined. The little ad hoc court convicted all five men—not of murder, but of assault and rioting. Livid at this latest flouting of Chinese law, Lin ordered a blockade of the Pearl River and an embargo on all food and water sold to the British. Taken together, these incidents revealed the perception among Anglo-Americans that Chinese society was a "lawless" and violent one. The Chinese, in the minds of Anglo-American traders, were no longer an ancient "high" civilization, but rather supposedly inferior "barbarians." Indeed, a short history of violence that began with the gunner aboard the *Lady Hughes* in 1784 and culminated in the torture and execution of Cohong merchants and opium traffickers in 1839 served as the basis for Anglo-Americans' critique of Chinese "legal despotism."[33]

Opinions about Chinese lawlessness and violence dovetailed with emergent racism. At Macao, Ellen Coolidge often sat outside on a verandah, while the "hum of voices rising from the street and flotilla of boats has something outlandish and displeasing to the ear," she reported to Heard. "It would be impossible," she continued, "to mistake the strange, uncouth ones and the jangling tones of the Chinese," which she equated with the "screaming of birds and growling and grunting of beasts," for the "modulated voices of civilized men." Later she toured the city with an acquaintance. Riding in a sedan chair through "all their part of town," Coolidge found her curiosity "gratified at the expense of my senses." She saw a "tangled set of narrow, filthy streets, literally swarming with a ragged, beggarly population" and "vile odours and such a tumult of human voices mingled with the barking of dogs, grunting of pigs and screaming of chickens." Many of the "little imps," she wrote, referring to the Chinese residents, "were actually afraid of me." Such views of Chinese racial inferiority, coupled with notions of the country's lawlessness, hastened the emergence of Anglo-American white supremacy at Canton. British and U.S. merchants increasingly believed that their intimate commercial ties were rooted in more than common material interests. What these traders shared was the racial identity that Ellen Coolidge had called attention to as she stood in the shadow of the Tower of London: Anglo-Saxonism.[34]

Yet outside the global community of China traders and their political allies in Britain and New England, few Anglo-Americans agreed that the Chinese were lawless "barbarians" or that war was justified. In Britain, abolitionists became anti-opium supporters. One pamphleteer charged that "there is no slavery on earth to name with the bondage into which opium casts its victim" and warned that "there is scarcely one known instance of escape from its toils, when once they have fairly enveloped a man." Opium, like slavery, deprived individuals of their manhood and moral and intellectual faculties—it "degraded" autonomous men, transforming them into addicts and dependents. William Gladstone, the son of a rich British West Indian enslaver and a future prime minister, condemned the war for opium in Parliament. Opioid dependance hit close to home for Gladstone—his younger sister Helen remained locked in the drug's throes. In urging his fellow MPs not to sanction a war in China, Gladstone asserted that there were no legal grounds for invasion. "A war more unjust in its origin, a war more calculated in its progress to cover this country with permanent disgrace, I do not know, and I have not heard of," Gladstone thundered.[35]

Americans were also critical of the war in China. Compromising Chinese sovereignty was bad news for anxious enslavers, who feared that the war might establish a dangerous precedent. In the wake of the abolition of slavery in the West Indies in 1838, U.S. enslavers worried that Britain might violate U.S. sovereignty and impose the law of abolition in slave states. These heightened fears compelled the planter class—and its representatives in Congress—to condemn the First Opium War. Britain's decision to "wage war against this venerable and peaceful people" was intended merely to "force on them the use of opium, the production of her slaves on the Hindu plantation, against the resistance of the Chinese government," excoriated South Carolinian John C. Calhoun in the U.S. Senate. For him, the logic for British aggression—China's arrogance and "barbarity"—was simply unfounded. Instead, Calhoun suggested, China was a "nation that has lived through generations of nations, and which was old and civilized before the governments of Western Europe came into existence." For American proslavery supporters like Calhoun, protecting U.S. sovereignty also meant condemning—and spotlighting—Britain's violation of Chinese law.[36]

But in Canton, surrounded by a haze of musket and cannon fire as the war stuttered on, Joseph Coolidge continued to sing a different tune. The Chinese were arrogant and lawless, he argued, and he supported Britain's war against them—if only to secure his own future commercial interests. The Qing Empire, he confided to Baring Brothers partner Joshua Bates, needed to be "humbled" by the British, since "they have the most exaggerated idea of their own strength and importance" and a "corresponding contempt for foreigners" and their trade. Coolidge was not speaking in the abstract, but rather from direct personal experience. As we shall see, the violence unleashed upon him by Chinese officials, coupled with the autonomy and wealth he enjoyed as a wartime trader, led him to conclude that the British military had just cause to invade China.[37]

In December 1839, Joseph Coolidge was on the outs. Russell and Company had no intention of welcoming Jefferson's grandson-in-law back into the firm, despite having assured him that letters of support from "merchants & men of business in America & England" could salvage his job. It was Houqua, the wealthy Cohong merchant through whom Russell and Company traded at Canton, who helped push Coolidge out. The only obstacle to the ouster was Coolidge's close relationship with Joshua Bates. The firm's partners, however, had "unbounded confidence" that Houqua "through his business can turn the obdurate heart of Bates" away from Coolidge.[38]

The Coolidges were furious at the news. "He has been foiled in his efforts at reconciliation with his partners," Ellen fumed, even though "he did every thing that a man of honour could do" and exhibited more deference than "I thought one of his impetuous temper to tolerate." Lonely and frustrated, Ellen wondered why she had traveled across the world to live away from her children on a half-deserted Portuguese island. But Joseph was determined to stay. Calculating his net worth at nearly two hundred thousand dollars, he refused to retire with a tarnished reputation. Instead, he hatched a plan. With only two commission houses functioning in Canton, Joseph told Augustine Heard, "There is ample room for more." His idea was to form a new partnership with Heard, who remained in Boston, to compete directly with his old business partners.[39]

Joseph Coolidge hoped to exploit the Sino-British standoff for his own gain. By January 1840, Parliament had voted to declare war on China, the British were expelled from Canton, and Coolidge was on his own trying to jumpstart the new firm of Augustine Heard and Company. Even as he watched foreign traders streaming out of China daily, Coolidge believed that the war was the ideal time for neutral traders like himself to make a fortune. Though the "Chinese seem to be expecting war," and Sino-British relations remained tense, Coolidge insisted that he would reap the most profit by remaining at his post. "I would not be frightened away from Canton," he wrote, since "I do not believe there will be any danger" and the "position of things" opened the door for myriad trade opportunities.[40]

Initially British traders had criticized their U.S. allies for signing the agreement with Commissioner Lin. But the British had not anticipated that the Americans' compliance with Chinese law would prove to be the "greatest advantage to all parties." By signing the affidavit, U.S. vessels were able to transship British goods and charge high commission rates, as no other foreigners remained in the port. Joseph Coolidge thrilled at U.S. ships "going up and down between Whampoa & Lintin taking Cotton and British goods up in frigates and bringing down Teas." Some U.S. traders even purchased English ships and "are freighting them as American vessels, having changed their names first," Coolidge reported. Now all he needed was a piece of the action—a British merchant who would trust him with trade, despite his sullied reputation.[41]

It may have been because of the global influence of Joseph Bates, or the sterling character of Augustine Heard, that the largest commission house in the China trade came knocking at Coolidge's door. He had heard a rumor that the firm's partners, the Scottish merchants William Jardine and James Matheson, were looking for an American agent to serve as their proxy in China. "Can we get their business?" Coolidge asked cautiously. Doing so would be a lucrative beginning for the new trading house. Against all odds, Coolidge landed the job. Trading on behalf of Jardine and Matheson was "a great feather in my cap, and will put dollars in my pocket," Coolidge declared confidently. "I am the confidential correspondent of Matheson," the head of the firm, and "authorized to go to a large amo. for him here," he boasted to Heard. If U.S. merchants continued the trade while the Chinese and British held to their standoff, and trade was "not again thrown open to the English, or wholly lost to them," then Coolidge could expect to make a hefty profit from his new commission.[42]

A huge proportion of profits came from the opium trade, which was "flourishing vigorously" during wartime. "Large quantities are coming in from Bombay and Calcutta," Coolidge disclosed to Heard, with Jardine and Matheson rumored to have made a million dollars in opium in a single month. But the punishment for the trade, Coolidge warned, remained in full force. The Chinese "cut off the heads of those who deal in it, when they can find them." This penalty did not deter Coolidge, who continued to traffic in opium, often writing secretive letters to Matheson that substituted "XXXX" for the word *opium*. In October 1841, he advised "Commanders of ships having *Indian Drugs* aboard" intended for the Scottish firm that an "increasing armed force in the river"—about two hundred Chinese gunboats between Whampoa and Canton—sought to "destroy the vessels under your command." He warned the ship captains to "be on your guard, and take any steps necessary for the preservation of the XX property." New hubs for U.S. transshipments of British goods also facilitated opium trafficking. In November 1841, Coolidge heard that "Teas may be shipped off thro. Macao, and payment taken in the Drug." Throughout 1841 and 1842, Coolidge continued to receive "applications for the Drug" in Canton and Whampoa, all of which he filled diligently.[43]

If only for the money, Coolidge was right to stay in Canton. British goods carried on board U.S. vessels were shipped through ports at Manila or Macao, translating into "magnificent profits, the like of which I think I cannot again accrue," rhapsodized Edward Delano of Russell and Company. Robert Bennet Forbes could only echo his colleague's amazement. "So good an opportunity will never be found during this century again," he declared. One of their firm's ships, the *Lintin,* had recently made twenty-five thousand dollars from a mere two voyages to Hong Kong and Whampoa.[44]

Americans' wartime business was a turning point for the China trade. "The truth is," Coolidge admitted, that "owing to the interruption of British trade, the American Houses have been doing an enormous business, and feel therefore very independent." In fact, he noted, U.S. merchants spoke with "contempt of the sort of business done formerly." In short, the traders' role as confidants and proxies of large British commission firms combined with their newfound knowledge of the scale and profits to be made in opium, tea, and manufactured goods showed what U.S. trade in Canton *could* be in the future: an independent commercial enterprise on par with Britain's. The scale of profits pulled in by firms like Heard and Company persuaded merchants that they were equal to their British counterparts. The status of U.S. merchants as dependent, junior partners appeared to be a thing of the past.[45]

But how long these soaring profits would last no one knew. Three months after Britain's declaration of war, tensions threatened to boil over. Though peace had seemed feasible during the winter of 1840, news of a British squadron being dispatched for China put everyone back on edge. From her post at Macao, Ellen Coolidge noted that "things have taken an entirely different turn from what was expected," and instead of the hoped-for peace and "open trade," the British were on the "eve of a protracted war" with the Chinese.[46]

Predictions about what would happen once British troops landed in Canton from India varied widely. Some thought that a show of British military might would be quickly followed by "submission on the part of the Chinese & that a commercial treaty will be formed between them without delay." But Augustine Heard held a more pessimistic view. A "nation like the Chinese will not suddenly relinquish the policy they have so long acted upon," he opined from Boston. They will "shield themselves from the attacks of the Eng. in the best manner they can & finally exterminate all foreigners & foreign trade." He advised that British troops should not underestimate China's strength: "China is very powerful." Joseph Coolidge tended to agree. Although the Chinese were "imperfectly armed," they also had "great resources, an immense population, and are peculiarly favored by the nature of their coast and country." Both men worried that Britain might overestimate its own imperial strength in waging a war with the vast Qing Empire.[47]

When a flotilla of British troops landed in China in June 1840, none of the Anglo-American merchants in Canton or Macao knew what would come next. But the first order of business, according to Lord Palmerston's directives, was to deploy the forces, comprised of Bengali volunteers, British Indian Army regulars, and East India Company fighters, and gain a foothold in the region. The island of Chusan (Zhoushan), located about halfway up the Chinese coast, appeared to fit the bill, and in July the British forces attacked. British naval warships soon flattened the Chinese junks guarding the harbor, capturing the port as well as the island's interior. Though disease broke out, the British lost no time in directing their troops southward, to the Pearl River, as well as northward to negotiate peace terms in Peking (Beijing). But Coolidge doubted whether the brief show of force at Chusan would be enough to achieve Britain's goal: the end of the Canton System and the signing of a formal commercial treaty. To avoid a costly and protracted war, he advised that British forces would only succeed "by striking terror at once, by the severity and rapidity of your blows." The British should act with "extraordinary vigor," using steamships and men of war to destroy undefended coastal cities. Only this, he argued, would "open the eyes of the Chinese, who are blinded by ignorance and conceit."[48]

As the denouement of their campaign, the British forces should proceed to Peking and demand an audience with the Qing emperor. If the "Son of Heaven" was not yet "ready to listen to reason," then the British should "repeat the dose" of violence. There was much at stake. "The security of your Indian Empire depends on your success in China," Coolidge warned Baring Brothers, and the "immense results to England of throwing open this vast country, with its industries and trading population, to the influences of free trade," justified "any measures necessary." He believed that the British military campaign should be brief and brutal, but its goal was not conquest. Instead, British forces would force the Qing emperor to accept the law of nations. Sanctioning Britain's violation of Chinese sovereignty was the best way to guarantee future U.S. security and profit, he reasoned.[49]

But Coolidge should have watched what he wished for. After failed negotiations in Peking, the British resumed their military campaign in 1841, fortified with hundreds of fresh Indian troops and more warships, at least one of them made of iron. Their goal: to wrest the valuable Pearl River Delta from Chinese control. When another round of peace talks collapsed after a battle at the mouth of the Pearl River in January 1841, British forces barreled upriver toward Canton, reaching the port by May. It was then that Coolidge fell victim to "outrage and plunder" during the "pillage of the factories" ahead of the arrival of British warships. A "disgraceful rabble" burst into the merchants' factories. Accosted by a group of soldiers who "rushed upon me with drawn swords," Coolidge would have been "cut . . . down," if not for "some of the factory coolies, who happened to be near and cried out that I was an American."[50]

Though he avoided the sword, Coolidge was taken prisoner. Shoved in front of a provincial Chinese judge along with his clerk and an American crew, Coolidge fell to his knees "in chains, bloody, and almost without covering." The judge interrogated Coolidge, asking "how many of these men were English," and "bidding me tell the truth that he might cut off their heads." The judge protested that Englishmen pretended to be Americans and demanded that "we ought to speak a different language, and wear a different dress" so he "might know us apart." Although Coolidge was not charged by the judge, he and his clerk, as well as several captured Americans, were nonetheless shuttled off to a "common prison," where they were chained together. In a dramatic twist, Houqua arrived and secured Coolidge's release, insisting that a mistake had been made. Brought through a "tumultuous throng" of soldiers who lopped off the tops of their sedan chairs with their swords, Coolidge and his clerk found themselves left among the ruins of their factory. No American ship came to their aid, but British soldiers soon forced their way through the city gates. "I cannot tell you with what feelings of good-will we looked upon every one of those red coats," Coolidge exclaimed. The damage to his property was extensive. The factory was mostly burned—his books, his clothes, and the contents of his office destroyed. Coolidge also lost his cow and his dog, along with his servant's "effects." In all, he claimed $33,620 in damages for the "outrage."[51]

After Coolidge's imprisonment, the British fleet sped up the coast, intending to capture several port cities before staging a blockade of the Yangtze (Yangzi) River. Although the conflict would drag on another year, into the summer of 1842, Coolidge's wartime experience of Chinese violence coupled with his newfound independent trading status shaped his vision for Anglo-American trade. Like many other U.S. merchants, Joseph Coolidge wanted to continue buying and selling opium, silk, and teas in China—not as a junior partner to British houses but as an equal commercial agent. And the China in which he would operate would not be outside the international system but rather squarely within it. U.S.–China traders outlined these goals to Secretary of State Daniel Webster in 1842, following the Sino-British Treaty of Nanking, which stipulated that China cede Hong Kong island, open five new ports to foreign trade, abolish the restrictive Canton System, pay a $21 million indemnity to the British for the confiscated and destroyed opium, and allow British extraterritorial jurisdiction within Chinese borders. No longer would British opium dealers be subject to Chinese laws when trading in the Qing Empire. They could look forward to being governed by British laws—and British courts.[52]

U.S. merchants had one main goal: to secure equal trading status with Britain. "All we could ask," Robert Bennett Forbes told Webster, was "to admit our trade upon the same footing with the most favored nation & we think it would be impolitic to accept anything less." Since China wanted "no political intercourse with Foreign Nations," the only way for the United States to get what it wanted was either through "armed compulsion" or a "politic desire to offer to us voluntarily what has been forced upon them by others." Forbes suggested the latter as a viable diplomatic strategy. For leverage, Forbes and other traders suggested that Webster refer to the willingness of American traders to comply with Chinese policy; they had, after all, signed Commissioner Lin's bond in 1839. A few merchants diverged from Forbes's demands, pleading that Webster expand the American consular presence and augment the U.S. naval fleet in China—all with the aim of protecting U.S. commerce. But the most common refrain from petitioners was commercial parity with Britain. Webster followed their lead. The main goal, Webster asserted in a speech he wrote for President John Tyler, was to "secure the entry of American ships and cargoes" on "terms as favorable as those which are enjoyed by the English merchants." British officials had done the heavy—and coercive—lifting in forcing the Chinese to enter the international system with their 1842 treaty. But U.S. merchants and diplomats sought to capitalize on China's new adherence to international law to extract their own trade agreement.[53]

Following British precedent, U.S. officials succeeded in securing most favored nation status through the Treaty of Wanghia in 1844. But Caleb Cushing, the U.S. diplomatic envoy, went a step farther. Cushing wanted Americans to be co-imperialists in China. To accomplish this, Cushing negotiated an American right of extraterritoriality. By imposing legal jurisdiction within China, the United States, like its British counterpart, compromised Chinese sovereignty, relegating the Qing Empire to "semicolonial status." In fact, America's path to equality with Britain on the world stage also meant replicating its diplomatic policies and imposing an unequal (and racist) legal regime on supposedly "inferior" nonwhite peoples, including the Chinese. It also depended on creating a tiered system of states in the world: white and Christian nations at the top, and "weaker" nonwhite, non-Christian nations ranked beneath them. While U.S. Revolutionary leaders may have viewed Britain as an impediment to their commercial independence and equality after 1776, it was clear—at least in the context of the First Opium War in China—that Britain facilitated U.S. empire building in Asia during the long nineteenth century.[54]

The Coolidges did not remain in China long enough to witness this new era of U.S. trading parity and imperialism. Ellen left in 1840, eager to be reunited with her children. Joseph departed in 1844, leaving several Boston-based agents to manage the firm in his stead. Now that he had salvaged his reputation and earned a "competence"—the term China traders used to indicate that they had amassed enough wealth to retire—Joseph had little need to remain in Canton. But even as he toured Europe with Ellen and visited his children at their boarding school in Geneva, he could not stop thinking about the East. He wanted to be "back again in China" where the "great struggle in wh. all men are engaged" was "more absorbing than anything to be found" in England, where he was living in 1844. It had been the British Empire, not the United States, that acted as a conduit to that "absorbing" place—a low-lying delta where some of the most valuable, and baneful, commodities in the world exchanged hands.[55]

Nicholas Trist

Imperial Power in Cuba and Mexico, 1839–1848

IN 1835, NICHOLAS TRIST, THE U.S. consul in Havana, steamed southward to Cuba. As the island came into view, he drew his wife's attention to the increasingly close ties between the Spanish imperial outpost and the United States. Cuba, Trist observed in his letter to her, had taken "a start in civilization and improvement" and in five years' time would "not be recognizable by former acquaintances." Commerce was exploding, with lines of steamboats "being established in every direction, and to the U. States." In just a short time, he thought, "it will be but a step to & fro." And Trist would be well positioned to take advantage of the opportunity of a lifetime. As he exclaimed to his wife, "There are a thousand chances for making money here." Indeed, one of the primary ways to generate cash in Cuba was by investing in sugar plantations or in the illegal slave trade between the island, the western coast of Africa, and the Gulf Coast.[1]

Nicholas Trist's stint in Cuba was the beginning of a diplomatic career, largely facilitated by Andrew Jackson's patronage, that spanned the 1830s and 1840s. Married to Thomas Jefferson's granddaughter Virginia Jefferson Randolph in 1825, Trist read law with his grandfather-in-law at Monticello before taking up a post in Washington. After serving as U.S. consul from 1833 to 1841 and then briefly as chief clerk in the State Department, Trist was appointed a special envoy to Mexico in 1847 and 1848. But none of these postings brought him fame or fortune. Instead, his work in Cuba and Mexico did quite the opposite, making him a pariah within the Democratic Party as well as the target of a congressional inquiry in 1840, culminating in a recall by the president in 1847.[2]

Nicholas Trist's diplomatic blunders spotlighted a major issue of the era: Anglo-American competition for dominance over the Caribbean and

John Neagle, *Portrait of Nicholas Trist,* 1835. (© Thomas Jefferson Foundation at Monticello.)

Latin America. American strategies, especially among proslavery Democrats, for bringing these areas more squarely under U.S. control ranged from annexation and "union" to robust and preferential trading. Britain's imperial strategy in Latin America was more uniform, relying upon "debtor diplomacy," free trade, and abolition. The dissolution of the Spanish Empire presented an opportunity for Britain: its giant merchant bank, Baring Brothers, extended loans to revolutionary governments with the tacit expectation that new republics would abolish the slave trade and ally themselves with the British Empire. As one member of the British Foreign Office touted in 1839, Latin American republics owed "their recent emancipation from dependence" to "the efforts and influence of this country."[3]

Initially, from his vantage point in Cuba, Trist declared that U.S. independence and equality in the world depended upon limiting British influence in the Americas. When British officials questioned U.S. involvement in the illegal slave trade and tried to enforce adherence to Article 10 of the Treaty of Ghent (1814), Trist cried foul, accusing Britain of trampling on the law of nations and brazenly violating U.S. sovereignty. But less than a decade later, he changed his tune, suggesting that Britain could serve as an umpire in a vastly unequal international order. In the midst of the Mexican-American War, Trist believed that British power could be directed to help preserve the sovereignty of "inferior" states. With President James K. Polk at the helm of a "wicked war," Trist suggested that a former enemy—Britain—could best bring about peace and preserve Mexican nationhood in the face of unwarranted U.S. aggression. Unlike Joseph Coolidge, who believed that British power could be used to *create* inequality in the international system, Trist took the inequality of nations as a given but suggested that it was still incumbent upon "great nations" (that is, Anglo-Saxon Protestant nations) to protect and preserve the sovereignty of nonwhite and non-Christian states.[4]

Still, Trist failed to notice that the British Foreign Office hoped to exploit his efforts in both Cuba and Mexico to curb American proslavery expansion. In Cuba, the Court of Mixed Commission, an Anglo-Spanish body tasked with prosecuting illegal slaving voyages, hoped to highlight Trist's alleged role in the slave trade as evidence of Americans' rampant—and illegal—trafficking in African captives. And in Mexico, eager to prevent President Polk from getting his hands on the country and expanding U.S. slavery all the way to the Pacific, British diplomats pressured Trist to extract a more equitable peace treaty that would stop U.S. empire building at the Rio Grande and secure Mexico as an antislavery ally.[5]

In 1839, Nicholas Trist found himself in a spot of trouble when he was charged with aiding and abetting an illegal slave ship in Havana—not the famous *Amistad,* but a more obscure slaver called the *Venus.* Somewhat mysteriously, the story of the vessel began in a Baltimore shipyard, where it was built and fitted out for sea. Constructed in Fells Point, the *Venus* was a clipper ship, "a noble corvette . . . pierced for 18 guns . . . built in this city on foreign account . . . [that] must outsail anything that floats." One newspaper suggested that the *Venus* was built as a warship for the Mexican government. Another reported that it was a merchantman, commissioned by an owner in the West Indies. But of course, the *Venus* was neither—it was a slave ship.[6]

After departing Baltimore in July 1838 flying the American flag, the *Venus* moored in Havana, where ownership was transferred to a noted Cuban slave trader. During a nineteen-day layover, the *Venus* probably underwent a transformation, fitted out with new platforms and iron shackles. The ship took to sea again in August, still flying the American flag, and ostensibly bound for Bahia, in Brazil. But by November the *Venus* had anchored in Lagos, on the West African coast, with over 1,000 captive Africans loaded into the hold. After the slaves were on board, the *Venus*'s identity was swapped, and its ownership transferred again, this time to an agent of the Cuban slave trader. The Portuguese flag was then hoisted, and a new name painted on the hull: *Duqueza de Braganza.* A hundred miles south of Lagos, a British anti–slave trade sloop sighted the *Duqueza* and engaged in hot pursuit, but without luck, as the ship was soon "out of sight." During the long voyage back to Cuba, more than 100 of the African captives died—only 860 lived to be sold at Havana, earning about three hundred thousand dollars for the *Duqueza*'s owners.[7]

By the time Nicholas Trist arrived in Havana, the illegal slave trade was deeply enmeshed in the Cuban plantation economy. Cuba had become, along with the United States and Brazil, a primary engine of plantation slavery, a source of New World produce, and a consumer of African captives. By 1844, Cuba was exporting nearly 170,000 tons of sugar and 180,000 pounds of coffee annually, harvested and processed by nearly half a million enslaved Africans. Beginning in the 1810s and 1820s, New England capitalists hoped to corner this exploding market for themselves, buying up Cuban slave plantations and investing in the transatlantic "Cuba-Baltic circuit" that linked Havana, Boston, and Saint Petersburg, Russia. Eventually becoming the second-largest U.S. trading partner, by the 1820s Cuba was exporting sugar, coffee, and cigars to American ports, while U.S.

producers sent beef, pork, and spermaceti oil to Havana. The scale of this exchange and investment soon led to the creation of an "informal empire," particularly in the wake of the Monroe Doctrine (1823), which some scholars have interpreted as being based less on securing hemispheric liberty than on protecting U.S. investments in Cuban slavery and the illicit traffic in African captives.[8]

But U.S. involvement in human trafficking in Cuba did not sit well with British imperial officials hoping to rein in the trade, not just in the wake of abolition in 1808 but also after British West Indian slave emancipation in 1838. By this time, Victorian Britons were deploying abolitionism as part of overseas policy. Britain's newfound role as an antislavery empire was also convenient for ambitious politicians and naval commanders, who used the law of abolition to police and control the Atlantic Ocean.[9]

Part of the British officials' strategy to curb the illegal slave trade was to create a naval blockade on the coast of Africa, thereby stopping slavers and preventing the "demand of slaves from being supplied to any great extent." They also cultivated alliances with leaders in Brazil and Cuba, some of whom, like General Gerónimo Valdés, the governor of Cuba, held antislavery leanings, while other local politicians, often bribed by wealthy slave dealers, supported the continuance of the trade. Between 1839 and 1840, British officials in Havana calculated that nearly 15,000 slaves were imported into Cuba alone. And the British Foreign Office estimated that between 1840 and 1867, approximately 222,834 African captives were forcibly smuggled into Cuba.[10]

Britain also maintained a bilateral court in Havana to prosecute illegal slaving ships. These Courts of Mixed Commission—created in conjunction with other European powers through treaties—were stationed at crucial hubs of slave trading in the Atlantic world: Sierra Leone, Angola, South Africa, Brazil, Surinam, Jamaica, New York, and Cuba. The courts could confiscate ships, equipment, and merchandise, and release human beings from captivity. But they had limited impact, since they could not jail or fine slavers' crews and owners, and because the confiscated goods were often repurchased by slave ship captains at prize auctions.[11]

Captains and slave ship owners adopted creative strategies to avoid capture and prosecution. For example, Cuban enslavers exploited the unclear distinction between newly imported African enslaved people and "ladinos," or Caribbean-born slaves. It was difficult for British commissioners to prove that an enslaved person was one or the other. One official described the smugglers' evasive tactics in 1839: enslaved people were imported from Africa, falsely identified as ladinos, sold in Havana, and then reshipped on board schooners or American steamers to elsewhere in Cuba, or to more distant places like Texas. This is what had happened in the *Amistad* case of 1839, which revolved around the question of whether forty-nine members of the Mendes tribe captured in Africa and fraudulently labeled ladinos in Cuba were free people or slaves under Spanish law.[12]

Slavers also evaded British authorities in Cuba by flying the flags of nations that had not signed anti–slave trade treaties with Britain, thereby preventing naval officers from boarding and searching suspected slave ships. In Cuba, illegal slavers most commonly flew the Portuguese and U.S. flags, since neither power had "admitted the search by British Cruizers." The only way to put a stop to the trade, British officials argued, was to add an amendment to the law of nations, defining the slave trade as piracy. Still, as long as slave trading was not uniformly condemned by all nations in the international system, loopholes would abound for slavers to exploit. In the meantime, in Cuba at least, British anti–slave trade advocates hoped that both a "continuous chain" of British naval cruisers encircling the island and the Courts of Mixed Commission would help curtail the trade.[13]

British officials were also keen to use the Court of Mixed Commission to halt American proslavery imperialism. As early as the 1830s, British diplomats were debating whether U.S. officials would use annexation as a political tool to acquire new territory in Latin America. In Cuba in 1839, one official warned of the "Texian policy of extensively colonizing this island by subjects of the United States," who "are daily acquiring more territory in this Spanish colony by extensive purchases." Indeed, that Cuba should become "another state in the banner" of the United States appeared all but inevitable. But British court commissioners claimed that the inexorable machine of American expansion could be halted. If there was a force that could "prevent this Island from falling into the hands of America," he declared, it was the "counteracting effects" of the court.[14]

As the scandal surrounding the slave ship *Venus* unfolded in 1839, the commissioners of the Mixed Court, encouraged by the foreign secretary, believed they had hit upon one way of "counteracting" U.S. influence—by taking Nicholas Trist to task. They intended to do this by asserting that in aiding and abetting the owners of the *Venus,* he had violated international law: the Treaty of Ghent. The Anglo-American agreement that had ended the War of 1812 included a vague clause gesturing toward a joint effort to suppress the slave trade. Article 10 stipulated that both nations "shall use their best endeavours" to promote the abolition of the slave trade. British officials hoped to use this law to condemn Trist's alleged role in the *Venus* affair. But proving that the U.S. consul had not utilized his "best endeavours" to curb the slave trade would be more difficult than they imagined. To do so, they would have to convince U.S. diplomats that the Court of Mixed Commission had the legal authority to police and enforce the 1814 treaty in Cuba.[15]

Two commissioners in the court at Havana, Campbell Dalrymple and James Kennedy, tested their strategy in the winter of 1839, when the ship formerly known as the *Venus* was first spotted in the Havana harbor. The commissioners pushed Trist to board the ship, now called the *Duqueza* and flying the Portuguese flag. But Trist flatly refused, asserting that he could not board it without proof that it was a slaver—and although hearsay evidence of slaving was clear at the Havana docks, no one would provide evidence in court against the Cuban slave traders. Dalrymple and Kennedy tried again, pressing Trist for information about British subjects as well as "several American citizens" involved in facilitating the *Venus*'s slaving voyage and invoking the Treaty of Ghent to lend authority to their requests. It was "perfectly consistent," the two men suggested, with the "respect" that the "agents for each country" felt for each other, that Anglo-American diplomats should abide by the treaty and share information that might contribute to the "common purpose" of abolition. At the least, Trist should grant their requests for information on U.S. slave trading because of the Anglo-American "peculiar relationship."[16]

Trist dug in his heels. Sitting down at his desk to pen the first of two diatribes to the commissioners, he declared that they did not understand international law; they were ignorant of the "first truths regarding international independence." Trist dismissed the commissioners' invocation of the Anglo-American "relationship," stubbornly reminding them that since 1776, the "only relation in which they stand to each other is that of two independent nations." The court, he continued, had no authority to police American diplomats—or citizens. There was no "official relation" between the U.S. consul and British commissioners. Instead, the commissioners could act "in no other capacity than that in which they had been recognized by the Spanish," since it was the Anglo-Spanish treaty "which alone entitled them to be here at all." Their role was "purely judicial" rather than diplomatic. Thus, a U.S. diplomat and two British jurists were incompatible "agents," preventing them from collaborating to enforce the Treaty of Ghent.[17]

At first, the commissioners tried to turn a deaf ear to Trist's tirade. They simply repeated their request for information based on rumors about Anglo-American involvement in the *Venus*'s transatlantic journey to and from West Africa. Kennedy and Dalrymple thought that the matter deserved "immediate investigation" by Trist, either by lodging inquiries with the governor, General Valdés, or by questioning the commander of the U.S. warship anchored in the Havana harbor. Even a cursory examination of the logbook and crew could not have "failed to elicit" information about which U.S. citizens might have been aboard the *Venus* during its trek east to Lagos, whether the *Venus* was indeed pursued by a British cruiser off the African coast, and the date when the ship was divested of its "American character" and sold. At the least, Kennedy and Dalrymple thought Trist should be alarmed at the "gross abuse" of the U.S. flag.[18]

The commissioners refused to be cowed by Trist's accusation that their request exceeded their authority. Kennedy and Dalrymple had no wish to interfere in another nation's business, with one exception—human rights violations. When it came down to it, the illegality of importing nearly nine hundred captives from Africa, Kennedy and Dalrymple argued, trumped everything else. "Our objects are too high, and our conviction of their rectitude too strong, to allow us to be turned from our course by taunts of any kind," they shot back at Trist. However, though the British officials did not admit it, the "rights of humanity" they invoked were not accepted as universal. Though British lawmakers had sought to use treaties—of which the Courts of Mixed Commission were a product—to try to impose the British law of abolition within non-British slave-trading jurisdictions, the question of whether Britain held legal authority within other sovereign entities remained contested.[19]

Trist's next response was a long time coming—probably because it took him several weeks to compose his searing, 260-page critique. About halfway through the essay, Trist admitted that Britain and the United States were obligated to comply with the Treaty of Ghent, but he took issue with Britain's use of Article 10 as a ploy to "effect the conquest of weaker states, or establish over their governments a control irreconcilable" with the law of nations. To him, the present action of the British government was not a sincere effort to end the slave trade, but sprang "solely from a desire to promote its own political and commercial power by inflicting injury upon other states." Here was Trist's big point: British jurists were using the court's power—and its pro-abolition stance—to violate weaker nations' sovereignty, thereby upholding British interests while also promoting a hierarchy of states in the international system.[20]

Dumbfounded by Trist's "extraordinary production," the commissioners promptly forwarded the 260-page opus to the foreign secretary, Viscount Palmerston. Kennedy and Dalrymple charged that the U.S. diplomat had been moonlighting as the acting Portuguese consul in Havana, a post that had been vacant for two years. Allegedly, Trist had granted fake bills of sale and provided "irregular assistance" to slavers, furnishing them with signed blank forms "to be filled up at their convenience." Essentially, in acting as the Portuguese consul, Trist had protected "Piratical vessels" that were sailing in breach of the law of nations, the commissioners suggested.[21]

But Dalrymple and Kennedy were on shaky ground. As Secretary of State John Forsyth had pointed out during the *Amistad* case, "however unjust and unnatural the slave trade may be, it is not contrary to the law of nations." Indeed, the trade was illegal only in "so far as each nation may have made it so by its own acts or laws." Still, Dalrymple and Kennedy were set on ensuring Trist's downfall. The U.S. consul's racist, proslavery beliefs, combined with his alleged role as acting Portuguese consul, the commissioners seethed, proved that he was an apologist for the slave trade, an abettor of enslavers, and "ready to violate the clearest provisions" of international law.[22]

Yet the commissioners had overlooked an important point when considering Trist's guilt. It was clear that any man who spent weeks composing a 260-page treatise could find little time to conduct business in the Havana harbor. Indeed, Trist delegated most of the daily consular tasks to his clerk, preferring to spend most of his time in his office or at home, buried in his law books, writing long letters, or worrying obsessively about his health. Some Americans complained that "going to Havana now they never could see the Consul." U.S. ship captains and their crews would occasionally spot "a handsome young man with black, curled whiskers who they supposed to be the Consul." But the man whom U.S. merchants—and slave ship captains—most often saw was a nineteen-year-old clerk named Peter Crusoe.[23]

The British Foreign Office lost no time in conveying its accusations about Trist's role in the illicit slave trade to Washington. Forwarded correspondence between the U.S. consul and the British commissioners as well as the results of the Mixed Courts' reconnaissance in Havana did little to improve Trist's image at home. Feeling the pressure to contain a growing scandal within his administration, President Martin Van Buren moved quickly, appointing Alexander Everett, the former U.S. minister to Spain and a keen supporter of Cuban annexation, to investigate the Foreign Office's charges in Havana. Everett, a native Bostonian, sailed for Cuba, not just to delve into Trist's alleged slave trafficking but also to gauge the pro-American leanings of Spanish Cubans. While in Cuba, Everett concluded that the "interference of the British in the slavery question" had created support for "union with the U.S."[24]

Everett's dream of incorporating Cuba into the United States made his confidential report on Trist's activities all the more revealing. Aware of the collusion between U.S. merchants and Cuban slave dealers but not wanting to cause trouble, Everett's solution was to spread the blame as widely as possible. He accused everybody he could think of—U.S. merchants, shipbuilders, ship captains—of playing a role in the illicit traffic. When Everett did get into specifics, he pointed the finger not at Nicholas Trist but at his young clerk, Peter Crusoe. Born in Gibraltar to British parents, Crusoe had gotten his first break in U.S. diplomacy in Rio, where he worked for the consul and picked up some Portuguese. In 1838, Crusoe went to work for Trist in Havana, selected for the post because he was a polyglot with "somewhat pleasing manners." Drawing only a small salary, Crusoe flaunted an expensive wardrobe that attracted suspicion from everyone but his boss. Even the acting consul, who stood in for Trist while he defended himself before Congress, raised an eyebrow at Crusoe's waistcoats.[25]

Acting consul John Morland suspected that Crusoe was up to no good—procuring "sums of money from the slave traders by employing his position" with the U.S. consular office to "facilitate in some way their operations." After speaking with Morland, Everett concluded that the clerk had stolen the blank shipping forms already signed by Trist and later sold them to Portuguese slave dealers. When Trist was made aware of Crusoe's role in the slave trade, the information "had no effect in shaking his confidence in" Crusoe. In fact, while Trist was away in Washington for the better part of a year, he gave Crusoe the "whole charge of the Consulate in his absence." Everyone but Trist seemed to know that Crusoe was "a man of disrepute and extravagant habits."[26]

Trist rambled through his congressional appearance, but in the end he got away with little more than a slap on the wrist—and a tarnished reputation. The incoming Whig administration, however, jettisoned Trist from his post in 1841, leaving him to languish in a Havana boardinghouse with his family. It remained to be seen whether Trist, relegated to political exile until 1845, would learn from his mistakes. For his part, Foreign Secretary Palmerston had already witnessed Trist in action, and he counted on the disgraced consul to unwittingly aid British strategy during the Mexican-American War.[27]

In April 1847, a man calling himself "Docteur Tarro" checked into the Hôtel d'Orléans. Arriving from Virginia, Tarro had endured nearly 250 miles of railroad travel, 100 miles of post coaches, and a steamboat journey from Montgomery, Alabama, to Louisiana. When Tarro set off in yet another steamer, this one bound for Vera Cruz, in Mexico, he was certain no one knew who he was. Yet Tarro's true identity had already been revealed, a slipup that annoyed President Polk, who had created Nicholas Trist's incognito with the aim of negotiating an end to the Mexican-American War. "The success of Trist's mission," Polk confided in the pages of his diary, "must depend mainly on keeping it a secret" from the Whig opposition in Congress as well as the Mexican government.[28]

The press had already gotten wind of the disguise. Though Jefferson's grandson-in-law maintained that he seldom reported on his movements, his family "saw enough about him in the news papers" to be aware of his new role in Mexico. So well known was Trist's assignment that both soldiers and journalists spoke openly about it. In fact, he was later the subject of a popular pulp novella, *The Mexican Ranchero*, which depicted him as the man who would finally end the war in Mexico.[29]

Trist had Andrew Jackson to thank for his covert new diplomatic mission. It was Jackson who tracked him down in Cuba and offered him a new lease on political life, convincing Polk, the pro-expansion Democrat narrowly elected to the presidency in 1844, to hire Trist as the chief clerk of the State Department. But on his return to Washington from his outpost in Cuba, Trist hardly seemed up to the task. Overwhelmed by Polk's micromanagement and the oversight of an entire government agency, Trist complained that "by the time I get away from the office, I am *broken down* for the day." He was soon relieved of the daily tedium of his State Department assignments when Polk, hoping to end a war that he never thought would extend beyond a mere skirmish, sent him to Mexico as a special emissary in 1847.[30]

Polk had chosen Trist not because he was a skilled negotiator or an influential party operative but because he was a nobody. "Such is the jealousy of the different factions of the Democratic party," Polk explained, that "it is impossible to appoint any prominent man or men without giving extensive dissatisfaction to others." Trist was not Polk's first representative to go to Mexico. Previously, the U.S. minister to Mexico, John Slidell, had tried to negotiate a boundary between Texas and Mexico, but the Mexican government refused even to meet with him, much less negotiate. A few months later, in an attempt to force Mexico's hand, Polk sent U.S. troops to the contested Nueces Strip, a sliver of land located between the Nueces River and the Rio Grande. When Mexican forces attacked a makeshift U.S. fort in April 1846, killing about a dozen Americans, Polk used the violence as a pretense for war.[31]

But the U.S. conflict with Mexico initiated by Polk and his allies had little to do with a desire to extend America's cotton empire into Mexico. It had much more to do with California. Though Polk, himself an enslaver, wanted to settle the contested border between Texan slaveholders and Mexican authorities in the Nueces Strip, he was interested in Mexico only insofar as it presented a conduit to the Pacific. "I had California & the fine bay of San Francisco" in view, Polk noted as early as 1845. California's coast, not northern Mexico, would be the real prize of the war. Acquiring land bordering the Pacific Ocean, the Democratic *Union* opined, "gives us some of the finest harbors in the world . . . with an immense commerce opening upon us with the richest nations of Asia." With northern Mexico in American hands, U.S. cotton planters would have a new outlet for their slave-grown produce in the Pacific world.[32]

Polk and other Democrats hoped to outmaneuver Britain, which was also bidding for California. "Great Britain had her eye on that country and intended to possess it if she could," Polk remarked, but assured his cabinet that the United States would not "willingly permit" that territory to become "any new colony planted by Great Britain or any foreign monarchy." Even the Mexican government was aware of Polk's designs. Almost a year before the war broke out, one British diplomat reported that "Mexico is abt to send an expedition into the Californias to protect them" as the "Govt greatly fears the intentions of the United States upon them" and the "sale of these provinces to England is talked of if she would purchase them." The acquisition of California was the main goal of the war, but Polk had good reason to keep public and political attention trained on the Nueces Strip.[33]

From the outset, Polk and his secretary of state, James Buchanan, tried to control the narrative of the war. The two allies engineered the conflict so that the United States appeared to be on the defensive, shielding Texas's boundary—which they imagined as the Rio Grande—from a Mexican invasion. Both men took great care to prevent the war from being interpreted as one of conquest, a perception that would not only delegitimize it but also potentially make the violence unpopular among Whigs and jeopardize Polk's reelection. It was thus essential that Mexico be perceived as the aggressor. As Ulysses S. Grant, who served as a lieutenant in the U.S. Army under General Zachary Taylor in Mexico, later recalled, "We were sent to provoke a fight, but it was essential that Mexico should commence it." Consequently, the United States could assure the world that no alternative remained but war.[34]

The conflict with Mexico was intended to hinge upon self-preservation, the first law of nations. But to maintain this line of argument and avoid a potentially costly and unpopular conflict, Polk and Buchanan would have to position the United States not just as the victim but also as the peacemaker. "Devoted" to "honorable peace," Polk postured that he was "determined that the evils of the war shall not be protracted one day longer than shall be rendered absolutely necessary by the Mexican Republic." Polk decided that the quickest way to ensure peace was to have a man on the ground in Mexico, ready to draw up a treaty at any moment. As Polk told Nicholas Trist, "If you can but succeed in restoring peace, you will render a great service to your country and acquire great distinction for yourself." Though Polk did not know it, these words would guide Trist's actions in Mexico for the next year.[35]

By the time Trist landed at Vera Cruz in 1847 disguised as Dr. Tarro, the war had threatened to deviate from the script manufactured by Polk and Buchanan. In the north, General Taylor and his four-thousand-man army defeated Mexican forces in battles at Palo Alto, Resaca de la Palma, and Monterrey. In the west, General Stephen Watts Kearny and his fifteen hundred army regulars took possession of New Mexico and fought through the Mexican province of Chihuahua. Later, General Winfield Scott would capture Vera Cruz and march inland, eventually occupying Mexico City. But even with these military successes in hand, the Mexicans still refused to surrender.[36]

Reports of atrocities committed by American regulars and volunteers against Mexican troops and civilians mounted. U.S. forces routinely killed, scalped, raped, and robbed Mexican men and women. As the *St. Louis Republican* lamented, "Let us no longer complain of Mexican barbarity—poor, degraded, 'priest ridden' as she is," when U.S. troops committed their own barbarous acts against Mexicans every day. A British consul reported the "gross disregard of the courtesies of civilized war" and complained of the "ignominious conditions which they [U.S. forces] attempted to impose on a brave enemy." While the regular army was "fairly disciplined," the volunteers were a different story. When one thousand Texas Rangers, whom the official called the "worst part of the population of Texas," landed at Vera Cruz, they were "let loose on the unfortunate inhabitants of the rural districts of this neighbourhood, whom they shoot, and whose property they destroy without mercy." The consul warned that the conflict was turning into "a war altogether of extermination." In a private meeting, Buchanan even confided his fears about the war to Lord Palmerston. He "avoided speaking on the subject of the war with Mexico" except to share that the "President & his Minrs. are much embarrassed at the present state of things."[37]

When Nicholas Trist arrived in Mexico in the spring of 1847, there was no sign of peace. General Scott's march into the Mexican interior was already yielding devastating results. With the Mexican army routed at Cerro Gordo and the city of Puebla falling to U.S. forces by early summer, the capture of Mexico City appeared imminent. Trist begged Scott to halt his advance, arguing that the further encroachment of U.S. troops hurt the "prospect" of a treaty. Scott, who viewed Trist's arrival as a usurpation of his own power, refused to open a backchannel with the Mexican government on the envoy's behalf and remained wary. But seeing the carnage and the inequity of the war firsthand, Trist declared that "this is a state of things which cannot last forever." Desperate to begin treaty negotiations with the Mexican government, he approached British diplomats.[38]

A year earlier, Polk and Buchanan had declined Britain's offer to help mediate an end to the war. Just as in Cuba, British imperial officials were pouring resources into the fledgling nation of Mexico in an attempt to stop American proslavery imperialism. Baring Brothers had helped finance Mexico's independence from the Spanish Empire in 1821, and in exchange the new Mexican government had committed to close ties to the British Empire as well as the abolition of slavery. With war imminent in 1846, Mexican president Mariano Paredes turned to the British Foreign Office, wanting to know whether Mexico "might count upon the assistance of England in her present perilous condition" and "prevent this Country from becoming the prey of the United States."[39]

British officials declined military involvement, but they did pledge to informally arbitrate a peace settlement. Lord Palmerston advised British diplomats to "use your good offices upon every favourable opportunity" to help settle the conflict "with as little sacrifice to Mexico as may be possible." So when Nicholas Trist, isolated and rebuffed, approached British agents in Mexico, they attempted to use him—as they had done in Havana years earlier—to curtail U.S. imperialism. British minister Charles Bankhead worked quickly, forwarding Buchanan's peace terms to the Mexican government. He also dispatched his own emissary, Secretary of the Legation Edward Thornton, to work as the primary intermediary between Trist and Mexican officials.[40]

In July and early August, Trist's peace negotiations faced two major obstacles: an imminent assault by U.S. troops on Mexico City and the internal political strife that threatened to tear Mexico apart. This chaos was in part the handiwork of Polk and his administration. A year earlier, Polk had facilitated the return of exiled Mexican general Antonio López de Santa Anna—of the Battle of the Alamo infamy—from Cuba. In exchange for a hefty payoff, Santa Anna pledged to make peace and cede the Mexican territory that Polk wanted. But instead of making good on his agreement, Santa Anna installed himself as president of the republic and commander of its army, promptly leading his troops into battle against the Americans. Santa Anna's appointment, which had been viewed with suspicion by many Mexicans, intensified political rivalries. His followers, the Santanistas, exploited the enmity between the various political factions that had sprung up within the federalists and centralists, each of whom mobilized its own troops—sometimes against each other. These divisions presented Trist with a quandary. Santa Anna had little support in the Mexican Congress, but he was close to commanding dictatorial powers. Yet it was through Santa Anna alone that "any chance whatever of establishing peace present[ed] itself."[41]

To negotiate a peace, Trist would have to avoid being mired in the factions that beset the government. Still, he remained bullish about his prospects after U.S. and Mexican forces agreed to an armistice in August. "The negotiation of the treaty," Trist told Buchanan, "I look upon as next to certain." The difficulty lay in ratification. Whether the various Mexican factions could overcome their rivalries and accept a joint treaty remained to be seen. The British minister to Mexico, Charles Bankhead, doubted such an outcome. It would be useless to tell the government not to throw away "so valuable an opportunity of releasing themselves from their perilous position." The Mexicans "cannot be convinced of their inability to compete with their neighbor," Bankhead wrote haughtily, because "their self-conceit and regard for the success of local and unimportant political intrigues, bear down all truly national or patriotick feelings." In Bankhead's eyes, factionalism would trump nationalism, thus spelling the end of Mexican independence.[42]

As Trist waded into initial peace talks with Mexican officials, he encountered an unanticipated problem. Mexico's demands for peace were shaped by the officials' perceptions of the cause of the war. During the August armistice, Trist outlined the terms approved by Buchanan: a $15 million indemnity paid to Mexico in exchange for the cession of all land stretching west from the Rio Grande along the thirty-second parallel. The ministers rejected this offer. They refused to cede New Mexico, the Nueces Strip, or California, though they did agree to accept Texas's annexation to the United States. For the Mexican commissioners, the actual cause of the present conflict was the Texas Revolution of 1835–1836. Indeed, though many foreign nations had established diplomatic relations with the new Texas Republic after 1836, Mexico had refused to recognize its independence. And when the United States acted, under President Tyler's direction, to annex Texas in 1845, Mexican officials viewed the move as tantamount to war.[43]

Even so, in the summer of 1847, Mexican officials decided to agree to the U.S. claim to Texas, an action that "removes the cause of the war," which "should at once cease." With this, Mexican leaders rejected Buchanan's ploy for additional territory. Since neither New Mexico nor California pertained to the Texas Revolution, they could not be a part of the 1847 peace deal. If the United States wanted this territory, it could gain title to it solely through conquest or purchase. But as the Mexican commissioners reminded Trist, "It would be repugnant to every idea of justice, to wage war against a nation for no other reason than her refusal to sell territory."[44]

The Mexican officials' counterproposal did not meet any of the U.S. demands, but Trist forwarded the request to Washington anyway. Buchanan and Polk were livid, blaming him for not pushing their terms more forcefully. Mexico's response was intolerable, Buchanan fumed, since it would force the United States to "abandon that portion of our country where Mexico attacked our forces and on our right to which the Whigs have raised such an unfounded clamor." What Buchanan did not acknowledge was that Mexico had called the Polk administration's bluff. A murky and problematic cause of the war could only mean a messy and contested outcome.[45]

Unsurprisingly, the U.S.–Mexico peace talks collapsed after only two weeks. An end to the armistice soon followed. General Scott and his troops resumed their march westward toward Mexico City, with their columns under constant attack by Mexican guerrilla fighters. To protect themselves, U.S. forces began "burning every home & village on that line of road." Though Scott sustained losses to his convoy, he and his troops stormed the gates of Mexico City in September. Santa Anna fled with his forces and resigned, leaving Scott to occupy the city, while the Mexican government relocated to Querétaro and appointed a new president, Manuel de la Peña y Peña.[46]

Nicholas Trist and the British diplomats continued to lobby for peace. He believed that persuading Mexican officials to accept Buchanan's version of the proposal meant persuading them that the United States had a right to land not just in Texas, but also in New Mexico and California.

Thornton, however, disapproved of Trist's "long and, I think, rather labored argument." Thornton suggested to Lord Palmerston that the important point was Trist's offer to reopen negotiations and "renew friendly relations" between the United States and Mexico. Nonetheless, to extract the vast Mexican territory that Polk and Buchanan wanted, Trist knew he had to persuade Mexican officials to change their minds about the cause of the war. It was not about Texan settlers' imperialistic ambitions, he tried to suggest, but rather about Mexican aggression on U.S. soil.[47]

It was possible that Trist did not grasp how ludicrous this claim appeared to the Mexican commissioners. Or perhaps he was simply seeking to fulfill his duty to a sitting U.S. president, trying to fit a square peg into a round hole. To achieve Polk and Buchanan's land grab, Trist was at a loss: how might he deploy international law to legitimize blatant U.S. imperialism? The only way for the United States to legally seize half of Mexico's territory, he concluded, was to argue that the conflict was a "just war" waged against an aggressive neighbor. In a long letter to his Mexican counterparts, Trist imparted a convoluted history lesson. After gaining independence and recognition in 1836, Texas then gained admission to the American federal union in 1845, entitling it to U.S. protection against invasion. But Texas could be protected only if its borders were defined, and, according to Texans, its southern border was the Rio Grande. Even so, Trist maintained, a boundary could not exist except by "agreement and recognition" of the "two coterminous nations." Despite President Polk's overtures to the Mexican government to determine a boundary and avoid a "collision," that government had refused to negotiate, much less recognize Texas.[48]

Here Trist's argument began to wobble. The cause of the war, he declared, was Mexico's "pertinacious refusal" to establish a border, and because of that, confusion over the Nueces Strip had ensued. Mexican forces crossing the Rio Grande in early 1846 "constituted a hostile invasion" against which U.S. forces quickly retaliated. But this was not conquest, in Trist's telling. It was "retention of territory" that "a neighbor, by forcing you into a war has compelled you to occupy, after every possible means has been exhausted by you to preserve peace." This legitimated a title by conquest in which "any member of the great family of nations may appeal to the certainty that it will be pronounced good" in the "eyes of a candid world." The United States had assumed the "character of a generous conqueror" who sought to reconcile the right to retain a "portion of his conquests" with the interests of Mexico by offering "pecuniary relief"— a multimillion-dollar indemnity. Added to that, since the land that the United States claimed in New Mexico and California was "remote and uninhabited," its loss would be "little felt" by Mexican officials, who maintained nominal and "purely sterile" authority over the districts.[49]

Back in Washington, a young Whig named Abraham Lincoln seized upon the stumble in Trist's argument. A "just war" could be proven only if Mexico had invaded *uncontested* U.S. territory. President Polk had hit hard on this point in late 1846, soon after persuading Congress to declare war on Mexico and appropriate resources to the tune of fifty thousand volunteers and $10 million. In his annual message to Congress, Polk insisted that Mexican forces had "invaded our territory, and commenced hostilities by attacking our forces." It was Mexico's fault, not America's, for starting an offensive war and "shedding the blood of our citizens on our own soil." Later in the speech, Polk did, in fact, acknowledge the contested nature of that "spot" on the Nueces Strip; he alluded to John Slidell's failed mission in 1845, which had sought to "adjust all questions in dispute" and address "questions of boundary" in that very territory.[50]

In late 1847, Lincoln, a freshman representative from Illinois, analyzed Polk's message and three others in what became known as the "Spot Resolutions," hoping to answer a simple query: Was the land where American blood was "spilled" ever under the government or laws of the United States? Though Lincoln found Polk's logic "like one in the half insane excitement of a fevered dream," he concluded that the answer to his question was no. "The soil was not ours," he explained to his former law partner, since "Congress did not annex or attempt to annex it." There was no "invasion" of U.S. territory since the Nueces Strip still belonged to Mexico. The danger of the situation, he warned, was an executive that could "make war at pleasure." Other Whigs in Congress shared Lincoln's alarm, and those in the House eventually voted to censure Polk in early 1848 for "unnecessarily and unconstitutionally" waging war against Mexico.[51]

As the war dragged into the autumn of 1847, the prospect for peace remained dim. After holding office less than two months, President Peña y Peña resigned, hoping to negotiate directly with Trist, and Pedro María de Anaya was appointed interim president in his place. But factionalism continued to plague the Mexican government, which favored a variety of strategies: a guerrilla war against U.S. forces, complete annexation by the United States, or intervention by France or Britain. The main obstacle to a peace treaty, however, remained the deeply divided Mexican Congress, which did not have a quorum. Without it, lawmakers could not appoint ministers to negotiate for peace, much less ratify a treaty.[52]

In the middle of this turmoil, Polk and Buchanan recalled Trist to Washington. Polk and his cabinet decided that if the U.S. envoy remained in Mexico any longer, the government there would become convinced of his government's desperation to end the war, paving the way for a peace treaty favoring Mexican terms. With Mexico City in U.S. hands, Polk believed that he held all the cards. He also set new sights on acquiring an even larger chunk of Mexico than originally proposed. Polk suggested that the negotiators demand control of Sonora, Baja, and the entire Gulf of California. Other members of his cabinet, including Buchanan, openly supported acquiring all of Mexico.[53]

But key Democratic supporters differed. Andrew Jackson Donelson, Trist's West Point classmate and a nephew of Andrew Jackson, urged Buchanan to "make peace as soon as you can." The war would "break our party down if we go into the elections with it on our shoulders." Donelson was convinced that there was a "mistake about the value of the country west of the Rio Grande," which was not "worth ten cents the acre, and is infinitely below standard of any agricultural section of our present Union." Unless Buchanan and Polk wanted to cede power to the Whigs in the coming election, peace, according to Donelson, was the only option. But Polk would not budge. Even under heavy criticism, the president determined not to make any more overtures for peace. If Mexico desired an end to the conflict, then any new terms would have to be directed to General Scott and sent to Washington.[54]

Back in Mexico, both Scott and Trist recoiled at the scope of Polk's new ambitions. In their opinion, there were only two options for the United States. One was that Mexico "should be abandoned and a certain length of frontier taken possession of." The second was permanent occupation by U.S. forces and subsequent annexation. Deploying a racist argument that would later be widely circulated by Polk's Whig opponents, Scott deemed that occupation and acquisition of most—if not all—of Mexico was impossible. Out of eight million Mexicans, he observed, "not more than one million" were of "pure European blood." Rather, an "exceedingly inferior" indigenous and mixed-race group comprised a majority of the population. Annexation, Scott charged, would portend a dangerous future: "mixing up that race with our own." Scott's fellow Whig politician Henry Clay reaffirmed this belief, questioning whether Mexico and the United States could be "blended together in one harmonious mass, and happily governed by one common authority." History, Clay warned, showed the "difficulty of combining and consolidating" both "conquering and conquered" peoples.[55]

But with his recall on the horizon, Nicholas Trist made no more pretensions that the war was anything but one of conquest. With Polk off his back, Trist admitted that it was impossible to argue that the conflict was a "just war." Truth be told, the "iniquity of the war" troubled him and was a "thing for every right-minded American to be ashamed of." Deferring an official announcement of his return to Washington, Trist resolved, with assistance from British diplomats, to continue to try to strike a deal with Mexican authorities, with "as little exacting as possible from Mexico." However, President Anaya had just taken power, and he had yet to nominate and approve commissioners who could negotiate with the U.S. envoy.[56]

His patience exhausted, Trist threatened to give up and go home. In November 1847, he wrote to Peña y Peña, admitting that his negotiating authority had been revoked. If Peña y Peña, Anaya, and other advocates of peace wanted to end the war, they needed to approach General Scott. Not more than two weeks later, Trist changed his mind. "For good or for evil," Trist confided to Thornton, "I am now resolved and committed to carry home with me a Treaty of Peace." To him the question had become "What is my line of duty to my government and my country?" Because "Peace is the earnest wish of both," Trist felt morally obligated to continue at his post, no matter what the cost. But the treaty would need to be based on the original proposal, and nothing less, the "boundary" being the Rio Bravo and the thirty-second parallel, which extended to the Pacific.[57]

Trist knew he would need to act quickly. If the opportunity was not seized while Mexico's Liberal Party was still in power, then every "chance for making a Treaty at all will be lost for an indefinite period, probably for ever." Mexico's tenuous political situation—and the threats to peace—were underscored by the increasing power of the Liberal Party's enemies. The "puros" wanted to continue the war, believing that Britain would soon come to Mexico's aid. And the pro-monarchist faction had already sent messages to several European states, with some asserting that Prince Leopold of Belgium would be "a very fit person to occupy the Mexican throne." Santa Anna, for his part, "had no hopes for saving his country but by establishing a monarchy."[58]

Trist's decision to stay in Mexico might have been a final chance for Mexican authorities to secure peace, but it was also a last opportunity for Polk, Buchanan, and other Democratic war hawks to control the narrative of the war. If Trist left Mexico empty-handed, then the "character" of the war would be "altogether changed, entirely reversed," he told Buchanan. What had been a "purely defensive war on our part" would "become a war of conquest" driven by "no other motive than acquisition." The conflict, Trist asserted, would be viewed as illegitimate in the eyes of the world, particularly because of the "weakness & defencelessness of Mexico." In a war of conquest, there were only two potential outcomes: the "subjugation of its inhabitants" by the U.S. government or the use of military power to enable Mexico to establish "a government for themselves."[59]

Both these options, Trist thought, would jeopardize sovereignty. Like Scott, he believed that annexing Mexico would create an "incalculable danger." The reason was simple. Americans were white and the United States was "above all others" among the "nations of the earth." Mexicans, by contrast, were nonwhite and thus inferior. The "unhappy People" of Mexico "do not so much constitute a Nation at all," Trist suggested, as an "incoherent collection of fragments of the human family." Consequently, Mexico occupied the "very lowest point" on the "scale" of nations, "beneath even the one proper to the Indian tribes within our borders." Indeed, Mexico's "existence as a Nation is limited to the one single fact, that their independence is recognized by the rest of mankind." Without a peace treaty that allowed Mexico to retain at least half of its original territory, Trist suggested, the nation would be unable to preserve itself, and soon descend into anarchy.[60]

Trist's argument pointed to recent Mexican history. Beginning in the 1830s, Native Americans unleashed a campaign of violence in northern Mexico, decimating the settler population, crippling the economy, and creating "deserts" where towns and farms once thrived. As the historian Brian DeLay has argued, Mexico's seeming inability to defend its northern borders against "barbarians" was taken to further justify the U.S. invasion of Mexico. In other words, it was Mexico's failure to repel Native peoples that compromised its sovereignty, breaking it into "fragments," as Trist asserted.[61]

Trist remained in Mexico for several more months, eventually securing peace with the Mexican commissioners—with British diplomatic assistance—in what became the Treaty of Guadeloupe-Hidalgo. Through this 1848 accord, which broadly followed the contours of Buchanan's original proposal, the United States acquired about half of Mexico's territory, including the much sought-after California, where gold had been discovered a few weeks earlier. But conveniently for Polk, Trist's treaty also rendered the primary issue at home—whether the Mexican-American War had truly commenced on U.S. soil—a moot point. The new agreement erased any doubt about borders by creating a "boundary line with due precision upon authoritative maps," Polk declared to Congress, establishing "upon the ground landmarks which shall allow the limits of both Republics."[62]

Without Trist's continued efforts and British diplomatic interference, there might not have been a peace in 1848. Still, his actions in Mexico were guided by a perception of the international system as vastly unequal, with states like Britain at the top, and weaker, nonwhite states like Mexico at the bottom. This hierarchy of nations enabled more powerful nations to prey on weaker ones, violating their sovereignty with impunity— exactly what the United States had tried to do in Mexico. As Trist explained it, his motivation for peace was the "iniquity of the war, as an abuse of power on our part." This mirrored what had happened in Cuba a decade earlier. Britain had tried to take advantage of America's weaker status, bullying it into collaborating to end the illegal slave trade. Trist believed that both cases constituted blatant violations of the law of nations, abuses that he highlighted publicly and passionately. But in the case of Mexico, Trist tried to use British power to limit America's, hoping to preserve some semblance of Mexican independence.[63]

Trist's defiance of an official government recall in 1847 left him ostracized and politically untouchable. Fifteen years later, penniless and languishing as a clerk for the Philadelphia, Wilmington & Baltimore Railroad, Trist was still waiting for the government to pay him $14,559.90 for his assignment in Mexico. After voting Republican in 1860, Trist, once a staunch Democrat, remained hopeful that Lincoln would take steps to reimburse him his lost wages, but the wartime president took no action.

Finally, his wife took up her own pen, drafting an appeal to a wealthy entrepreneur who had benefited from the 1848 treaty, in the hope that he might send some money. In this letter, Virginia Randolph Trist paraphrased her husband's arguments for defying his recall and remaining in Mexico, offering the most explicit explanation of his struggle to protect Mexican sovereignty. "Could these Mexicans have seen into my heart at that moment," she summarized from her husband's recollections, "they would have known . . . *my* feeling of shame as an American." Ultimately, her effort was unsuccessful. It was not until 1871 that Charles Sumner, a Massachusetts Republican who had once been caned and bloodied on the floor in Congress, would push through legislation that finally compensated Trist for his lost State Department salary.[64]

PART TWO
Slavery

THREE

Thomas Jefferson Randolph

Slave Leasing and the Railroad in Virginia, 1826–1852

A COLD WIND RIFLED THROUGH THE crowd gathered on the West Lawn of Monticello, failing to deter a flurry of raised hands. Before them, a twenty-six-year-old man named Israel Gillette was standing on the auction block—one of nearly 130 enslaved people owned by the recently deceased Thomas Jefferson to do so on that wintry January day. One man in the crowd, the Virginia lawmaker and future secretary of the navy Thomas Walker Gilmer, made the winning bid, offering five hundred dollars for Gillette, a former household and textile worker, and postillion for Jefferson's horse-drawn carriage. After learning his fate, Gillette could only watch in horror as dozens of his family members also ascended the auction block, including his parents. His elderly father, the estate appraisers declared, was valued at a mere fifty dollars, while his mother was deemed "worth nothing." As horrific as the sale was for Gillette, he also described it as the inevitable outcome of bondage—the auction was the "usual course" of those "born slaves," including his four children.[1]

For African Americans, the death of their enslaver devastated families and dictated futures, the tragic effects of which would ripple across generations, and still impacts lives today. Between 1826 and 1865, African Americans sold away from Monticello were forcibly taken to Arkansas, Missouri, Kentucky, Alabama, and across Virginia. As Peter Fossett, a man once enslaved at Monticello, later recalled, the forced separation of families meant that "we were scattered all over the country, never to meet each other again until we meet in another world." Indeed, when Fossett was sold "like a horse" in 1827, he faced decades more of enslavement, which he met with decades more of resistance, owing to his fierce resolution to "get free, or die in the attempt." Only five African Americans, out of the approximately two hundred people Jefferson owned in 1826, gained their freedom through the terms of his will, including two of his own children.[2]

Much of the rest of Jefferson's property, with the exception of his Palladian villa and land, was also sold. Jefferson's white descendants were among the buyers. His daughter Martha Jefferson Randolph bought a tureen, mahogany table, clock, thermometer, and several prints for $234. His granddaughter Cornelia Randolph purchased China cups and saucers for $1.50. Jefferson's grandson-in-law Joseph Coolidge spent $167 on engravings, paintings, and three Houdon busts—of George Washington, John Paul Jones, and Voltaire. Another grandson-in-law, Nicholas Trist, shelled out about $16 for odds and ends, including a writing table and a "shower bath." In addition to a coffee roaster, a George Washington medal, a pair of globes, and other items, Jefferson's grandson Thomas Jefferson Randolph (known by his family as Jeff) bought sixteen African Americans, including several members of the Granger family, for $6,200.[3]

Born at Monticello in 1792, Jeff Randolph was the eldest child of Martha Jefferson and the Virginia planter-politician Thomas Mann Randolph, Jr. As a teenager—and at his grandfather's behest—he studied botany, natural science, and anatomy in Philadelphia, though he showed little aptitude or interest in intellectual pursuits. Back home in Virginia, Jeff took a shine to farming, eventually assuming management of his grandfather's enterprise at the Monticello home farm, one of four "quarter farms" that comprised the entire five-thousand-acre estate, in 1815. Two years later he took control of two other Monticello tracts, Lego and Tufton, and rented the farms' enslaved people from his grandfather. Jeff later married Jane Hollins Nicholas, daughter of Wilson Cary Nicholas, a former Virginia governor.[4]

Jeff Randolph often found himself bearing the brunt of family problems, such as the estrangement of his mercurial and insolvent father and the violent alcoholism of his brother-in-law Charles Bankhead. After Randolph managed to purchase his father's Edgehill plantation, located three miles from Monticello, at a foreclosure auction, his grandfather died, leaving Randolph responsible for paying off a debt that had ballooned to $107,000—about $3.2 million in today's money. The estate sales that Randolph ordered in 1827 resulted in the sale of nearly a hundred people from Monticello and an additional seventy people from Jefferson's Poplar Forest plantation in Bedford County, but netted only about $50,000. And the

Charles Willson Peale, *Portrait of Thomas Jefferson Randolph*, 1808. (© Thomas Jefferson Foundation at Monticello.)

1829 sale of thirty-one enslaved people at the Eagle Tavern in downtown Charlottesville generated just over $8,000. Still, these three auctions left a little less than half of Thomas Jefferson's original debt still to be paid.[5]

Although nearly all wealthy Virginia landowners owed debts, the scale of Jefferson's "pecuniary embarrassment" and the threat of insolvency jeopardized the Randolph family's status. "If a man is poor and slothful he had better go and hang [himself], as the only evidence which he can give of being useful to his fellow man is by getting out of the way,"

Randolph told his mother. In an era in which indebtedness was conflated with dependence and servitude, Randolph's comment pointed to the desperation with which he viewed his financial situation. Suicide, he suggested, might be more "useful" than continuing to bear the burden of a debt he could not possibly discharge. It was thus imperative that Randolph find a way to pay off the inherited debt, becoming an independent property holder and "master" once more, or else get "out of the way."[6]

Initially, in the 1820s and early 1830s, Randolph developed strategies to monetize Jefferson's legacy and launch his own career in state politics. He planned to edit and then sell an edition of his grandfather's letters, netting big profits in the process. When this deal fell through, he turned to the Monticello mansion itself, believing that a "relic" of the third president would fetch an enormous sum. But the house and surrounding lands sold for a paltry $7,500 in 1831. Desperate for cash in the mid-1830s, Randolph deployed a new strategy—monetizing the labor and bodies of African Americans. As an investor in and contractor for the Virginia Central Railroad (later named the Blue Ridge Railroad), Randolph took full advantage of the economic opportunity that various massive infrastructure projects brought to Virginia, reaping huge profits from hiring out dozens of enslaved men and boys. In the end it was the railroad that made "family fortunes appear to be taking a turn" for the better, allowing Randolph to pay off debts and restore his status as an independent property holder, a free and equal member of the planter class.[7]

Beginning in the 1840s, Randolph's lucrative role as a railroad contractor linked him to a new, industrialized form of slavery taking shape in nineteenth-century Virginia, one that relied on large numbers of enslaved African Americans to labor in ironworks, in coal and salt mines, and on canals, turnpikes, and railroads. Contemporary political economists had not anticipated this development. The "rise of cities" in Virginia, declared the William and Mary professor Thomas Roderick Dew, meant that "less slave labor and more free labor will be requisite." Baltimore, Dew pointed out, exemplified this process—industrialization was "fast making Maryland a non slave-holding state." But Dew's proto-industrial free labor system failed to materialize in Virginia. Even in a state where it was too cold to grow cotton, slavery exploded, the enslaved population surging from 287,959 in 1790 to 448,987 in 1840. Likewise, the rapid commercialization of slavery—leasing, mortgaging, insuring, and buying and selling human beings—demonstrated not just the institution's survival but also the speed and scale of its expansion.[8]

A spate of new infrastructure projects in the 1840s and 1850s, especially railroads and turnpikes, increased the demand for enslaved workers to clear land and blast through rock, build roadbeds, and lay tracks. Chartered in 1836, the Virginia Central Railroad (originally the Louisa Railroad) snaked northwest from Richmond through Henrico, Hanover, and Louisa counties before terminating in the hamlet of Gordonsville. Though it was intended to link the Shenandoah Valley to the eastern part of the state via Harrisonburg, the state legislature amended the charter in 1847, extending the railroad from Gordonsville to Charlottesville. In 1849, the General Assembly chartered yet another rail project—the Virginia Central Railroad—to construct tracks and a series of tunnels that extended westward to Waynesboro. Though historians of capitalism and slavery have emphasized that the expansion of the cotton empire in the Mississippi River valley fueled demand for captives in the Upper South, the contours of the slave market in Virginia were also shaped by large-scale infrastructure projects within the state.[9]

The railroads, which passed near Jeff Randolph's plantation at Edgehill, buoyed his finances not just through slave leasing—which generated an eye-popping $70,000—but also because new turnpikes and railroads drove up land prices. His twenty-five-hundred-acre estate at Edgehill was valued at $58,359 in 1841 before jumping to $74,437 in 1852 and finally topping out at $89,475 on the eve of the Civil War. Randolph may have failed to monetize his grandfather's legacy, but he soundly succeeded in profiting from the bodies of African Americans, drastically improving his family's fortunes by 1860.[10]

After 1826, Thomas Jefferson's indebtedness and the sale of nearly two hundred enslaved people created an image problem for the Randolph family, threatening to derail their moneymaking strategy. During both the 1827 estate sale on the West Lawn of Monticello and the 1829 sale at Eagle Tavern in downtown Charlottesville, Jeff Randolph tried to alter the public perception of what was, in reality, the rapid liquidation of his grandfather's property. He and his siblings reaffirmed their commitment to keeping enslaved people "in the family," or at least out of the internal slave trade. For example, Randolph deflected offers from Deep South slave buyers.

When a Georgia planter proposed buying all of Jefferson's human property to settle a new cotton estate, Randolph flatly declined.[11]

According to Mary Randolph, Jeff's sister, what made the Monticello auction less "distressing" was that the enslaved people "with one exception I believe, are all sold to persons living in the State," with many in "this neighbourhood or the adjoining counties." By suggesting that Jefferson's white grandchildren did everything in their power to ameliorate the circumstances—selling African Americans to Jefferson's friends and contacts *within* Virginia—Jeff and Mary tried to salvage the family's good name.[12]

There was also the problem of Thomas Jefferson's financial ruin. Many white Americans saw his vast plantation landholdings, hundreds of enslaved people, grand Palladian villa, and uncontrolled spending as excessive and self-indulgent. Jefferson, by his own hand, had dug himself into an abyss of debt, many critics asserted. The third president's impoverished circumstances connoted not just dependence but also a kind of hubris and moral failure. In the wake of his death, it became publicly clear that overspending had been Jefferson's Achilles' heel. Randolph and his family members were keen to prevent this from becoming a flaw that marred Jefferson's legacy—and threatened their ability to profit from it.[13]

The mounting of a cogent defense of Jefferson's "pecuniary embarrassment" began almost immediately after his death. In 1826, Ellen Wayles Coolidge met one of her grandfather's devotees in Boston, who asked "how it came that having received from his father a large property, marrying an heiress & receiving for many years a regular salary from the public Treasury," Jefferson would have "fallen into the distress" which forced him to "sell his estate by lottery." Here the Boston admirer referenced Jefferson's ill-fated 1824 scheme to use a public lottery to pay down his debts and save his property, hoping to sell just over eleven thousand lottery tickets for ten dollars each, a hefty price tag for the day.[14]

This chance meeting convinced Ellen of the necessity of putting pen to paper. In collaboration with her mother, Martha Randolph, she reimagined Jefferson's financial situation as a "lost cause." Martha wrote the initial essay, then sent it to her daughter to "select what would be proper" and "what to with hold from the public." Ellen composed a whittled-down version of her mother's treatise, recasting Jefferson as a selfless patriot whose devotion to his country "prevailed over all considerations of personal interest." Ellen also absolved Jefferson of any agency in his own financial demise—since he had inherited his debt, he was simply a victim of economic forces beyond his control. Though the essay was never published, it still found its way into print: in the fall of 1826, John Thornton Kirkland, president of Harvard University, delivered an address on the "literary characters" of John Adams and Thomas Jefferson at the American Academy of Arts and Sciences in Boston. Ellen Coolidge "furnished the materials" on Jefferson, and Kirkland "used, in great part . . . her own words."[15]

But Jeff Randolph thought that his grandfather's refurbished image could also help finance his descendants. In the winter of 1826, Randolph was roving the drawing rooms of the Washington elite. After chatting with some representatives from Louisiana who spoke admiringly of his grandfather, Randolph thought he had happened upon a potential buyer of some Jefferson memorabilia. Presumably because of Jefferson's role in spearheading the Louisiana Purchase of 1803, the Louisiana State Legislature agreed to purchase his "bust by Caracci" for five thousand dollars in bank shares. The annual draw (interest) of four hundred dollars, Randolph calculated, would "produce a good deal of comfort" when combined with income reaped from yearly subscriptions to an edited volume of his grandfather's letters—a collection he was already beginning to assemble. In Randolph's estimation, the road to better "fortunes" would be short; he predicted that at the "end of two years our resources will have been collected and increased." After liquidating Jefferson's land and enslaved people, and then by selling Jefferson's letters and a bust, Jeff and the rest of the Randolph family hoped to "become inhabitants once more of Monticello" without public assistance.[16]

But this turned out to be only partially accurate. South Carolina lawmakers pledged ten thousand dollars in bank stock to support Martha Randolph and her dependents. Privately, the family hoped that other states would follow suit, offering financial support in recognition of Jefferson's public service and patriotism. "I do not suppose that the example of South Carolina will be followed by any of the other states," Mary Randolph lamented, but the state "will have done enough to lighten our burthen and perhaps to secure a subsistence" which might have been "difficult or impossible with our own unaided means." Her private admission that the "maintenance of our very large family" could not be achieved "unaided," showed the depths of their financial despair, as well as the importance of concealing it from the public.[17]

Other family members were more vocal about their desire for state support. Despite "sixty years of devoted services," Cornelia Randolph moaned, Jefferson's "children were left in beggary by the country to whom he had bequeathed them." She seemed unaware that neither the states nor the federal government were in the habit of supporting the descendants of public servants. If anything, states offered funding to indigent war widows who petitioned for assistance. When the public got wind of the Randolphs' private desire for state funds, few would look kindly upon an elite landowning family—whose patriarch had earned a substantial salary in his lifetime—scrounging for public support. Later, only one other state joined South Carolina in pledging bank shares to the Randolphs: Louisiana.[18]

As part of his effort to raise more money and prevent the sale of Monticello, Jeff Randolph had begun pushing for the publication of his grandfather's letters. His peers, however, warned against being too hasty. The famed orator and Massachusetts congressman Edward Everett implored Randolph to wait, advising that a well-chosen selection of letters might yield as much as $100,000. But Randolph was in the market for a quick return. When an Albany publishing house expressed interest in publishing forty thousand sets of Jefferson's writings, Randolph jumped at the chance. The deal soon fell through, and Randolph decided that his only option was to print the first edition at his own expense. He approached F. Carr and Company in Charlottesville, later complaining that the arrangement would leave him the "miserable pittance of $2 per copy." But then a Boston-based publisher, Bowen and Gray, agreed to print three thousand copies of the volumes for $6,000.[19]

Several leading politicians, including Everett, offered to help Randolph select letters for inclusion in the new collections, but the Randolph women performed most of the work. They spent hours poring over the letters and transcribing them for the printer, squabbling about which letters would be chosen and whether they would be edited. Martha Randolph whined that it would be "sacrilege" to "alter or add to the writings" of her father. Nicholas Trist warned that "if proper care were not exercised in the selection of the material," the "consequence" could be very damaging.[20]

But Jeff, who acted as the informal managing editor of the volumes, eventually won out. He argued in favor of letters that would generate the most popular interest "with a view to promote their sale." Randolph evinced little concern that his plan might backfire, but that was exactly what happened when the volumes hit the press in 1830. Jefferson's negative impressions of popular politicians and war heroes like Henry Lee and the marquis de Lafayette, in addition to his unpopular religious beliefs, cast the third president "in the most unfavorable light possible—indeed in a bad, very bad light," wrote Randolph's brother-in law Nicholas Trist. Still, what seemed even worse was that the volumes' sale hardly made a dent in the outstanding debt.[21]

The consequences of Randolph's miscalculation were swift and calamitous: Monticello would need to be sold. "There remain $30.000 of the debts still to be paid," Cornelia told her sister Ellen, and "he (brother J.) has made nothing from the publication of the manuscripts" of Jefferson's letters. Although Jeff initially thought the mansion and surrounding land could fetch close to $12,000, he had trouble finding a buyer; Virginia property was much less valuable than new cotton land in the Southwest. Monticello had also essentially been abandoned since the dispersal sale of 1827. "Numerous parties" of trespassers paraded around the vacant property, especially at night, stealing "every thing and any thing they fancied." Freed members of the extended Hemings family still living at Monticello, including John and Priscilla Hemmings and Wormley Hughes, were often reduced to the roles of guards and gatekeepers of the rapidly disintegrating mansion.[22]

In the end, the only person who expressed any interest in Monticello was an eccentric local druggist, Dr. James Barclay, who planned to turn the property into a silkworm farm. Before summer's end in 1831, Barclay had purchased the Monticello mansion and five hundred surrounding acres for a mere $7,500. "You will say it was a dreadfull sacrifice," Martha Randolph confided to her daughter, but the "debts are pressing, the place going to ruin, and no other offer." Barclay would retain possession of Monticello for only a few years, however. By 1834, his silkworm experiment had proven a bust, and Barclay handed off the property to a Jewish officer in the U.S. Navy, Uriah Phillips Levy, for $2,500.[23]

But making money was not the only reason for trading on Jefferson's reputation. Beginning in the 1820s, Jeff Randolph tried to exploit his familial connection to the third president to help launch a career in state politics. His political ideas were far from new—in most cases he simply repeated his grandfather's proposals, believing that this would be the best path to boosting his reputation and social status. Things began haltingly, however. Randolph lost his first two bids for a seat in the Virginia legislature, in 1829 and 1830, but finally triumphed in 1831. Between 1833 and 1845, Randolph and Valentine Southall—a planter and lawyer who had once been a frequent visitor to Monticello—would essentially alternate as the elected representative for Albemarle County in the Virginia House of Delegates.[24]

Few members of Randolph's family could understand his political ambitions. His mother-in-law wondered how Randolph could "justify the neglecting of his own business" at Edgehill plantation, not to mention his wife. Another Virginian, Ann Maury, believed Randolph "well qualified to shine in social life," but thought it a shame that he "should desire to be a politician" when he so clearly excelled at farming. But Randolph was hopeful that a political career—sustained by recycling Jeffersonian ideas—would catapult him into more exalted circles. Wielding more power and political influence would also increase Randolph's chances of making money. Without additional income, he feared, the extended Randolph family might need to sell up and head west.[25]

When Randolph did assume his seat in the House of Delegates, in 1831, it was in the wake of the Nat Turner revolt. A few months before, in the Tidewater, Virginia, Turner and a band of nearly sixty African Americans had beaten, stabbed, and shot about fifty-five white people. The response from white people to Turner's uprising was swift and brutal: men hunted down and killed around forty Black people, and after the trials of the insurgents, a further thirty people were executed. On the heels of a large manhunt, Turner himself was hanged and skinned, the spectacle of his death intended to deter other insurrection attempts by enslaved people and free African Americans.[26]

In Randolph's view, the Nat Turner revolt demonstrated how prophetic Jefferson had been when he wrote that failing to abolish slavery would lead to a deadly race war. Randolph simply restated this prediction, telling the House of Delegates that there was "one circumstance" that would be "inevitable in the fullness of time; a dissolution of this union." And in a proposal that cribbed heavily from the "ex post nati" scheme first outlined in Jefferson's *Notes on the State of Virginia* (1782), Randolph laid out a gradual emancipation plan that would remove infants from their mothers—and enslavers—in 1840, with full freedom and deportation commencing in 1858. The only way to avert a race war was to "remove" free and enslaved Blacks beyond the borders of the United States, he argued. Seeing himself and Jefferson as cut from the same antislavery cloth, Randolph declared that he was an "avowed abolitionist, indifferent as to the means, but inflexible as to the purpose." Randolph read his antislavery proposal, which took two hours to deliver, to the Virginia legislature. But the delegates, unmoved by Randolph's reassertion of Jefferson's antislavery scheme, voted down the plan, 73 to 58.[27]

Despite the unpopularity of his speeches on slavery in 1832, Randolph managed to eke out reelection later that year by 95 votes. While his mother-in-law, Peggy Nicholas, considered him a "Mad Man" for running at all, she conceded that he was still popular among "good Republicans" in the poorer, western part of the county. Faced with another political crisis during his new term in Richmond, Randolph again decided to fashion himself as a repository and guardian of his grandfather's ideas. The exigency in question was the Nullification Crisis. In 1828 many southerners, particularly South Carolinians, had bristled in reaction to the passage of the so-called Tariff of Abominations, a protective duty meant to protect U.S. manufacturing that they deemed baneful to southern agriculture. Even though President Andrew Jackson lowered the tariff, South Carolinians pronounced it unconstitutional, threatening to secede if the federal government tried to force compliance.[28]

Randolph was outraged at South Carolina's actions. The crisis, he told his childhood friend William Cabell Rives, was "a struggle against a new principle": the "right of constitutional peaceable secession at will by any state desiring it." He decried South Carolinians' invocation of the Virginia and Kentucky Resolutions of 1798—penned anonymously by Jefferson and Madison in response to the Alien and Sedition Acts—to legitimize their call for secession in 1832. "Mr. Jefferson never entertained such an opinion," Randolph declared emphatically. In a speech before the state legislature, Randolph asserted that Jefferson's Revolutionary era principles— the limits on federal authority within the states—were "as unlike the new doctrines as the pure truths revealed in the Sermon on the Mount."[29]

Several legislators scoffed at Randolph's speech. One lawmaker declared that Randolph "completely overthrew all the established principles of Mr. Jefferson, whom he conclusively proved to be a fool." Another delegate criticized Randolph's efforts to consider himself the "repository of Mr. Jefferson's sentiments & principles." He advised Randolph to surrender the "keeping of his grandfather's fame to the American people" and to stop criticizing South Carolina, whose legislature had given the Randolphs thousands of dollars after Jefferson's death. Meanwhile, the Virginia debate ended in a draw. While the legislature decreed that the "Principles of '98" did not authorize secession, neither did they legitimize federal intervention in state affairs.[30]

The unpopularity of Randolph's speeches in the 1830s on antislavery and federalism, and the Randolphs' inability to sell either Jefferson's house or his edited letters at a profit seemed to indicate how marginal Jefferson and his white descendants had become. In 1833, Martha Randolph observed that "Virginia is no longer a home for the family of Thomas Jefferson." Even Monticello seemed to reflect her family's steep decline. The estate was "so totally changed" that it resembled a "mass of ruins," the once manicured West Lawn plowed up and planted in corn, its august oaks and chestnuts chopped down for firewood. Indeed, she lamented, no sign of Jefferson remained, save the newly sculpted "monument" that was his tombstone.[31]

Feeling marginalized in Virginia, the Randolphs decided that there were "good reasons for quitting the state" and eyed better prospects out west. Peggy Nicholas hoped the family would relocate to far western Virginia, near what is present-day Wheeling, West Virginia. Predicting the outbreak of civil war, Nicholas believed that Virginia would become the main battleground in the contest; she urged her daughter Jane to leave before the violence began. Jane's brother suggested that the family settle in Louisiana, while her sister advocated joining Robert Owen's New Harmony experiment in utopianism in Indiana. For her part, Jane, still shaken by the violence of 1831, was willing to go anywhere that outlawed slavery, and floated the prospect of Cincinnati.[32]

But her husband set his sights on land beyond the Mississippi River. He "had resolved to sell his plantation, pay the debt, and move to Missouri with the remains of his property," Martha revealed. There, Jeff planned to finally make good on his grandfather's antislavery ideas. As Martha noted, it was "Jefferson's tenderness for his negros, who were all good and attached to the family," that "determined his choice of a slave state." Missouri's geographic position would enable Randolph to gradually emancipate his enslaved people. From "being surrounded by free states," Randolph suggested, enslaved men and women "will in time dissapear by degrees."[33]

In theory, Randolph's emancipated human property could gradually move northeast, into Illinois, or north, into the unorganized Missouri territory, or even to Wisconsin, where Eston Hemings and his family would later settle and "pass" into white society in 1852. But whatever the possibilities in the West, Randolph believed that the problem of slavery could no longer be solved in eastern slave states like Virginia, where the African American population was increasing so quickly that enslavers were reluctant to consider any emancipation proposals whatsoever.[34]

Jeff Randolph never got to the West. Instead, he remained at Edgehill, the patriarch and enslaver of dozens of human beings, including the families of descendants of those who once lived at Monticello. During the 1830s and 1840s, Randolph abandoned his grandfather's antislavery ideas, relinquishing any belief that bondage was a moral evil, that it created a system of vast inequality, or that its only solution was gradual emancipation paired with colonization. Randolph attributed this turnabout to the rise of white and Black activists who espoused immediate abolition and the inclusion of African Americans in the United States as citizens. Manumitting and then deporting the "colored race" was a strong "cause" in Virginia that continued to "gain ground steadily," he recalled of the early 1830s. But this progress, he suggested, ended with the rise of northern abolitionism, and in particular the publication of Harriet Beecher Stowe's *Uncle Tom's Cabin* in 1852.[35]

George Randolph, Jeff's younger brother, a midshipman and later a Richmond lawyer and Secretary of War for the Confederacy, agreed that a sea change occurred in the 1830s. "In Southern hands," George argued, abolition was a "measure of reform, recognizing the legality of slavery, and looking forward to its peaceful extinction by the will of the master." But "under Northern auspices," it "promised to be a bloody and violent revolution proceeding from the slave." In Jeff and George's telling, proslavery emerged in Virginia only as a kind of last resort, as the best means of warding off northern and Black abolitionists' threats. Knowing full well that "no abolition can succeed in our day and generation without violence and bloodshed," the Randolphs threw their support behind the majority viewpoint: proslavery. By the 1840s, faced with paying off the remainder of his grandfather's debt, Jeff abandoned his strategy to monetize Jefferson, and instead embraced new projects that monetized African Americans, including slave leasing to the railroads.[36]

Rockfish Gap was an auspicious place. In August 1818, Thomas Jefferson had ascended the steep incline of Afton Mountain, taken in the sweeping views at the crest of the Blue Ridge, then hurried to a meeting with an array of Virginia dignitaries, including former president James Madison, at a tavern to decide the future location of the University of Virginia. Two decades later, in 1839, a Frenchman also looked down from Rockfish Gap, surveying the same jaw-dropping views that Jefferson had once witnessed— the rolling hills of the Piedmont to the east, the flat green expanse of the Shenandoah Valley unfurling west.[37]

That Claudius Crozet was in Virginia at all was largely the handiwork of Jefferson's friend, the Revolutionary War hero the marquis de Lafayette. Crozet stood on the nineteen-hundred-foot-high cleft in the Blue Ridge not as a tourist but as a railroad engineer. Born the same year as the outbreak of the French Revolution, Crozet had studied at the École Polytechnique before Napoleon came to power. Serving as an artillery officer in Napoleon's army during the invasion of Russia, Crozet received some reprieve in capture—he was imprisoned at the estate of a Russian nobleman. After Napoleon's defeat at Waterloo, the war-weary Crozet set his sights beyond Europe, on the infant United States. With Lafayette's recommendation tucked under his arm, Crozet secured a position at West Point as professor of engineering in 1816.[38]

Virginia politicians soon took note of the stout, irascible Frenchman. The state's newly formed Board of Public Works—which oversaw the construction of "internal improvements" such as canals, turnpikes, and railroads—intermittently hired Crozet to serve as its chief engineer between 1823 and 1857. While many Virginians supported canal-building projects that would connect the state's waterways and augment trade, Crozet dismissed them. If pressured to choose, a "railroad was undoubtedly the system I should prefer," he declared in 1831. Nearly two decades later, in 1849, Crozet got his wish: he was tasked with leading Virginia's effort to clear and lay seventeen miles of track that would later become the Virginia Central Railroad. It was a small but crucial piece of a much larger infrastructure project in Virginia. Three other railroad companies were collectively laying hundreds of miles of track that would traverse the Blue Ridge and the Allegheny mountains, thereby linking the Atlantic Ocean to the Ohio River and the American interior.[39]

Building a tunnel beneath Rockfish Gap—as well as laying tracks on either side of it—was a monumental task. Clearing land, constructing railroad beds, and blasting through mountains would require the mobilization and recruitment of hundreds, if not thousands, of workers. Yet Crozet never considered native white Virginians as a potential source of labor. Instead, he turned to Irish immigrants living in the Shenandoah Valley who had fled the deadly Great Famine in Ireland in the 1840s. Paid a pittance, these nominally free laborers constructed four main railroad tunnels—the Greenwood, Brooksville, Little Rock, and Blue Ridge.[40]

The argument driving Crozet's decision to use immigrant labor was twofold. On one hand, the work was notoriously dangerous. In an era before dynamite, men were invariably killed when using gunpowder to blast through rock. Some laborers saw their limbs blown off while others witnessed their friends and family members engulfed and killed by a poorly planned explosion. Still other men perished in rockslides—the exploded rock fell like an avalanche, crushing and suffocating many to death. On the other, the Irish workers were considered more expendable than valuable human chattel. Not only did the Virginia Central Railroad have to take out insurance on each enslaved laborer it leased, it also was responsible for paying owners for any "damage" to their human property, including injury or death. As a result, Crozet directed that leased-out enslaved people only clear land and lay tracks, both considered far less risky than tunnel work.[41]

About three hundred leased African Americans ultimately worked on the Virginia Central Railroad in the 1850s, and Crozet came by these laborers in a variety of ways. Many enslaved men and women were hired locally from Albemarle County enslavers. Some of the enslaved people forced to cart earth, clear brambles, and build culverts did not hail from Albemarle County. Several of the captives were brought from Richmond and Washington, D.C.—two important commercial centers not just for slave selling but also for slave hiring. Crozet's railroad enterprise plugged into a larger slave dealing network that linked his seventeen-mile public works project in the Blue Ridge to slave scouts, slave dealers, and hiring agents—and Virginia's broader slave economy.[42]

Slave hiring had become a pervasive and highly profitable enterprise in Virginia by the time railroad construction began in 1849. Indeed, slave dealers offered a wide range of services that depended upon the commodification of Black people. In Richmond in the 1840s and 1850s, slave trading firms often advertised themselves as auctioneers, slave traders, and hiring agents. As the sheer number of Richmond slave hiring agents indicates, leasing was widespread. While some enslavers contracted directly with individuals or companies to lease out their human property, many rural farmers and planters sent their enslaved people to Richmond agents, who took a 5 percent cut. In turn, these dealers leased enslaved people at the Richmond hiring grounds in late December. Annual contracts, secured on credit, usually began on New Year's Day.[43]

When visiting Richmond in the 1850s, the landscape architect Frederick Law Olmsted remarked on a "villainous-looking white man" standing in front of a group of African American men and boys. Soon a "stout, respectable man" carrying a golden walking stick emerged from a storefront down the street. Walking briskly, the wealthy-looking man led the enslaved people in single file, the slave trader bringing up the rear. Olmsted concluded that the men and boys were "slaves that had been sent into the town to be hired out as servants or factory hands." He also deduced that the "respectable" man was the "broker in the business." What Olmsted witnessed was the rapid adaptation of the U.S. slave system to shifting economic demands—slave hiring was predicated upon a need for temporary labor to complete infrastructure projects like turnpikes, railroads, and canals, or to work in emerging industries like salt and coal mining.[44]

At times, Crozet tried to lease people directly. In 1853, after strikes by Irish workers left him with a labor shortage, Crozet was desperate to hire enslaved people to work in the Blue Ridge Tunnel. He wrote to two well-known slave dealers in Richmond—George W. Toler and John R. Cook—who operated their business on the west side of the Virginia Central Railroad tracks, probably transporting human beings in the rail cars. Toler and Cook informed Crozet that enslavers "generally object to hiring for the Tunnel" since the work was so dangerous. Word had spread of an earlier accident in the tunnel—part of the ceiling had collapsed on three Irish workers, disabling and nearly crushing them to death. Toler and Cook were not optimistic about satisfying Crozet's needs; only a few men might be rented for the year, they said, and even those would cost upward of $200, a much higher sum than the $130 annual rate paid for leased enslaved people performing non-tunnel work. Crozet was willing to pay the exorbitant sum, but he realized that Toler and Cook would never be able satisfy his labor needs. Disappointed, he began looking elsewhere.[45]

Most often, Crozet relied on local knowledge and labor supply— Albemarle planters, innkeepers, and railroad contractors who owned enslaved people, or knew of people who did. One such man was George Farrow, the owner of the 525-acre Brooksville plantation and inn, which sat at the eastern foot of Afton Mountain. Crozet kept an office at the inn and sometimes slept there, as he did at many other taverns along the railroad route. A Fauquier County native who later worked as a deputy sheriff and jailer in Prince William County, Farrow was deeply implicated in Virginia slave markets. Not only had he mended and purchased the leg irons, handcuffs, and chains used to restrain Black fugitives who were captured and then incarcerated, he also had ties to the Yellow House, the notorious slave pen in Washington, D.C. Though the structure had the appearance of a "quiet private residence," explained Solomon Northrup, who was kidnapped and enslaved there in 1841, it had "execrable uses." Indeed, Northrup declared, it was "a slave pen in the very shadow of the Capitol!"[46]

Farrow leased captives to the railroad for large sums of money. Sensing the weakness of Crozet's position as he faced dire Irish labor shortages in 1853, Farrow and his brother-in-law agreed to lease thirty people to work in the tunnel. Later that year, Farrow and another railroad contractor, William Sclater, decided to source enslaved people from the Yellow House slave pen. Probably chained and shuttled down to Virginia, Yellow House enslaved people like Bob, Horace, and Jefferson were destined for dangerous tunnel work. In 1854, these men largely labored in the dark, clearing up loose rock after explosions and pumping out the torrents of water that pooled on the ground, forced to grow accustomed to a new world of peril and anxiety. Every working day, they heard—and felt—the deafening cacophony of the never-ending explosions and smelled the "old-strong-sour-wet smell particularly sickening" of lingering gunpowder in the "tunnel house."[47]

Crozet tapped into a network of Virginia planters, including Jeff Randolph, to lease enslaved people. In all, Crozet leased African Americans from fifty-two enslavers, the vast majority of whom hailed from Albemarle County. Crozet may have met Jeff Randolph as far back as 1838, when he was first surveying the land from Charlottesville to Gordonsville, following the contours of the hills and rivers with his "compass book" and a sharp pencil. Crozet skirted around ravines and pressed through dense tree lines of hickory, pine, oak, and chestnut near Edgehill plantation. Walking on Randolph's land, he hugged the Rivanna River until he came to Shadwell, Thomas Jefferson's birthplace, where he encountered a gristmill and a "cotton factory," part of which had been constructed in Jefferson's lifetime. But it would not be for another decade, under the auspices of the Virginia Central Railroad, that Randolph and Crozet would again cross paths.[48]

By the late 1840s, Randolph was no longer a neighboring planter evincing curiosity in Crozet's infrastructure projects. A small-time investor and subscriber to the railroads, Randolph had recently teamed up with another Virginia resident of a more modest background: Richard Omohundro. A Fluvanna County native with close links to the tobacco and slave trades, Omohundro had his fingers in many pies. Together, the two men planned to marshal enough capital and enslaved labor to complete the entire stretch of the Virginia Central Railroad.[49]

There is little to suggest how Jeff Randolph and Richard Omohundro became acquainted or why they decided to partner on the Virginia Central Railroad contract in 1849, except for a paper trail of railroad shares. The two men each bought a handful of stocks—Omohundro purchased five and Randolph ten—of the Louisa Railroad, first chartered by the Virginia Assembly in 1836 with the intention of linking Richmond to Gordonsville. More than a decade later, the track was extended from Gordonsville to Charlottesville, where it passed around Randolph's land. The stocks—a majority owned by the Virginia Board of Public Works—did not hold enormous value in and of themselves. But being shareholders of the Louisa Railroad helped men like Randolph and Omohundro get a foot in the door. Their modest speculation introduced them to a lucrative world of capital investment projects and railroad-building schemes that depended on the mobilization of millions of dollars and thousands of temporary laborers.[50]

Omohundro in particular had long envisioned his fortune as tied to Virginia infrastructure projects. After the Staunton and James River turnpike was completed in 1824, the town of Scottsville, perched on the James River, became its terminus. Virtually overnight, a sleepy town was transformed into a bustling commercial center and tobacco shipping port. Omohundro established himself at the center of it all, becoming one of the first inspectors at the new tobacco warehouse. But Scottsville's star soon faded with the advent of the railroads in the 1840s, and Omohundro conveniently jumped ship. By 1850, he was serving as the station agent for the Gordonsville depot of the Louisa Railroad, a position that put five hundred dollars a year in his pocket. His proximity to Randolph's plantation— Gordonsville was fewer than fifteen miles from Edgehill—meant that the men may have overlapped in this context as well.[51]

Omohundro also had deep ties to the internal slave trade. His brother Silas first cut his teeth in the domestic slave trade as an agent for Franklin & Armfield in Alexandria, buying and selling people on commission. Silas Omohundro soon relocated to Richmond, and by 1846 he had opened a compound in the heart of Shockoe Bottom: a slave jail, a house, and a boardinghouse. Incarcerating nearly two thousand people between 1851 and the start of the Civil War, Silas Omohundro reaped incredible profits from his jail, charging fees for the enslaved people who were awaiting sale or enduring punishment. His boardinghouse, on the other hand, made thousands of dollars from traders in town for slave auctions. And of course, Silas Omohundro sold enslaved people, often in partnership with other traders, including his brother Richard. During the 1850s, Richard and Silas Omohundro sold scores of people to the Deep South from Virginia. Richard Omohundro's close familial connections to the slave mart in Richmond—and elsewhere in Virginia—convinced Randolph that he would be a good prospective partner for the railroad project. If anyone could locate and lease enslaved people for the railroad, it was surely a member of the Omohundro family.[52]

Randolph's appetite for railroad building was first whetted in 1847. Striking a deal with the chief engineer of the Louisa Railroad, he pledged to complete four sections of roadbed that passed in front of his plantation. The task delegated to Randolph's enslaved force, which probably came from his Edgehill estate, was grading and masonry. Enslaved men and boys worked the better part of a year to level the roadway, stabilize it with rocky embankments, and build culverts over gullies and streams. One of Randolph's daughters, Ellen, appeared to have visited the worksite daily, reporting on the laborers' progress to her presumably absent father. "We go down regularly every Sunday to see how things progress and you ought to hear how learnedly we talk of dumping carts etc.," Ellen boasted. In the spring of 1848, she observed that "Pa's railroad work is coming on bravely," though "Culvert No. 8 is not much more than half done, and I don't think they have nearly enough stone for it." Where the enslaved workers would find rocks more than five feet long to lay atop the drains was "more than she could tell."[53]

The road that Jeff Randolph's enslaved people built ended at the Rivanna River, where a crew of engineers was laying a "magnificent" bridge constructed almost entirely of iron. Though no record survives of the money Randolph was paid for work done by his captive labor force, the Louisa Railroad did record that the entire railbed construction between Gordonsville and Woodville, just west of Charlottesville, cost $234,847, or nearly $12,000 per mile. The enslaved men and boys may have been among the fifty-seven "coloured hands on the road," for which the Louisa Railroad paid $4,190. Still, hired enslaved people were not the only African Americans involved in the railroad project. Twenty-five men, some white and some Black, labored at Hanover Junction, outside Richmond, and seven men of color worked on the trains themselves as agents, enginemen, and firemen. African American labor was critical to a company that boasted five locomotive engines, four passenger coaches, two baggage cars, and ninety-one "burden" cars, probably used to transport enslaved people, livestock, and supplies up and down the tracks.[54]

When Virginia Central Railroad officials solicited requests for proposals to complete the tracks between Woodville and Waynesboro, on the western side of the mountains, Jeff Randolph was only too happy to throw his hat into the ring. Randolph and Omohundro's pitch was one of sixteen forwarded for consideration. The lowest bid came from John Kelly, the man who later won the contract to complete the Blue Ridge Tunnel with Irish immigrant laborers, at $244,451. And the bid demanding the highest payout came from one A. S. Orensby, who proposed the fantastic sum of $362,783.[55]

Randolph and Omohundro were in the middle of the pack, though they declined to bid on sections five and six of the track—the two portions that would go through the base of the mountain at Rockfish Gap. It is likely that neither man wanted to risk the lives of valuable human chattel in perilous tunnel work, calculating that a contract worth $168,105 would suit them just fine. That Randolph and Omohundro bid on the entire line is significant, for it points to their confidence in marshaling hundreds of hired enslaved people to complete all sections of track. Even if Randolph and Omohundro had decided to mobilize their own enslaved workforces to complete the project, they would have needed more labor—and who better to provide it from Richmond than Silas Omohundro?[56]

In the end, Crozet and the Board of Public Works declined all bids. Instead, each bidder received a contract for one or more sections. Randolph and Omohundro landed a contract for sections seven and eight, worth approximately $70,130. But when Omohundro bowed out of the deal at the last minute, Randolph was aware that he had lost not just a partner but a critical link to slave dealers. Desperate, Randolph searched for a replacement, soon turning to Christopher Valentine, an overseer and plantation manager living in Louisa who had just quit his current employer, as an alternative. Though another planter was "pressing me to decide whether I will take charge of his plantation or not," Valentine was holding out for Randolph. "I am . . . wating to hear whether you get a contract on the Rail Road or not, in the decision of my arrangements for next year," Valentine wrote impatiently in the autumn of 1849.[57]

About a month later, hearing that Randolph had in fact won the contract for a "portion of the Blue ridge road," Valentine made plans to move his family to Albemarle County. Struggling to complete work for the plantation in Louisa before moving—he was trying to plant wheat during a string of fierce thunderstorms—Valentine hoped to begin work on the railroad as soon as possible. He was as good as his word, much to Randolph's relief. By December, Valentine was busy locating supplies to start work in earnest in the spring, purchasing several items from Omohundro. He bought four horses, eight carts, and a wagon for $190, which, he told Randolph, was "rather better than I expected to find."[58]

Leasing enslaved people proved more difficult. "I have not engaged any hands positively, and do not believe I can, until the regular hiring," Valentine wrote dejectedly from Louisa in December 1849. And even if he could find them, he feared having to pay a rate in excess of $100 a year. Apparently, Valentine had heard, "they were offering $120 for hands in Richmond to go on the Danville Road" (the Richmond and Danville railroad) creating fierce competition for enslaved labor. Alternatively, Valentine could try to lease African Americans in Albemarle County. But in Louisa, at least, "there is prejudice in this neighborhood against Railroads

with both Masters and hands," and, Valentine suggested, "we may do better in your neighborhood than we can here."[59]

Enslavers had probably witnessed the deaths and injuries of enslaved
people hired out to the Louisa railroad, and had little interest in renting
out their valuable chattel to work under such dangerous conditions. And,
importantly, African Americans were themselves reluctant to do such work;
there is archival evidence of planters rejecting offers to hire their enslaved
people for that reason. While it is possible that in the end Randolph
and Valentine hired enslaved people from Richmond or local Albemarle
County planters, a likely scenario is that they did not hire from anyone
at all. Randolph may have decided to utilize his own captive workforce on
his contracted sections of the Virginia Central Railroad. In fact, many of
the African Americans he forced to labor on the Virginia Central Railroad
may have once belonged to his grandfather, or at the least been their
descendants.[60]

The U.S. census supports this theory. In 1840, Randolph was recorded as the owner of sixty-nine people. A decade later, in August 1850,
the enslaved population at Edgehill had mysteriously declined—to forty-
six people. But that October a separate census listed Randolph and Valentine as jointly owning thirty-two individuals. Given these numbers, as
well as the absence of any large slave sale at Edgehill around this time, it
seems likely that Randolph simply diverted many enslaved people to work
on the railroad. Of the thirty-two listed as laboring under Randolph and
Valentine in 1850, twenty-seven were men and boys ranging in age from ten
to forty-five. There was also one twenty-five-year-old woman—probably a
cook—along with four children who may have been hers. Separated from
their spouses, children, parents, and siblings at Edgehill, these enslaved
people literally lived at work, probably housed together in a makeshift
shanty along the roadbed.[61]

They were not without constant white supervision. Perhaps a few
hundred feet away, in a smaller wooden shack, Valentine lived with his
wife and children. As the sections of track were laid, the enslaved were
allowed infrequent visits home. According to Randolph's contract with
the Virginia Central Railroad, he and Valentine claimed the "privilege of
passing free on the cars such hands as may be visiting their wives." But the
enslaved workers could not "go oftener than once in two months and not

more than five at a time." The completion of the railroad, not the integrity of the men's families, remained the priority.[62]

In the spring of 1850, the twenty-seven men and boys had nineteen acres of work ahead of them. Their task: clear 2.7 miles of roadbed between the new Greenwood Tunnel and a plantation known as Blair Park. The first order of business was to cut a path through the forest—the force cut down trees, dragged stumps out of the cloying red soil, and pulled away endless knots of bramble. Shouldering pickaxes, saws, and shovels, the men and boys would have performed this grubbing work at the height of summer, the heat and humidity boring down on their bodies. But removing the trees and underbrush only revealed the irregularity—and difficulty—of the terrain. Randolph and Valentine's sections were not far from the base of Afton Mountain, and even on comparatively flat land, ravines and gullies sliced deep into the landscape. Creating a level surface for the tracks would not be easy. Using the carts and horses purchased from Omohundro, the enslaved workers hunted for rock to fill in the ravines, creating an embankment that would stabilize the road.[63]

But there was little rock to be found. "One of the greatest difficulties in this work, has been the want of building stone and good brick clay," Crozet complained. Since no good quarry had been discovered, the Edgehill men and boys were forced to resort to the more-brittle slate. But not all ravines could be filled with rock, since some "discharge at times large volumes of water." Atop the gullies, the enslaved men and boys built culverts up to a hundred feet in length and embankments between thirty and seventy-five feet high. If grubbing and hauling rock required incredible physical strength, then building the culverts necessitated extraordinary skill. As stonemasons, quarryman, and stonecutters, the enslaved workers constructed fifteen culverts along sections seven and eight, some requiring mortared stone and others carefully cut segments of rock laid into an arch.[64]

But Valentine's letters to Randolph revealed that the men were doing more than scouring the hills for rock—they were also blasting it. In the early summer of 1851, Valentine had "received from Scottsville since I saw you 100 kegs powder, 2 boxes fuse, and the steel iron hammers." These supplies reveal the most dangerous aspect of the work—blasting through solid rock to create a cut for the roadbed. The men would have hammered deep holes in the rock by hand, filling them with gunpowder before lighting a fuse and then ducking for cover. The volatility of gunpowder would have made it difficult for the enslaved men to predict the size and direction of the blast. The explosion might indeed make the correct cut through the rock, but just as easily, it might kill them all.[65]

In theory, Randolph was the primary contractor for the Virginia Central Railroad, but Valentine's letters indicate that he was often absent. Only months after work began, Randolph was not even in Albemarle County. Named a delegate to the Virginia Constitutional Convention of 1850–1851, Randolph rushed off to Richmond to take his seat on the Legislative Committee, where he tried his hand at "straightening out the finances of the State." Though the convention met its goal of achieving greater equality between the eastern and western portions of the state by expanding suffrage and western representation in the legislature, Jeff and his younger brother George had found much to complain about by the summer of 1851. There was the unbearable heat, swarms of mosquitoes, and the lack of a quorum at many of the sessions, something that George, a young lawyer in Richmond, deemed outrageous.[66]

Meanwhile, dozens of miles west, Valentine attempted to keep the railroad project on track. He was often desperate for Randolph's presence— and bankroll. "I have been looking for you for some time to come up and see how our work is going on," Valentine wrote in the early summer of 1851, "tho' I have looked in vain so far." He hoped Randolph would be able to leave the convention long enough "to come up soon, as I am doing my best with the work." Valentine confessed that he was "pretty nearly out of money" and implored Randolph to "bring some or send it as soon as you can." Valentine was on the hook for food rations for the entire enslaved workforce—he had promised to pay for fifty barrels of corn by the end of the month and had no funds to do so.[67]

Randolph may have been a largely absent contractor, but his actions showed him to be a shrewd investor. If he did mobilize his own enslaved people from Edgehill to complete sections seven and eight, as the evidence suggests, then his profits from the $70,130 payout from the railroad would have been much greater than if he had relied on outside labor from local planters or slave dealers like Silas Omohundro in Richmond. And because Valentine was never listed as an official partner or contractor for the two sections of railroad, Randolph need not have felt compelled to split the profits. Either way, between 1848 and 1852, Randolph deftly exploited the needs of two separate railroad companies to generate enormous personal profit, all at the expense of dozens of enslaved men and boys. Unlike his schemes to monetize his grandfather's legacy in the 1820s and 1830s, the railroad did yield dividends that probably wiped out most of the remaining debt Randolph had inherited from Jefferson.[68]

On the eve of the Civil War, Jeff Randolph, no longer teetering on the edge of bankruptcy, had become an independent property holder and an equal member of Virginia's white elite. The commodification of enslaved people had facilitated his remarkable rise in wealth and status in the 1840s and 1850s. But the tide would soon turn. After Virginia's secession from the federal union in 1861, Randolph invested in the Confederacy, purchasing eighty thousand dollars' worth of Confederate bonds. After the war, in 1866, Israel Gillette, formerly enslaved at Monticello, visited Virginia from Ohio as a free man. He encountered Jeff Randolph at Edgehill, a mere four miles from where Gillette was "born and bred." Gillette described Randolph as old, impoverished, and "outwardly surrounded by the evidence of former ease and opulence gone to decay." Indeed, the once "proud and haughty" Randolph had lost "nearly all his personal property of every kind," including the families he had once enslaved. The "rebellion stripped him of everything," Gillette concluded, "save one old blind mule."[69]

Meriwether Lewis Randolph

Slavery and Land Speculation in Arkansas, 1835–1838

IN THE SPRING OF 1835, THE APTLY named Meriwether Lewis Randolph went west. Traveling by wagon and boat to what had once been Caddo, Osage, and Quapaw lands, Randolph arrived in Little Rock in May. Originally part of the Louisiana Purchase, the Arkansas Territory fanned westward from the Mississippi River, wedged between the Missouri Territory and the state of Louisiana. Randolph had traversed the low and muddy Arkansas River by steamboat, docking in the territorial capital with eighteen other first-class passengers, thirty individuals on deck, and several tons of backlogged mail. Abuzz with land surveyors, speculators, and settlers, Little Rock was "filled with strangers, and the taverns overflowing" while "not a house can be rented" because of the influx of new migrants.[1]

But the white men and their families who steamed west or crowded the rutted and mud-clogged roads from Memphis to Little Rock did not come alone. They also brought enslaved people. In the space of a week, reported the *Arkansas Gazette,* "not less than 300 negroes" had arrived in town, either to serve their enslavers or to be sold. During 1835 alone, the paper estimated that between 1,500 and 1,800 enslaved people "have been carried out of the county by emigrating parties." Many hailed from Virginia. "No less than forty families in the great county of Albemarle have removed or intend removing," the *Gazette* boasted, a figure that included Jefferson's white grandson Lewis, as he was called. Because the cheap land that these Virginia families hoped to purchase at land offices was in fact heavily timbered backcountry, enslaved African Americans were viewed as critical to establishing a robust plantation empire in Arkansas. White settlers forced Black captives to clear the hardwood and pine, drain the land, and prepare it for cotton cultivation. White people also sold, rented, or mortgaged their human chattel—all in the name of profit, progress, and territorial development.[2]

In the space of two years, Lewis Randolph claimed an astonishing 27,145 acres of federal land in Arkansas. But how he came by these parcels—and what he did with them—sheds light on early land speculation on the periphery of America's cotton empire. A closer look at Randolph's schemes between 1835 and 1837 illuminates the varied ways that Jefferson's grandson commodified both land and enslaved African Americans to maximize short-term profit. Initially, the cash-poor Randolph bought cheap acreage on behalf of local investors, taking a cut of the land purchases as payment. But he soon expanded this business model outside Arkansas, hoping to persuade entrepreneurs tied to the slave and opium trades on the East Coast to invest in even larger land parcels, with Randolph again receiving payment in the form of land. But Randolph had no intention of simply reselling his newly acquired parcels—at a much higher price—at the first chance he got. Instead, he developed his "wilderness" into inchoate cotton plantations, cultivated by an enslaved labor force, to increase the value of his holdings. Though Randolph did not live long enough to realize his ambition, the "creative destruction" he practiced offers an important window into U.S. empire building in the early trans-Mississippi West.[3]

In the early nineteenth century, slavery's expansion and the rapid growth of the U.S. cotton empire across the Southwest presented an enormous opportunity for poorer or middling white men like Randolph. Speculating on stolen Native land in the Southwest Territory (present-day Alabama and Mississippi) and in the southern portion of the Louisiana Territory created a route to wealth and prominence, enabling white men without fortunes to become independent and equal property holders. As the historian Michael Blaakman has pointed out, "To a far greater degree than their revolutionary-era forebears, nineteenth-century planters and investors were drawn to land speculation by faith in slavery's continued profitability and its power to make land lucrative." Between the late 1790s and 1840, land jobbers gambled that the Lower Mississippi River valley would become integral to a rapidly growing cotton empire, and the engine of global capital. Tragically, these speculators were not wrong—slave-grown cotton and the expropriated Native land on which it was cultivated fueled enormous economic growth in the space of a few short decades, making the U.S. economy a world leader by 1860.[4]

Lewis Randolph found himself at the center of the Arkansas land craze not because of credentials acquired back in Virginia but because of his connection to Andrew Jackson. On paper, Randolph appeared to have a clear advantage over other white elites of the period: he was from a storied Virginia family and a grandson of Thomas Jefferson. But he was also one of the youngest sons of the mercurial and bankrupt Virginia politician and planter Thomas Mann Randolph, Jr., who remained estranged from his family for years before dying at Monticello in 1828. Added to that, Lewis and his family found themselves saddled with—and unable to pay—their grandfather's massive debt. The Randolphs scraped together enough tuition money to fund Lewis's studies in ancient languages, moral philosophy, law, and mathematics at the University of Virginia in 1826 and 1830, but he proved a poor student.[5]

His mother, Martha Randolph, hoped he would become a lawyer— the profession that would best confer money and status on one of her youngest sons. But Lewis's "mind is considerable unsettled as to his profession for which he has conceived a great disgust, not at all lessened by the circumstance of it's being so completely overdone that none but lawyers of the first standing make bread by it," Martha reported. If he refused to study law, then Martha thought her wayward son's best hope for improved circumstances lay in an advantageous marriage. Lewis did become engaged, in 1833, to a "warm hearted generous tempered girl," but Martha objected "on the score of his want of fortune"—and the bride's as well. Elizabeth Martin may have been without a dowry, but she brought something else to the marriage that Lewis Randolph needed: political connections. Martin was the niece of President Jackson's recently deceased wife, Rachel Donelson.[6]

Jackson made a deep impression on the young Lewis Randolph. Born in 1810, Randolph had been too young—or too lacking in intellectual ambition—to forge a particularly close bond with his grandfather. As he confessed to his sister, he respected Jefferson's Revolutionary era ideas and actions, but he considered himself squarely in Jackson's camp—he was an avid supporter of the racialized democratic populism that Jackson preached. Later he would tell his brother-in-law that Jackson was his "best

Miniature Portrait of Meriwether Lewis Randolph, 1905. (© Thomas Jefferson Foundation at Monticello.)

friend & benefactor" and even named his only son after the president. Randolph landed his first job, a clerkship in the State Department, because of Jackson's preferment. But the president knew that Randolph had grander ambitions than an office job in Washington.[7]

Randolph had long thought that his future success depended on leaving Virginia. In 1832, he made the mistake of visiting Monticello, a year after the house had been sold to the Charlottesville druggist James T. Barclay. As Randolph ascended the little mountain, the "prospect sickened" him "to the heart." Corn was growing all over the mountaintop, even on the "verge of the Lawn & front yard." Where there had once been groves of aspen and fields of Scotch broom, now were only "red gullies & black dead trees." The "savage," Randolph seethed, referring to Barclay, "had burnt them." The "monument" created by Jefferson—the iconic house and lawn—had been replaced by other shrines of "the destroying hand of the Gothic barbarian." Only the graveyard, "that sacred spot," remained "untouched." It had been "spared," protected by the "arm of the Law." Otherwise, Randolph wrote sarcastically, "I cannot say, that the plough share would not have visited its walls & violated the sanctity of that soil."[8]

Yet even if the graveyard and the remains within it stood both timeless and sacred in Randolph's eyes, nothing else on his grandfather's mountaintop did. "I most sincerely pray," he noted dramatically, that "before I leave the neighborhood my eyes may be gladdened with the sight of the House wrapped in flames." The sale of the Monticello house brought home to Randolph, as it did to his mother and many of his siblings, the fact that the era of Jefferson—and the pinnacle of his power and influence in Virginia—was over. But unlike them, Lewis Randolph was not interested in remaining in Virginia to restore Jefferson's image or his family's fortunes.[9]

And neither was Randolph's cousin, Francis Eppes. The son of Maria Jefferson and John Wayles Eppes, he inherited Jefferson's Bedford estate, Poplar Forest, in 1826. But he had little interest in taking up residence in what he perceived to be a rapidly changing—and declining—state in the union. "Yankee notions, and Yankee practices," Eppes puffed a few months after Jefferson's death, had "poisoned our atmosphere" and altered the "public mind." Moreover, the scale of emigration of "old Settlers from the State" and the "more equal distribution of property" threatened the survival of founding era families like the Randolphs. In sum, Eppes concluded, the "liberality and generosity, and patriotism of the old Dominion, is in the wane." In light of the increasingly dire situation in Virginia, Eppes urged, the Randolphs should be governed by no "maxim" save self-preservation, even at the "expence, of every principle, of honour, and generosity, and justice."[10]

Eppes's wife, Mary, predicted that tobacco would no longer turn a profit in Virginia. "Tobacco is the only thing which can be made here, and after vast labour and expence, in raising and manufacturing the vile weed, and acquiring both skill and judgement in the business, to find still that no profit must be expected, is disheartening indeed," she lamented. Mary was eager to leave the "worn out fields" and "this unfinished leaking hull of a house" at Poplar Forest. Francis proposed abandoning our "gullies to the yankee pedlars, who covet them so much" and moving to Florida, Kentucky, Tennessee, or Missouri, where "I can make more money." Francis preferred eastern Florida, near Tallahassee; he had heard that the "best land is worth $4 pr acre and Cuffee hires, for one hundred and sixty dollars pr annum!!!" Francis Eppes did sell Poplar Forest—the "gully" in Bedford County—and headed south with his family and enslaved people, including several Hemings descendants, to plant cotton in Leon County, Florida.[11]

Initially, Lewis Randolph thought that he too might travel south, perhaps following in Eppes's footsteps. The month following his ill-fated visit to Monticello in 1832, his mother reported that Randolph "talks of going to Florida when he gets a licence [to practice law] of which *he* has no doubt though he is far from being thoroughly read." But he changed his tune after traveling to New York a year later. Enamored of the Hudson River valley during a visit in 1833, he urged his siblings to consider moving there. "The Hudson stands unrivaled in the history of rivers," he rhapsodized, "the scenery on the bank various & beautiful beyond conception, the streams crowded with sails, the country on either side in the highest state of cultivation, and literally thronged with villages, towns, and cities." He noted that "an air of wealth, industry, prosperity, and happiness reigns throughout the whole country entirely new to one from the sinking South." To Randolph, at least during his 1833 trip, upstate New York, not Virginia, represented the cutting edge of progress and profit in postrevolutionary America.[12]

But in the end, it was neither the North nor the South that sustained Randolph's attention—it was the West. In 1834 a member of Congress tried to tempt Randolph to Indiana, where, as a "Register of a Land office," he could expect to rake in about three thousand dollars a year. A further attraction of the post, Randolph revealed, was that the responsibilities were "trifling" and the position would be the "best stepping stone to political advancement." Although the offer to go to Indiana fell through, western federal lands had piqued Randolph's interest. Even when choosing a wife—the blue-eyed and auburn-haired niece of President Jackson—he did so with the West in his sights. Elizabeth Martin, he reported, "was hale, hearty, & handsome," and he warned against rousing her "mettle for she is Western to the backbone."[13]

A year later, it was Jackson who facilitated Randolph's move west. The president, Randolph's mother gushed in 1835, had just appointed her son secretary of the Arkansas Territory, a post that came with an annual salary of a thousand dollars plus "perquisites making it some thing more." The position would also, Martha Randolph suggested, allow Lewis "time to practise his profession (the law)." Technically, Lewis would serve under Governor Robert S. Fulton, military secretary to Jackson during the First Seminole War and later a jurist in Tennessee and Alabama. But it was Elijah Hayward, commissioner of the General Land Office, who really delineated Randolph's new job: inspecting the land offices throughout Arkansas, paying particular attention to the Mississippi River port town of Helena, "which is the special, if not exclusive occasion of your appointment." Officially, Randolph's duty was to oversee land claims, but he also hoped to do what so many others had done out West: make a fortune in land speculation. As his mother implied, this was the primary "perquisite" of his new post.[14]

When Lewis Randolph arrived in Arkansas, land sales were the engine of development in Little Rock and the surrounding country. In the mid-1830s, at the height of a cotton boom, Arkansas land sales were coming to market after remaining dormant for two decades. In 1815, the General Land Office had initiated surveys of a massive district that included present-day Illinois, Missouri, and Arkansas, but the sheer size of the area slowed the arduous process of surveying, platting, and selling those lands. The inspector general of the district, William Rector, first directed military bounty surveys—intended for veterans of the War of 1812—in eastern Arkansas before turning his attention toward surveys of what would become public land. It was not until 1822, three years after the Arkansas Territory was established, that the first government land offices opened in Little Rock and Batesville. Surveying and land sales continued to proceed at a glacial pace, with only 62,500 acres sold between 1821 and 1830. In 1832, the "quantity of public lands remaining unsurveyed" compelled Congress to redefine Arkansas as a standalone surveying district.[15]

President Jackson's appointment of a locally based surveyor-general, James Sevier Conway, hastened the process of surveying roughly 17 million acres of expropriated Native land in Arkansas. Though the Arkansas landscape had already been divided up on paper into "townships" of 36 square miles and "sections" of about 640 acres, it had yet to be mapped by surveyors. Conway hired and dispatched teams of private surveying crews, each group charged with taking detailed notes of the physical landscape, as well as calculating measurements and boundaries. By 1837, nearly all of the exterior boundaries of Arkansas's 1,440 townships had been surveyed.[16]

Land sales boomed after the surveying push. In 1836, Arkansas claims reached their peak—one million acres were sold out of the territory's four land offices. As the *Arkansas Gazette* reported, the sale of public lands "by private entry are very brisk," with over $30,000 received in a single day. With the help of an auctioneer "whose skill enabled them to facilitate the sales very much," speculators would immediately liquidate their purchases at private auction for a minimum of $2.50 per acre, with coveted "front lands" bordering on navigable streams fetching even higher prices. Interest was directed at the southern part of the territory, where cotton would grow best. The northernmost parts of Arkansas, framed by the rugged Ozark Mountains, were too cold for temperate crops. For this reason, Lewis Randolph kept his eye on the southwestern part of the territory and the rivers that flowed there.[17]

Land hunters and surveyors on the federal government's payroll identified the Arkansas territory as "empty" space in the public domain. As the surveyor Caleb Langtree noted of the landscape of southern Arkansas, "I cannot but observe the wild & desolate looking appearance of the place," where the "forest trees are large & blackened by the overflow, long grape vines & rattan vines hung in disorder on all sides." Nothing, Langtree surmised, "indicated the presence of man." But despite what Langtree implied, many men—and women—claimed Arkansas as their ancestral home. Since the turn of the nineteenth century, indigenous Arkansas tribes, including the Caddo, Osage, and Quapaw, had been forced to cede their lands, first to other Native peoples, and then to white squatters and settlers. After the Louisiana Purchase, Jefferson had eyed Upper Louisiana, which included Arkansas, as a possible new "homeland" for southeastern tribes. Members of the Cherokee, Choctaw, Chickasaw, Creek, and Seminole soon found themselves forcibly pushed west of the Mississippi River to make way for white settlements.[18]

The arrival of thousands of refugee bands from the eastern United States placed tremendous pressure on indigenous Arkansas tribes. In 1824 the federal government forced the Quapaw to relocate to new lands along the Red River, in present-day Louisiana. The next year, the Osage found themselves deprived of their ancestral lands and "removed" to a reservation in Kansas. About a decade later, their homeland overrun by displaced Delaware, Shawnee, Cherokee, and Choctaw peoples, the Caddo relinquished rights to their Arkansas lands, intending to move to Texas. But their autonomy was short-lived—after enduring horrific violence at the hands of Texan settlers, the Caddo were forcibly placed on a reservation along the Brazos River in 1855. Though it was deemed "Indian Country" during Jefferson's presidency, settlers and the U.S. imperial state had quickly transformed Arkansas into cotton country by the late 1830s. As a result, the forced deportation of Native people was in full flow—and on tragic display—when Lewis Randolph arrived. After landing in Little Rock in 1835, Randolph may have seen indigenous or refugee tribes, goaded on and watched over by federal troops along an old, rutted military road that wound through Arkansas, but he remained silent about the stolen Native property that he and other settlers had re-envisioned as U.S. public land.[19]

Randolph's new role as secretary of the Arkansas Territory enabled him to profit from these newly "empty" public lands, allowing him to rub shoulders with knowledgeable land hunters and surveyors as well as deep-pocketed investors and planters. These men later recruited Randolph to use his insider knowledge of land surveys to speculate on large parcels, for which services he received a cut. Randolph purchased land for both William McKim, a well-to-do investor, and John T. Jones, a wealthy land speculator who was amassing huge tracts of land in southern Arkansas. For Jones, he bought 1,039.3 acres in Columbia and Lafayette counties, both of which lay on the southernmost Arkansas border, near Louisiana. And for McKim, Randolph patented 1,455.6 acres in Lafayette and Nevada counties. In total, Randolph purchased 5,015.96 acres. The location of these parcels suggested that McKim and Jones both reckoned that the southernmost parts of Arkansas would be ideal for cotton. In less than two years, Randolph speculated on thousands of acres of cheap government land, which buyers hoped to resell to aspiring cotton planters at a steep profit.[20]

Randolph tried to disguise his imperial ambitions in letters home to his sisters and mother. He portrayed himself as an impoverished frontiersman, a kind of down-on-his-luck Daniel Boone character. "My face is sharp and lean enough to split a north wester," he told his sister, and "my arms resemble a couple of bench legs." He was also embarking upon a seemingly humble—and individual—project: "I went into the woods to fell a forest & provide a home for us." Yet Randolph's words were misleading. He had embraced a muscular imperialism borrowed from Andrew Jackson in the Arkansas backcountry that was predicated on white supremacy and the "mastery" of dozens of enslaved laborers. Leaving his family under the care of territorial governor Robert Fulton at Little Rock, Randolph struck out for Clark County, southwest of the capital.[21]

That Randolph came into possession of land in Clark County was no accident. Retaining two supposedly knowledgeable land surveyors who in turn retained a group of land hunters, he deemed the property fronting the Terre Noir Creek "first rate bottom land." Even though Randolph had not examined the land himself, he trusted the surveyors' judgment. He jotted down a few notes from the land hunters' reports in his memoranda book: "Sections 29 & W ½ of 28 in Town 10 S. 19 W best quality, most desirable" while "S. 14 & W ½ 13 same T. equally good."[22]

Later, Randolph elaborated upon why Township 10 South seemed so ideal. The uplands, "lying most favorably for cultivation," were undulating rather than steep. The sandy soil, ten to fifteen inches deep, was a "dark mulatto" that approached gray near the ridgeline. The land was forested: black oak, hickory, and sweet gum grew thickly, with some pine, mulberry, post oak, and grape vines "intermixed." And the township, though riven by "springs of good water," was far away from disease-ridden swamps. The land also produced corn and cotton "in great abundance," and was "fine stock country." In short, the sections presented "every inducement to settlement" and possessed "every advantage to be found in our country." Convinced that the land was valuable, Randolph claimed eleven sections at the Washington, Arkansas, land office. He then gave eighty-eight acres of his new property as "compensation for the selection" to the land hunters.[23]

Randolph himself directed the clearing of his land, employing the indispensable labor of enslaved African Americans. He soon reported that the "negro cabines are built" and the "great house" was under way. When the house was "habitable," Randolph said, he intended to "settle down" as a planter. But the uncultivated and uninhabited Arkansas pine woods remained proximate—almost too much so. From the new house, he could hear the "crying of the panthers," the "growling of varmints of different kinds," and "as for wolves they are as gentle as house dogs & deer browse in the very yard." Randolph worried about whether his new wife would adapt to life in the woods. During her stay in Little Rock, Elizabeth Martin Randolph had become the "belle among the hunting shirts" and was "much taken with the metropolis and fascinated with the gaiety of the city." Her husband feared that she would "pine on the Terre Noir" in southeastern Arkansas.[24]

Cash poor, Randolph struggled to make ends meet. He turned down his sister's offer of money but later accepted sixteen dollars from his brother Jeff. Lewis insisted that he would instead "be dependent upon the 1/3 hire of Mama's negroes," which amounted to sixty or seventy dollars per year. These two enslaved African Americans were Ferrell and Stephen, men originally owned by Martha Randolph and rented out in Virginia to support her sons. The leased labor of the enslaved men would, as Lewis put it, "clothe me" and provide income to support his wife and his young son, Jack. Empire for white families in Arkansas was financed by the enslaved labor of African Americans in Virginia. If he had more money, Lewis said that he would "lay it out in law books I daily read," though he was not optimistic that he would be able to buy such books (or become a lawyer) for years to come. Displaying the self-pity that exemplified the always aggrieved planter class, Lewis maintained that he was suffering the "innumerable wiles of poverty," his clothes fraying to rags, his health in decline, and his wallet empty.[25]

Lewis Randolph may have been without cash, but he was hardly a lone frontiersman on the margins of the United States. He had recently gone into partnership with another Arkansas land speculator, John S. Nicholas, and the plantation to which Randolph referred in his letters home was to be managed by both men. The forest that he "felled" in Clark County was actually thousands of acres recently purchased from the federal government. And his new house was designed to be a replica of his grandfather's mansion at Monticello. Moreover, he was not merely chopping down pine and hardwoods in the Arkansas "wilderness"—he was directing enslaved people to clear the forest, build their own homes (and his), prepare the soil for cultivation, and plant dozens of acres of corn and cotton. His was an inchoate plantation empire being forged on a muddy tributary of the Arkansas River, a waterway that emptied into the mighty Mississippi. But he knew that making his ambition a reality meant securing more capital.[26]

In the early spring of 1836, Randolph headed for the East Coast, stopping in Charlottesville, Richmond, and Boston. In these places, Randolph met with investors tied to the opium trade, the domestic slave trade, and transatlantic commerce. He took his nephew Thomas Mann Randolph Bankhead with him, a youth keen to learn the ropes of land speculation. Lewis Randolph's business trip proved a wise move. In 1836 the population of Arkansas had swelled to more than sixty thousand inhabitants, meeting the threshold for statehood and admittance to the federal union. But the end of the territorial government also meant the end of gainful employment for Randolph—he was out of a job that supplied him with a steady income. He toyed with the idea of moving elsewhere in cotton country, perhaps even to Mississippi. "I think Lewis will go there when Arkansas becomes a state," his wife predicted, since "it holds out more inducements for one of his profession than any other state in the West."[27]

President Jackson soon delivered more bad news. "I had great perplexity and dificulty" on the "subject of appointments in Arkansa," Jackson admitted. He had appointed Benjamin Johnson federal district judge since he was "Senior & well recommended," while he selected another man, Thomas Jefferson Lacy, as the district attorney after "deep reflection." Jackson conceded to Randolph that Lacy's position had been "intended to be given you," and promised that if Lacy refused the post, Randolph could have it. The president also reassured Randolph of his continued support. "You may rest assured it will always afford me pleasure to promote your welfare," Jackson wrote. Nevertheless, passed over for a federal position, Randolph concentrated on expanding his land speculation enterprise in Arkansas. To do that, he needed more money.[28]

By February 1836, Randolph was in Boston, having a cup of tea with an opium trader. His brother-in-law Joseph Coolidge had engineered a meeting with Augustine Heard. Coolidge "thought well of the speculation," and agreed with Randolph's predictions for Arkansas lands. "There is every prospect that these lands will rise rapidly in value," Coolidge told Randolph, and even if cotton production "outruns the demand," the "old half escheated lands of the settled states" would inevitably "give way to the vigorous sale of the new." Although Coolidge was sorry to miss out on Randolph's scheme, various "impediments" prevented his involvement. So Coolidge offered to introduce Randolph to Heard, one of New England's leading China merchants (and Coolidge's future business partner). In 1834, Heard had returned to Boston, his health deteriorating because of the oppressively hot, humid conditions of southern China. When Randolph met him two years later, Heard was a millionaire and a partner of Russell and Company, a leading commission house in the U.S.–China trade.[29]

The partners of Russell and Company were no strangers to diverting money reaped from the lucrative—and illegal—opium trade in China to buy cheap land in the western United States. For years, in an effort to diversify its assets, the company had been investing in two things: railroads and land speculation in places like Wisconsin, Ohio, Illinois, and Kentucky. Heard persuaded fellow China traders Samuel Russell and John Murray Forbes to join him in a scheme to buy Arkansas land. Forbes seemed a little less convinced—he only ponied up $1,200 while Heard and Russell pledged $5,900 each.[30]

At the end of the month, Heard sent Randolph a letter authorizing him to buy up to $15,000 worth of "investments in Arkansas Govt lands." With federal land prices at $1.25 per acre, Heard could purchase up to twelve thousand acres for his money. In return, Heard wrote, Randolph would receive a 25 percent cut for "buying, selling, & doing every thing relating to the purchases, such as surveying &c." Heard was relying on Randolph's "thorough knowledge of the country, its capacities & comparative advantages" to make a sound investment. Though he declined to provide Randolph with detailed instructions, Heard did recommend "proceeding upon the safest ground, & avoiding operations that may promise the greatest result, if, from any cause, they may be attended with additional hazard." At the same time, Heard pledged the "fullest confidence in leaving the whole business" to Randolph's skill, convinced that Jefferson's grandson would "render it a profitable speculation."[31]

With Heard on board, Randolph traveled south, hoping to drum up more money in Virginia. In March, Randolph drew up a contract with four Richmond entrepreneurs, two of whom had been known to his grandfather. The Richmond merchant Bernard Peyton had been a close business associate of Jefferson, who called the merchant "one of the best friends in the world." Joseph Marx, a German trader who emigrated from Hannover to Virginia in the 1790s, was a prominent merchant, land investor, and banker, becoming the director of the Farmers' Bank of Virginia in 1812 and of the Richmond branch of the Second Bank of the United States in 1819. As head of the latter bank, Marx often corresponded with Jefferson, particularly on the subject of his defaulted, cosigned loan with Wilson Cary Nicholas. The two other partners were prominent Virginians. Wyndham Robertson, born across the James River from Richmond in 1803, was the descendant of tobacco barons and influential politicians. When he signed his name to the contract for the Arkansas scheme in 1836, Robertson was serving as acting governor of Virginia. The last man in the partnership was George E. Harrison, a prominent planter and heir to a Virginia dynasty.[32]

In March 1836, all the men save Bernard Peyton, who withdrew from the scheme, pledged to buy 8,846 acres of Arkansas land through Randolph for the total sum of $12,360. Rather than buying land directly from Randolph at a generous markup, the three Richmond men were securing Jefferson's grandson as a land agent to patent sections on their behalf. Harrison, Robertson, and Marx expected Randolph to ensure that "separate titles" were promptly issued in each man's name. The deal also contained a significant perk for Randolph—approximately 2,250 acres of land.[33]

The investors whom Randolph secured in Boston and Richmond represented an expansion of the business model he had established in Arkansas. Whereas he had previously relied on local money men to bankroll land purchases, his 1836 trip east demonstrated that Randolph was building a national network of speculators willing to fund land purchases in Arkansas. After meeting with Heard and Marx, Randolph had secured approximately $27,360 to buy land on behalf of the eastern buyers. In return for his services, Randolph would be paid in land rather than cash. Back out west, Randolph funneled the investors' money directly into land purchases, totaling 21,716.11 acres in southern Arkansas. Ignoring parcels north of Little Rock, Randolph knew that his investors had only one reason to back his scheme: reselling cheap government land to prospective cotton planters.[34]

But Randolph's trip east also yielded a new strategy to profit from Arkansas land—one that focused on securing capital to transform the territory's pine woods into profitable cotton plantations. To this end, he formed a new partnership in Richmond with two other powerful Virginians, James Lyons and John Heth. Born the same year that Jefferson became president, Lyons hailed from Hanover, a hamlet just north of Richmond, along the Pamunkey River. After graduating from the College of William and Mary, Lyons threw himself into the practice of law and elite Richmond society. When the marquis de Lafayette made a tour of the United States in 1824, Lyons organized the Virginia leg of the trip. By the 1830s, Lyons had become a staunch Whig supporter, albeit a critic of protective tariffs and a central bank. He was also an enslaver and investor, often partnering with Heth.

For his part, Heth was a coal magnate, his family having mined coal south of Richmond for decades, beginning with his father, Henry Heth, a native of England and a Revolutionary War veteran. Even the duc de la Rochefoucauld saw the pits on his postwar visit to Jefferson at Monticello, frowning at the operators' use of hundreds of enslaved people in the mines. In 1785 the elder Heth began operating Black Heath Mine in Chesterfield County, an enterprise that was little more than a few shallow holes dug in the ground. These evolved into deeper, bulb-shaped pits and then to small corridors held up by pillars of coal. By the time John Heth took over the business, in the 1830s, the pits had become deep underground tunnels, supported by coal, rock, and timber. The enslaved miners piled coal pieces into boxes atop mule-driven wagons. At Black Heath, between one hundred and two hundred African Americans, some owned directly by Heth and others hired from local owners, labored in the terrifically dangerous tunnels, where methane gas, heat, and loose coal made fire a frequent occurrence. Ever the entrepreneur, Heth began rotating his enslaved labor force between his business holdings: the Chesterfield coal mines and west-ern Virginia salt mines.[35]

It's unclear how Lewis Randolph met these two Richmond entrepre-neurs, but it may have been through another man, John Stuart Skinner, who was well known to Thomas Jefferson and his circle. A lawyer, editor, and publisher, Skinner grew up on a large plantation near the Chesapeake Bay, later becoming a notary public and jurist. But it was his work as a government agent during the War of 1812—inspecting European ships, overseeing prisoners of war, and acting as a purser in the U.S. Navy—that put him into contact with a slew of founding luminaries, including James Madison and James Monroe, and made him fantastically wealthy. In 1824, after entertaining the marquis de Lafayette in Baltimore, Skinner was selected to manage the enormous land tract—23,000 acres in northern Florida—given to the French Revolutionary war hero by the U.S. govern-ment. For his part, Jefferson knew Skinner primarily as an agriculturist. In the 1820s, Jefferson had written to him about a variety of crop experiments, as well as about making Parmesan cheese, a process the third president had observed while in Milan in the 1780s.[36]

John Heth was also acquainted with Skinner, and Skinner's land schemes probably whetted Heth's appetite for speculation. In the fall of 1836, Skinner hoped to convince Heth to invest in cotton lands with "friends." Skinner would purchase 4,000 acres, which "with some money, I should like to put in against negroes." Land, he noted to Heth, could "not be had" for less than $5 per acre. But Heth appeared reluctant. Re-sorting to peer pressure, Skinner said he had "no doubt when your friends hear that you are interested, and that you are about making an establish-ment in that vicinity," some of them would "be glad to secure, whilst they can, a plantation" of a section and a half (960 acres) or two sections (1,280 acres). In short, Skinner hoped to persuade Heth to invest up to $6,400. Heth may have gotten cold feet, however, and instead backed what seemed like a surer bet: an Arkansas land speculation scheme piloted by Jeffer-son's grandson. In either case, wealthy men in eastern urban centers were funneling cash into land- and slave-buying schemes in the future Cotton Belt.[37]

Heth, along with Lyons, agreed to partner with Randolph and John S. Nicholas. Their goal was straightforward: establish a new, profitable cotton plantation in southeastern Arkansas. The lengthy contract was drawn up by the lone lawyer in the group: Lyons. Both sets of partners brought something to the bargaining table. Randolph and Nicholas owned land in Clark County—six sections, or 3,840 acres valued at $21,120 (at $5.50 per acre). As Skinner had intimated earlier, western land clearly fetched a much higher price back east—more than three times the original cost. Agreeing to such an inflated valuation, Heth and Lyons would supply what the two land speculators lacked, a "force to cultivate." The Richmond men pledged $21,000 worth of human chattel: fifteen enslaved African Americans, whom the speculators would send west to "to settle on the said land." Upon returning to Arkansas, Randolph and Nicholas would serve as managing partners of the enterprise. Under their supervision, the plantation would be "cleared & opened for cultivation as soon as practicable" and planted in corn and cotton, though cotton was "to be the staple crop." The Arkansas partners would live on-site, hire an overseer, and practice "judicious management" of the enslaved African Americans.[38]

Randolph and Nicholas also agreed to serve as the plantation's agents, selling and delivering the crops, buying livestock and supplies, and managing the accounts. While Randolph and Nicholas were free to eat "all the edible products" on the plantation, the profits of the staple crops were to be divided equally among all parties. The four men were not playing a long game, however. The partnership was only slated to last five years. When it expired, the "whole property"—land, enslaved people, livestock, structures, and tools—would be valued and sold, the proceeds going directly to Heth, Lyons, Nicholas, and Randolph. Significantly, these men were not in the business of becoming Arkansas cotton planters. Their partnership simply represented a new kind of speculative venture, a second wave after the initial, feverish buy-up of federal lands. The four men were betting that the commodities at the center of their partnership—cotton, land, and enslaved people—would all skyrocket in value over the course of a few short years, especially in the wake of Arkansas statehood.[39]

The 15 people enumerated in the contract may have belonged to Heth, or the coal-mining entrepreneur may also have purchased them directly from the Richmond slave market, a hub of the sprawling domestic slave trade. Virginia enslavers sold an estimated 350,000 people in the city between the 1830s and the Civil War. Men, women, and children, all shuttled in from Virginia farms and plantations, were sold at Shockoe Bottom, along Wall Street, not far from the James River. But there was no single slave market; slave traders established "auction rooms," as the English writer Eyre Crowe noted. Enslaved people stood on auction blocks in "low rooms, roughly white-washed, with worn and dirty flooring," open to the street. Slave dealers announced sales by "pinning a manuscript notice of the lot to be sold" and "hanging out a small red flag on a pole from the doorway."[40]

Buyers proceeded from compartment to compartment down Wall Street, bidding on enslaved people. A prospective customer might make a "stalwart hand pace up and down the compartment, as would be done with a horse, to note his action." To determine the man's "ocular soundness," another might fix "one of his thumbs into the socket of the supposed valid eye, holding up a hair by the other hand, and asking the negro to state what was the object held up before him." Slave traders also groomed and grouped enslaved people to fetch high prices. In one compartment, white-aproned young girls huddled together on rough benches. In another were the "form of a woman clasping her infant" and a "muscular field-labourer." All these African Americans would ascend the auction block, goaded by the auctioneer, prodded by slave dealers, and sold to the highest bidder. Afterward, the "usual exodus" of men, women, and children "marched under escort of their new owners across the town to the railway station, where they took their places, and 'went South.'" But in the case of the Arkansas land speculation, Heth and Lyons's fifteen enslaved people headed west, probably forced overland.[41]

Lewis Randolph soon added a sixteenth person to his coffle. He had written to his brother Benjamin Franklin Randolph, a planter and doctor living in southern Albemarle County, about an enslaved woman owned by their mother. The person in question was Martha Ann Colbert, a member of the extended Hemings family. Lewis hoped to bring Colbert with him to Arkansas, where she would be a domestic worker for his wife. Martha Randolph was only too happy to consent. "I am very glad that she can be of use to Elizabeth, and feel no scruple in transferring her," Martha wrote, certain that Colbert "could not fall into better hands." Torn from her immediate family—her great aunt Critta Hemings Bowles, a free African American woman, and husband, Zachariah Bowles—as well as from her home on the Bowles's ninety-six-acre farm just north of Charlottesville, Colbert was taken nearly a thousand miles from central Virginia.[42]

Even Martha Randolph understood the consequences. Noting that "separating her [Colbert] from her family is an evil" she added, more coldly, that "it is one that we are all exposed to in this life." Yet she reassured herself that the separation would be "temporary," since she hoped that Lewis would "finally settle where I can sometimes see you and yours." Despite an awareness of the trauma she was about to impose on Colbert, she gave the young woman to her son, believing that his material interests— the "first and dearest objects of my life"—ranked above those of an enslaved woman and her family. Aware that the news of Colbert's departure for Arkansas would devastate her family, Martha tried to persuade her son Ben to break the news sooner rather than later, so "that it may not fall like a clap of thunder upon her at the moment of separation." Lewis soon arrived in Albemarle County with a wagon, the fifteen enslaved people from Richmond, and his nephew Thomas Mann Randolph Bankhead accompanying him. He probably forced Colbert to join the coffle before driving west.[43]

Starting a large plantation in the Arkansas interior proved no easy task. Both Lewis Randolph and John S. Nicholas had bet big on the value of these lands—a hundred miles from Little Rock, fronting a creek rather than a river. Soon after they took "charge of the Negroes" and arrived at the plantation in January 1837, the challenges became apparent. The Panic of 1837 was just setting in, causing a financial crisis that gripped both U.S. and international markets, shuttered banks, and contracted capital. Randolph hoped to depend on Native peoples still living in that part of the state for food and supplies. And yet, "it being the term of the bank panic," the speculators "could obtain nothing from the natives without gold or silver," paying the astronomical sum of four dollars per bushel in gold for corn. After purchasing the corn from Native farmers, Randolph was forced to send it to the nearest mill to be ground into meal, twenty-five miles away. Finding it virtually impossible to secure provisions in Arkansas and aware that they would run out of food by June, the business partners soon looked elsewhere.[44]

New Orleans seemed like the best choice, and Nicholas drifted down the Mississippi by riverboat in the early spring, later arriving at one of the most important trading entrepôts in North America. There he bought nearly five hundred bushels of corn, five hundred pounds of bacon, and

an array of other supplies. What followed, however, was a comedy of er-
rors. Nicholas instructed that the goods be shipped to a port close to their
Clark County lands—Cape Fabre on the Ouachita River—but the New
Orleans merchant misheard him, shipping the produce to Little Rock
instead. Randolph and Nicholas were faced with a tough choice: retrieve
the supplies and forgo at least part of a crop of corn and cotton, or travel to
Little Rock and stave off starvation. The men chose the latter, but it took
seven or eight trips to fetch all the supplies. Perturbed, Nicholas carted
two wagons, six mules, four oxen, and two enslaved men back and forth to
the Arkansas capital.[45]

By June, Randolph was feeling more bullish about his prospects. His
wife and son, who had been living in Little Rock with the Fultons, arrived
at the plantation, probably on one of the supply wagons driven by Nicholas. Elizabeth found a new "comfortable house," full of new furniture
shipped from Cape Fabre. She also discovered several newly constructed
outbuildings, including a kitchen, store room packed with supplies from
New Orleans, smokehouse, overseer's house, and "4 negro houses built
since the first of January." There was a vegetable garden, and "a prospect
of a fine crop of corn" of about fifty acres. In short, the land appeared to
be a recognizable and potentially viable plantation—a possibility that as-
tounded Elizabeth. Lewis was determined to spend the first year opening
the land and planting corn, devoting the second year exclusively to cotton.
That would leave him a further three years before the expiration of the
contract with Heth and Lyons to turn a profit. As an experiment, Randolph also planted four or five acres of cotton in early summer, just to "see
how it would grow." Unbeknownst to the inexperienced Randolph, May
was too late to plant cotton—the crop demanded a long growing season,
and most planters seeded it just after the threat of frost had passed. The
heavy rains, which tore through the fields, gullying them, did not help
either. By October, the cotton was a wet and wilted mess, the cold weather
having "carried it to mould and mildew."[46]

In the midst of the bad weather, Randolph decided to head south.
Unless he went to Cape Fabre, the plantation would not last through the
winter. In September he pushed off in a dugout canoe, paddling along the
Terre Noir creek. He expected to be gone only a few weeks, but it rained
constantly. Randolph soon fell ill, as did the rest of his family, including his
son Jack. Even Martha Ann Colbert was "as bad off as any of us." Young

Thomas Mann Randolph Bankhead served as a kind of impromptu nurse as sickness ravaged the household. "God knows what I should have done if it had not been for my nephew Tom," Elizabeth moaned. "He nursed Jack, Lewis, and I through our sickness, and has given me every consolation in his power." Elizabeth, Jack, and Martha Ann survived, but Lewis died at the end of September, age twenty-seven. "Lewis took leave of the troublesome world and had left me in keeping of his good name," wrote his wife, who hoped to leave Arkansas by mid-October and return to Tennessee. But she did not know where to turn. "My situation is a gloomy one," she lamented, as "I have no one to advise me and Tom is not yet of age and cannot act as administrator." Indeed, Lewis had left a tangled legacy behind—no will and thousands of acres of land without clear title.[47]

It became evident that the land in Township 10 South was worthless. "The land was not worth what it was represented to be," Elizabeth admitted. She discovered that Lewis had bought the property without ever having seen it. Instead, it was "selected and bought by the recommendation" of two Arkansas land agents. The parcels had been decreed "first rate" by land hunters who had first scouted the sections. Lewis Randolph bought the land in his name in the Red River district, in the town of Washington, convinced that the parcels would be ideal for cotton cultivation.[48]

Heth and Lyons were livid after learning that Randolph's landholdings had almost no value. Given the worthlessness of the land, Randolph and Nicholas certainly held nothing close to the value of fifteen enslaved people, a glaring problem since the entire premise of the partnership was the equality of investment. The Richmond businessmen charged that the "place had been mismanaged" and hoped to reclaim their human property and sell them as soon as possible. Frustrated, Elizabeth tried to wrangle a string of witnesses who were "acquainted with all the facts in relation to the purchase of the land" and could testify that Lewis Randolph had acted in good faith.[49]

In the meantime, Nicholas, as the only partner still alive in Arkansas, attempted to keep the plantation afloat. In the spring of 1838, he reported that the "wilderness" was fast becoming a productive estate. The enslaved workforce had cleared eighty acres during the winter, and Nicholas predicted that he would get a hundred acres of corn yielding two thousand bushels and eighty acres of cotton that would produce eighty thousand pounds of the silky fiber. He expected to lay out some capital to build a cotton gin and a gristmill, hoping to eliminate the need to travel long distances to process his crops. Even the "negroes have excellent health," he reported, though one child died in a fire and "was burnt to a cinder." But that, Nicholas insisted, was the only "melancholy incident" to mar the winter.[50]

His optimism about the plantation was short-lived, however. The property was too far north to grow cotton productively—Nicholas experienced "frosty mornings" well into April—and he found it "impossible to conduct the plantation" without proximate supplies and services, such as a blacksmith. Perhaps concluding that he was as ill-suited to cotton planting as the land, Nicholas decided to sell his stake in the partnership to Heth and Lyons for eight thousand dollars. Not long afterward, Lyons took the "negroes out of the state and sold them, and now says he wishes an order of Court to sell the land to reimburse his losses." Lyons probably thought the enslaved people could fetch higher prices in the Deep South, perhaps Louisiana. Lewis Randolph's widow was outraged: Lyons had "broken the contract by selling the negroes without consenting me in my own right." In retaliation, she and Thomas Mann Randolph Bankhead later tried to sue both Heth and Lyons in Henrico County, Virginia.[51]

There were further problems, this time concerning Augustine Heard's investment. Although Lewis Randolph had purchased the Arkansas lands for the three investors at Russell and Company, he had failed to title those lands in the names of Augustine Heard, Samuel Russell, and John Murray Forbes. Legally speaking, none of the opium traders appeared to have any right to the land Randolph had purchased on their behalf. Randolph's widow maintained that because the lands were bought in her late husband's name at two separate land offices—Washington and Little Rock—they now constituted her property. Heard was furious, charging that "all has not been done by her Husband that was agreed upon." He softened only slightly, offering to split the landholdings with Elizabeth Randolph, whom he believed, according to the initial contract, would be entitled to Lewis's share—a quarter of the lands.[52]

By September, Heard had engaged a small-time lawyer in Arkansas named John Field, sent him the original contract with Lewis Randolph, and directed him to "obtain a clear title." Six months later, Heard complained to Samuel Russell that there was still no "satisfactory account of our Arkansas interest." In fact, he had heard nothing from either Field or

Lewis's widow in months. "I do not like to think we are dealing with dishonest people," he ventured, and "yet things do not look right." But, surprisingly, Heard soon had a bit of good news. Field was indeed on the case, securing a "decree of Court which will be a good title." By May, Field hoped to leave Hempstead County, travel to Boston, and personally hand Heard proof of his land ownership in Arkansas. Yet Heard seemed oblivious of the fact that the value of the cotton lands had been grossly inflated. By all accounts, his thirteen-thousand-dollar investment in Lewis Randolph's land speculation scheme had not been a sound one.[53]

In the end, none of Randolph's land bets proved prescient. This was not to say that Arkansas did not become an important cotton-producing state. By 1860, more than two decades after Lewis Randolph had made the initial patents, cotton production was at an all-time high in Arkansas, with most of the valuable staple crop being produced along the state's eastern edge, near the Mississippi River. On the eve of the Civil War, Arkansas farmers and planters produced 367,393 bales of cotton (with each bale weighing five hundred pounds) valued at close to $16 million. Approximately 111,000 enslaved people comprised nearly 23 percent of the Arkansas population in 1860, many of them forced to plant cotton.[54]

But Lewis Randolph's purchases in the far interior of the state did not track with the ensuing cotton boom. In particular, the land he purchased in Columbia, Nevada, Hot Spring, Saline, and Conway counties remained far from the epicenter of cultivation in Arkansas. In general, the largest cotton-producing areas—where planters could expect a yield of up to two bales per acre—were in the Arkansas Delta region. Unfortunately for him, Randolph's land purchases were all far removed from the Mississippi River. Randolph's blood relative J. W. Jefferson criticized the interior of Arkansas when he and his Wisconsin regiment traveled through that country during the Civil War. What caught his attention were the plantations fanning out along the Mississippi River, particularly those near Memphis. After the war ended, Randolph's mixed-race cousin purchased several cotton estates, all of them located in the Arkansas Delta.[55]

Randolph, on the other hand, had always envisioned Arkansas land speculation as a means to an end. He never wanted to become a cotton planter—he was interested in the short-term gain to be had from flipping land in a place that would surely, he thought, become part of an extended U.S. cotton empire. Randolph intended to ride not one but two waves of speculation in Arkansas—first buying cheap federal land on behalf of other investors and retaining a cut, and then founding a cotton plantation that he could sell in a few short years at an exorbitant profit. Investing in land would provide him with the money he sorely lacked, allowing him to accrue independence and equal standing among white elites, while also allowing him to move on to a respectable profession—the law.[56]

In the early 1830s, as an impoverished grandson of the third U.S. president, Lewis Randolph believed he was out of options. With no inheritance in either land or enslaved people, and with his elder brother close to bankruptcy, Randolph thought that his only choice was to quit Virginia and head west, where he could imagine elevating and remaking himself. In the Southwest, slavery's capitalism created a unique opportunity for white men without fortunes; in a space seemingly destined to become part of the future U.S. cotton empire, men like Randolph could generate massive profits by investing in cheap land and enslaved people. Even after Randolph's death, his nephew Thomas Mann Randolph Bankhead remained in Arkansas, fashioning himself as a land speculator in his uncle's image. But as land prices rose and more of the Arkansas public lands were snapped up by investors and settlers, Bankhead looked southward, to new opportunities in Texas. In the 1840s, he moved his venture across state lines, betting that land in the newest state in the union would produce cotton. He reckoned correctly—slave-grown cotton plantations unfurled across East Texas, even along the Gulf Coast, where he himself died, a wealthy but childless man, in 1852.[57]

PART THREE

Race

Madison Hemings

Migration and Belonging in Virginia and Ohio, 1827–1873

IN 1805 A FATHER RECORDED THE BIRTH of his son in a slave roll. In the ensuing years, this same man would document the childhood and young adulthood of his child through a series of lists: who his mother was and his siblings, how much bread he ate, how many yards of wool or osnaburg cloth he was allotted each year, whether he received a bed or blanket to sleep on, where he lived, what work he performed and where on the plantation. Identified by his first name and birth year—lest the father confuse him with another enslaved boy who shared the same name—the son appeared twenty-two times over the course of twenty-one years. The records ceased when the father died. Only then was the son no longer known as his property, as a name in a plantation manual: "Madison 05." Only in his will, sketched out in the terms of his son's emancipation from bondage, did Thomas Jefferson finally acknowledge the full name of his child: Madison Hemings. But liberating his own son from enslavement conferred no legal status of inclusion, equality, or citizenship in the early nineteenth-century United States.[1]

Madison Hemings was not surprised that his father refused to acknowledge him as a blood relative, as a person, or as an American. As he later recalled, Jefferson was "not in the habit of showing partiality or fatherly affection to us children." By contrast, he was always "affectionate towards his white grandchildren"—the Hemings siblings' contemporaries on the Monticello mountaintop. The only capacity in which Jefferson viewed his mixed-race children with Sally Hemings was as his property and plantation labor force. On Mulberry Row, the main plantation street at Monticello, which ran perpendicular to the main house, Jefferson directed and surveilled his children's work, measuring their efficiency and productivity as their owner—and master. Madison, Eston, Beverly, and

Harriet Hemings were "mechanics," in Jefferson's eyes, laborers in whose "operations he took a great interest."[2]

Standing aloof in the dark corners of the smoky, crowded workshops where the Hemingses toiled, Jefferson was almost unknowable to his children. "Of my father," Madison later remembered, he knew little, save that his "temperament was smooth and even." That the Hemings children lived in such close proximity to Jefferson throughout their childhood— in cabins along Mulberry Row or in a room under the South Terrace wing of the mansion—and yet hardly knew him further demonstrated that their father viewed his children in much the same light as his other human property. From his deathbed in 1826, Jefferson remitted "my last, solemn, dutiful thanks" to two "servants": his children Madison and Eston Hemings. These were the last words communicated from a father to sons not named as such, but instead referred to as "apprentices" of their uncle John Hemmings.[3]

Madison Hemings became a free person for the first time in 1827, no longer subject to the oversight and mastery of an enslaver or catalogued as property in his father's slave roll. But liberty did not mean an escape from white surveillance in the slave state of Virginia. Indeed, all free African Americans were required to produce manumission papers and register at the county courthouse at regular intervals. In 1831, Madison Hemings was once again reduced to a name and physical description, this time as a liberated African American man: "5:7 3/8 Inches high light complexion no scars or marks perceivable." No longer recorded by an individual enslaver in a plantation journal, Hemings was now documented by a state official in the county minute book.[4]

Nor did his newfound liberty give Madison Hemings the right to legal residency in Virginia. In fact, on paper at least, it was mandatory for all manumitted African Americans to leave the state within a year. As an 1806 law stipulated, any person manumitted in that year or later who did not emigrate elsewhere would forfeit his or her "right to freedom" and could be "apprehended and sold" by the overseers of the poor—officials who administered poor relief in Virginia. But before he died, Jefferson had petitioned the General Assembly to permit his two sons, Madison and Eston Hemings, "to remain in this state where their families and connections are." The legislature granted Jefferson's request, and it was through this special dispensation—in addition to his enrollment on the "Free Negro

Register"—that Madison Hemings legally became a resident of Virginia. While some historians have argued that free Black registration and the 1806 act were only sporadically enforced before the Civil War, refusal to comply with these laws nonetheless left African Americans acutely vulnerable to re-enslavement and kidnapping in a state that was a primary hub of the internal slave trade.[5]

The register worked as a double-edged sword for African Americans manumitted before 1806. On one hand, it subjected them to a new form of white surveillance. But on the other, it afforded them a measure of protection and transformed their status before the law. Though men like Madison Hemings were not citizens—they could not vote or claim an array of legal privileges extended to white Virginians—they *were* property holders and legal residents of Virginia. In fact, registering with the court enabled free Black individuals to buy and sell property, witness marriages, record wills, and act as guarantors on loans. Appearing at the courthouse to conduct business other than submitting to the mandatory registration renewal enabled African Americans to become recognized and legitimate legal actors who comported themselves like citizens.[6]

In the free state of Ohio, where Madison Hemings and his family settled in 1836, African Americans were similarly surveilled and regulated by the state. Any free Black person wishing to settle in Ohio was required to present manumission papers for inspection, pay a five hundred dollar security bond guaranteed by two white Ohioans, and register at the county courthouse. Failure to comply with these mandates meant that immigrating African Americans were not entitled to legal settlement and could be banished from the state. Under Ohio law, unregistered African Americans were considered dependent "aliens" who could not purchase property or claim any kind of legal protection. While these laws, as in Virginia, were intermittently enforced, they still heightened the risk of African Americans' "removal" from Ohio.[7]

As the historians Annette Gordon-Reed and Lucia Stanton have emphasized, freedom from bondage allowed Madison Hemings to preserve his family and reclaim a personhood that had been stolen under slavery.[8] Still, Hemings was excluded from citizenship in Ohio and Virginia. Before the passage of the Fourteenth Amendment, citizenship was conferred by state governments—it was predicated on an individual's status as a legal settler, a category that implied whiteness, independence, and equality. Outside New England, state officials in the North, South, and West borrowed from the English Poor Law tradition to define African Americans as vagrants, paupers, and dependents, thereby providing a legal basis for the exclusion or restriction of Black migration and settlement. Even when African Americans did claim legal residency by complying with state law, as Madison Hemings did in Virginia in the 1830s, state officials defined them as noncitizens.[9]

State officials extended the right of immigration and settlement only to free African Americans who submitted to state surveillance and control. That free and slave states implemented similar exclusionary legislation was not lost on liberated Black Americans who hoped to make a new life outside the slave South. In the 1820s, John Malvin, an African American man born to a free mother and enslaved father in Virginia, traveled more than three hundred miles from his birthplace to southern Ohio. "I thought upon coming to a free State like Ohio, I would find every door thrown open to receive me," he noted, but "I found it little better than Virginia." Rather, Malvin "found every door closed against the colored man in a free State, excepting the jails and penitentiaries." So racist and oppressive were Ohio's anti-Black laws that Malvin briefly toyed with the idea of returning to Virginia.[10]

In this chapter I argue that between the 1820s and the 1870s, Madison Hemings employed creative strategies to resist state officials' attempts to categorize him as a "foreign" dependent noncitizen. But his strategies varied across jurisdictions and depended upon local circumstances. In the slave state of Virginia, Hemings consciously created a highly visible legal footprint. Though the state reduced his legal existence to a brief physical description in the register, he challenged that definition by exercising all the rights available to him as a free person of color. But in Ohio, Hemings refused to submit to state surveillance and control. Because state citizenship was predicated on whiteness, Hemings, a proud African American his entire life, did not aspire to that status. Instead, Hemings disappeared from the Ohio public record for about two decades, striving for what the scholar Koritha Mitchell has called "homemade citizenship"—Black belonging centered on the home and community that did not depend on white recognition. Only in 1856 did Madison Hemings reveal himself, purchasing land for the first time. And only in 1873, in the wake of the adoption of the Reconstruction Amendments that explicitly defined him as both independent *and* equal—as a citizen of the United States—did he finally tell his story, asserting that he was, and always had been, an American.[11]

In the August heat of 1827, Madison Hemings walked into the county courthouse in Charlottesville, across the street from the Eagle Tavern, the site where thirty-three of his father's enslaved people would be sold two years later. When he strode into court, he was not alone. A white man and blood relative, Thomas Jefferson (Jeff) Randolph, accompanied him, as did three other family members also manumitted according to the terms of Jefferson's will: Burwell Colbert, Joseph Fossett, and John Hemmings. As the executor of his grandfather's debt-ridden estate, Jeff Randolph was present to consent to the freedom of these men—all the "property of the said deceased and who were emancipated by his Will." Even though the emancipation of these African American men had been inscribed in a legal document written by the third president of the United States, a white man still had to vouch for the legitimacy of their freedom. All four African American men received their manumission papers and registered with the court that day—proof of their freedom, as well as evidence of their unequal status before the law.[12]

A few years later, in 1831, Madison Hemings was back at the courthouse with his uncle John Hemmings. The court clerk—who played a crucial and powerful role in how the state "saw" Black people—was responsible for noting down changes in the physical descriptions of free people of color. He itemized new scars, lost or damaged limbs, even gray hair. In 1831, after Madison Hemings "personally" appeared in court and produced "satisfactory evidence of his freedom," the clerk collapsed his entire personhood into a brief line in the ledger: a "man of colour" who was twenty-eight years old. The clerk also took down details about John Hemmings. Sally Hemings's half-brother was fifty-six years old, just over 5 foot 5 inches tall, and had a "high light complexion." Hemmings, the eagle-eyed clerk noted, also had a small scar on his right wrist.[13]

The hostility of white people toward free African Americans had a long history in Virginia, and those prejudices intensified after the turn of the century. In 1800, an uprising masterminded by an enslaved artisan and his twenty-five followers in Richmond electrified white society. The man was Gabriel Prosser, a well-read blacksmith who labored at many of Richmond's foundries, leased there by his owner. As an enslaved but highly mobile ironworker, Prosser probably pieced together the revolutionary events impacting his world: the upcoming presidential election between Federalists and their Democratic-Republican challengers, and the ongoing struggles of Black people in Saint-Domingue to overthrow slavery and the brutal plantation regime. Such news was exactly what white Virginians did not want enslaved people to hear. Free Black people around the Atlantic world created clandestine networks and inspired enslaved people to challenge white supremacy and assert their claims to freedom. In the 1790s and the first decade of the 1800s, a smattering of revolts or plots in Spanish Louisiana, the French and British Caribbean, and the United States—in addition to Britain's abolition of slavery in 1833—convinced white Virginians that security for slavery depended largely on cordoning off the state from both "foreign" and potentially incendiary information and from free Black people. Virginia officials took swift action, passing a series of laws intended to clamp down on Black people's mobility, literacy, and access to information as well as mandating that manumitted slaves leave the state within a year.[14]

In the 1820s and 1830s, Madison Hemings and other free people of color used these laws to construct a legal record of their own, creating paper trails that challenged the state's racist prescriptions. They took laws that characterized them as hostile and dependent aliens in need of surveillance and used them in an innovative way—to assert themselves as community members whose freedom and property deserved to be protected by the state. While Virginia law forced Hemings to appear at the courthouse every three years, he did so on a more regular basis of his own accord—to transact business usually associated with white Virginians.[15]

Like other free African Americans, Hemings understood that complying with the free Black register enabled him to become a legal resident of Virginia and claim an array of privileges and protections under the law. While the county minute books described free African Americans as mere bodies, deed and marriage records reflected them as they wanted to be seen—as people and property holders. African Americans' names often appeared repeatedly in these records, perhaps to constantly reaffirm their holders' status as non-slaves—and to demonstrate that they could engage in the same legal transactions as white people. When Madison Hemings got married or bought a parcel of land, he was exercising legal rights that had been denied to him as his father's chattel. Yet even as a free person with property rights, he could not claim state citizenship.[16]

Soon after registering with the court clerk in 1827, Hemings began constructing a more visible legal record of himself in Charlottesville. In 1830, he and his brother Eston pooled their resources and became land-owners for the first time, purchasing a city lot from John and Frances Perry for five hundred dollars. The lot the Hemings brothers bought was a half-acre, "more or less," lying just off the main thoroughfare connecting the downtown area, anchored by the courthouse square, and the University of Virginia. The lot included a house, and it adjoined another lot owned by the Perrys. Though the exact location of the house remains unknown, the Hemings' new neighborhood appeared, at least to white observers, as empty space, a kind of wasteland shunted between the town and the col-lege. As one white resident recounted, Main Street "had few houses, and only two or three business places on it." The road itself was rough and unpaved—deep mud stalled wagons there in winter.[17]

But Madison Hemings was hardly isolated. He had become part of a network of free Black property owners, many of them relatives. An aunt, Mary Hemings Bell, lived on a Main Street lot inherited from her white merchant husband, Thomas Bell. It was to this lot that Joseph Fossett—another Hemings family member—came to live after being freed under the terms of Jefferson's will. Fossett, a blacksmith by trade, converted Bell's granary into a house for himself, his wife, and several of their children. And Jesse Scott, a free Black musician married to one of Bell's daughters, was also a member of the Bell household. It was Scott who joined the crowd of bidders at the Monticello estate sale in 1827, purchasing his sister-in-law Edith Fossett (Joseph's wife) and her two youngest children for $505. And catty-corner from Mary Bell's lot stood a large wooden house belonging to the Jewish merchant David Isaacs and his wife, Nancy West, a free woman of color. In 1832, Eston Hemings married their daughter, Julia Ann Isaacs. Rather than the veritable no-man's-land described by the white onlooker, this was a vibrant, closely knit community of free Black and mixed-race property holders.[18]

The Perrys were not unknown to the Hemings family. A master brick-layer and carpenter, John Perry had completed numerous building proj-ects at Jefferson's Monticello and Poplar Forest plantations between 1800 and 1811. Perry was something of an entrepreneur, and working on farms, houses, and churches throughout central Virginia helped foot the bill for his extensive land purchases. In 1817 he shrewdly sold some of this land to the University of Virginia under the condition that he would win joinery and carpentry contracts during construction of the college. Later, Perry helped appraise Jefferson's estate, even trekking up the mountain for the 1827 sale, where he purchased a marble table on the West Lawn for $41. Two years later, he would be one of the slave buyers who crowded in front of the Eagle Tavern, ultimately purchasing three people: a woman named Lania and her child for $295, and a man, Washington, for $150. When Madison and Eston Hemings purchased the lot from Perry, they bought it from a man with whom they had a complicated connection. John Perry had worked for their father, just as they had done. He was also a woodworker, as the Hemings siblings themselves were gifted carpenters. But he was still a white man and an enslaver.[19]

Eston and Madison Hemings did not live in their new house alone. Their fifty-seven-year-old mother, Sally Hemings, shared it with them. For the first time in their lives, the family was able to live together of their own volition. Contrary to what the register implied, Madison Hemings was more than an unattached Black man. He was a member of a family—after 1830, a property-owning family. While enslaved to Jefferson at Monticello, Sally Hemings and her children had held a favored position on the mountaintop. "We were always permitted to be with our mother," Madison recalled of the privilege that set his siblings apart from other enslaved children on the plantation. Yet they remained Jefferson's chattel: they were, in Madison's words, "well used." Like Jefferson's other human property, the Hemings family was constantly shuttled from dwelling to dwelling on the mountaintop, whether to a small room under the South Terrace or one of the cabins along Mulberry Row. Simply put, the Hemings family never had a permanent home there. They were too busy taking care of Jefferson's. "It was her duty, all her life long," Madison remembered of his mother, "to take care of his [Jefferson's] chamber and wardrobe."[20]

After gaining their freedom, Madison and Eston Hemings brought their "mother to live with us." Unlike her two sons, Sally Hemings had not been freed by Jefferson's will. Jefferson's white daughter Martha Jefferson Randolph had instead given her enslaved cousin "her time"—unofficially manumitted her. For the next five years, in a state of unofficial freedom, Sally Hemings lived in a home owned by her children, unburdened of the "dread" of slavery. Yet her safety remained precarious. Without formal manumission papers, and without her name itemized in the register, she remained vulnerable and at risk. If a slave trader kidnapped her, she would have no recourse to freedom. And if Virginia officials caught wind of the fact that she had evaded registration at the courthouse, Sally Hemings could face sale on an auction block. To protect her, Madison and Eston Hemings worked to keep their mother invisible in the legal record. In fact, her name appeared only once after she settled in Charlottesville, in a special state census conducted in 1833.[21]

A year after buying the lot off Main Street, Madison Hemings signed his name to a legal document for the first time. In a hesitant scrawl, he wrote out his given name, then his last, spelling it first phonetically as "Hemins" before reshaping the last letter into a "g." The other man who signed the legal document, a free Black man named William Spinner, drew only an "X" in the space for his signature. The clerk, presumably white, wrote the man's name for him above the mark: "Wm. Spinner." Spinner, the bondsman for Hemings's marriage certificate, probably could neither read nor write, even though he was a property holder and the first free Black man employed by the University of Virginia. In offering a bond (or promise) of $150, Spinner and Hemings were providing a form of guarantee that there was no legal bar to the marriage—that neither the bride nor the groom was already married, that the couple was of legal age, and that they were not too closely related. Hemings's halting script and Spinner's "X" were probably the result of enslavers' and legislators' efforts to further restrict literacy among Black people.[22]

Reading and writing were never skills that Jefferson had endorsed or encouraged among the enslaved people at Monticello, not even for his children. No white person voluntarily gave Hemings any formal instruction. "I learned to read by inducing the white children to teach me the letters and something more," Hemings remembered. He had to persuade the white grandchildren—whom he observed playing with Jefferson while he stood at a distance—that he too deserved the chance at education. After his emancipation in 1827, Hemings's ad hoc schooling at Monticello ended, and for the next several decades he "picked up here and there" all of "what else I know." But the process of becoming literate must have been painstakingly slow, since it was not until 1873, when he dictated his memoir, that he declared, "Now I can read and write."[23]

While Hemings may have been barely literate in 1831, he nonetheless achieved something that no other African American family member had done before him—he got legally married. Whereas Jefferson had recognized slave marriages at Monticello, Virginia law did not. As a free Black man, Hemings, with the help of Spinner, provided a guarantee of $150 to become "held and firmly bound" to a free woman of color: Mary Hughes McCoy. This legal decree augmented Hemings's self-determined personhood. He was a free man, a property holder, and now a husband. Indeed, he and his siblings shared a crucial characteristic in freedom: "we all married and have raised families."[24]

But Madison Hemings's carefully constructed—and highly visible—legal identity soon came under threat. In 1831, the devoutly religious Nat Turner staged his uprising in the Virginia Tidewater. After the violence finally abated, white legislators lost no time in enacting new laws curtailing the mobility and education of free African Americans, and more aggressively enforcing the 1806 "removal" law. They also commissioned a special census, taken in 1833. As Martha Jefferson Randolph reported, the laws were "more exactly enforced and they [Black people] are denied the liberty of social intercourse by the restrictions with which it [one of the laws] is hampered." There were to be "no meetings, no night visiting, and upon those plantations which are at all disorderly, harassed with the night visits of the patrol, besides being watched at every turn." But members of the General Assembly also debated ways to end slavery. Soon after Turner and his co-conspirators were hanged—and in Turner's case, skinned—delegates, spurred by Jeff Randolph, entertained proposals to emancipate and then "remove" enslaved and free Black people from the state.[25]

In 1832, the Virginia legislature embraced calls for Black expatriation. Rather than focus on freeing enslaved people, the General Assembly turned its attention toward expelling the state's free African American population (including the Hemings family), which hovered around fifty thousand souls. The Nat Turner revolt had only made the state's colonization project more urgent. Most white people attributed racial violence to free Black people rather than enslaved people—they saw literate free people of color as the primary purveyors of information and instigators of rebellion. To alleviate the constant threat of bloodshed amid a rapidly increasing nonwhite population, legislators identified colonization to Liberia as the best way to "drain" their state of African Americans. In 1833, free people of color were given the option of being sent to Africa. Perhaps unsurprisingly, not one of the more than four hundred people of African descent in Albemarle County accepted the offer, including Madison, Eston, and Sally Hemings.[26]

One member of the extended Hemings family living across the Blue Ridge Mountains in Lexington did make the choice to leave Virginia. After being freed by enslaver John Jordan, Brown Colbert, his wife, and their two youngest sons made what would prove to be a fatal journey to Liberia aboard the brig *Roanoke* in 1833. Only one member of the family—eight-year-old Burwell Colbert—survived, perhaps living long enough to see Liberia transition from an American colony to an independent nation in 1847. As the descendant of one of Brown Colbert's sons who could not be freed from bondage in Virginia, Bill Webb observed that his ancestor must have had a "strong conviction for freedom" to set sail for Africa, although the "price he paid" for that belief was enormous.[27]

The Virginia legislature's colonization offer probably rankled with Madison Hemings. To make matters worse, the state also mandated that the Hemings family submit to more surveillance and control in the form of the special census. When the census taker arrived at the half-acre lot owned by Madison Hemings in July 1833, he encountered three free people of color. Madison Hemings, listed as twenty-nine years old, was a carpenter by trade. His wife, Mary, recorded as twenty-four years old, and his mother, deemed to be sixty-five, were listed as dependents in his household. The state official recorded that both Madison and Sally Hemings were manumitted in 1826, which was untrue—Madison became free in 1827 and his mother never officially gained her freedom. By contrast, Mary was recorded as "born" free. All three residents of the house were deemed "mulattoes" who were "not willing" to leave Virginia for Liberia. This tally represented the state's concerted effort to augment its long-standing catalogue of free people of color with more specific information. But this census also confirmed Madison Hemings as a head of household, landowner, and legal resident of Virginia.[28]

As racism and the threat of violence and deportation probably loomed large, Madison Hemings turned his attention north and west, to the free states across the Ohio River. He took pride in leaving of his own choice, rather than at the behest of state officials. "We lived and labored until 1836," Hemings later declared in his memoir, "when we voluntarily left the state." Other free African Americans would make the same decision in the latter 1830s, including Madison's brother Eston and Hemings family relatives Joseph and Edith Fossett.[29]

But Madison Hemings was not the first member of his immediate family to leave the state. His siblings Beverly and Harriet had departed Virginia more than a decade earlier. In 1822, his brother and sister had "walked away and staid away," leaving Monticello and possibly boarding a stagecoach north to Washington, D.C. Former overseer Edmund Bacon claimed that Jefferson had handed his daughter fifty dollars for the journey. It had allegedly been Jefferson's "principle," recalled Ellen Wayles Coolidge, "to allow such of his [Jefferson's] slaves as were sufficiently white to pass for white men, to withdraw from the plantation." It was "called running away, but they were never reclaimed," she explained. This "principle" apparently extended to his own children. When Beverly Hemings set foot in Washington, he was on paper, at least, a fugitive. Consequently, he made the decision to enter the nation's capital as something else: a white man. He soon "married a white woman in Maryland," Madison recalled, and Beverly's daughter was "not known by the white folks to have any coloured blood coursing in her veins."[30]

Harriet Hemings also went to Washington "to assume the role of a white woman." Marrying a white man "in good standing," she raised a family, and "so far as I know they were never suspected of being tainted with African blood." Madison avoided disclosing any details about his sister's identity for "prudential reasons." Even he did not know her precise whereabouts. "I have not heard from her for ten years," Madison lamented, "and do not know whether she is dead or alive." This grief-stricken line captures the true horror of "passing" for Black Americans: to protect their families and assert their place in white society, they adopted whiteness, a strategy that forced them to sever ties with African American family members forever. For all intents and purposes, they were invisible; only oral history and memoirs provided clues to their existence and whereabouts. All Madison could do was mourn—and remember—his lost siblings: he named two of his own children after Beverly and Harriet.[31]

When Madison Hemings packed up his family and belongings and

left for Ohio, he did so without his siblings, and without his mother. Sally
Hemings had died in 1835, of unknown causes. Madison may have remained in Charlottesville for as long as he did for his mother's sake—as
an unofficially freed person, she would have been at enormous risk outside
Virginia, and, in particular, in a free state that regulated African American
immigration. When he departed Charlottesville, he also left behind "a
son in the soil near Monticello." But like all of Jefferson's African American descendants, Madison Hemings believed that leaving Virginia was a
necessity—he saw no viable future for himself or his family in a slave state.[32]

No one knows which route Madison, Mary, and Sarah Hemings took on
their trek northwest, but one thing is certain: they crossed the great tributary dividing North and South, free states and slave states, the Ohio River.
They also set foot in a state that had only recently been carved from the
Northwest Territory—lands fringing the Great Lakes that had first been
occupied by Indigenous tribes, later becoming central to French and British imperial commerce before being ceded to the United States after the
American Revolution. Traveling nearly four hundred miles from their
home in Virginia, Hemings and his family settled in Pebble Township, in
Pike County, not fifty miles north of the slave state of Kentucky. Though
he was seven-eighths white, Hemings was unwilling to sacrifice his African American identity in Ohio. Rather than hide his Blackness—as he
could have done—he maintained it, suggesting that a primary reason for
abandoning Virginia was the threat it posed not just to his family's security
but also to his African American personhood.[33]

When Madison Hemings and his family crossed the Ohio River, they
did much more than cross state lines—they entered an entirely different
jurisdiction. The Northwest Ordinance, which placed lands originally
claimed by Virginia under federal authority, banned slavery from the
Northwest Territory in 1787. But this was not the result of newfound hu-
manitarianism on the part of the Continental Congress; instead, southern
states hoped to block the creation of slaveholding competitors north of the
Ohio River. Few white settlers—Anglo-American, French, and Spanish
inhabitants—in the territory welcomed the news. One settler, Bartholomew
Cardiveau, dismissed the "obnoxious resolution," telling the first territorial governor, Arthur St. Clair, that the law would "deprive a considerable
number of citizens of their property, acquired and enjoyed long before they

were under the dominion of the United States." But although the ordinance prohibited slavery, the act also restricted the immigration of people of color. Any enslaved person who escaped into this new zone of freedom could be lawfully "reclaimed and conveyed to the person claiming his or her labor or service." Fugitive slaves were unwelcome—and illegal—within the borders of the Northwest Territory. When Ohio became a state in 1803, it reaffirmed and expanded upon this precedent. The new state constitution outlawed slavery within its borders, denied voting rights to African Americans, and further restricted Black immigration.[34]

To be considered as a legal resident and free person in Ohio, Hemings would need to comply with a new set of state laws. Just as in the slave state of Virginia, he would need to register with the clerk of the court and present his manumission papers as proof of his free status. He would also be required to pay an enormous fee and locate two white male guarantors. Without taking these steps, Madison Hemings would not be entitled to legally immigrate to, settle in, or purchase property in Ohio. He would be deemed an "alien" without any legal protection for himself or his family.[35]

But these laws did not stop Hemings and other African Americans from migrating northwest. While many enslaved people sought refuge in Ohio, particularly from the neighboring slave states of Virginia and Kentucky, many free people of color from the southern states also crossed into Ohio and other western free states in the first half of the nineteenth century. This substantial mobilization of free African Americans was in large part the result of new legal restrictions in the slave states, such as Virginia's 1806 requirement that enslaved people who had been manumitted leave the state within one year or face sale or re-enslavement. But free people of color may also have headed to Ohio from northern states. Between 1827 and 1850, thousands of African Americans gained their freedom when slavery officially ended in New York, Pennsylvania, New Jersey, Connecticut, and Rhode Island, but they were nevertheless systematically disenfranchised and excluded from political participation.[36]

Madison Hemings and his family joined a wave of free Black migrants fleeing exclusionary legislation and outright hostility. But the West offered little refuge. In fact, violence toward—and marginalization of—free Black people was pervasive there. As one formerly enslaved man observed, the "African race" was perceived in one of two ways: as "being little above the brute creation" or as "some separate class of degraded beings, too deficient in intellect to provide for their own wants," who "must therefore depend on the superior ability of their oppressors, to take care of them." From the Great Lakes to the Pacific Coast, white legislatures passed a spate of anti-Black laws. Between the 1780s and 1860, every new state (whether slave or free) carved from federal territories, save California and Wisconsin, passed similar restrictive and racist immigration laws.[37]

Ohio was a case in point. The state constitution stripped African Americans of voting rights, a privilege that they had claimed under the territorial government. In 1803, the state legislature compelled "white able-bodied male citizen[s]" to enroll in the militia, implicitly excluding free Black men. And in 1804, an act "to regulate black and mulatto persons" required African Americans to register with county officials, prove their free status, and pay a fee of 12½ cents. An amendment to the law in 1807 underscored Ohio's evolving strategy of racial exclusion: new Black immigrants were required to locate two freeholders willing to post a $500 surety bond on their behalf to guard against their "dependence" on the state. The punishment for failing to register or posting a bond was "removal." Other anti-Black legislation prevented African Americans from voting, testifying in court against white people, serving on juries, or attending public schools. These laws, even when they remained unenforced, sent a clear message: free African Americans and Black fugitives were not welcome within Ohio's borders. However, even with these laws on the books, the free Black population continued to increase, rising from 337 in 1800 to 25,279 by 1850.[38]

These numbers created tensions among white Ohioans, many of whom feared the consequences of large-scale African American immigration. In 1819, an anonymous observer in Cincinnati complained that restrictive laws in slave states were "driving all their free negroes upon us," a population that he described as "perhaps as depraved and ignorant a set of people as any of their kind." Resistance to Black settlers became particularly pronounced in Cincinnati, a town on the Ohio River that lay directly across the water from slaveholding Kentucky. In 1829, prejudice toward recent Black immigrants reached a violent climax. African Americans had poured into the city in the 1820s, settling along the riverfront and swelling the Black population to more than 2,200 souls. Poor white people, including Irish immigrants, criticized the arrival of new competition for wage labor jobs on the busy Cincinnati docks. Their resentment, and the increasing numbers of Black residents, soon pressured city officials to act. The solution, lawmakers decided, was to enforce the 1807 law in earnest, declaring that "all black residents must enter into bond [the five-hundred-dollar surety]" after thirty days "or face expulsion."[39]

White colonization advocates in Ohio had long tried to foment resentment between free Black people and working-class white people in Cincinnati, hoping that such antagonism would spur the Black people to accept their colonization proposals. In 1826, Robert Finley, secretary of the Cincinnati auxiliary of the American Colonization Society, suggested that "if we could transport one hundred [African Americans] per year from this place I think the citizens would willingly contribute $1,000 per year." The nearly one thousand African Americans in Cincinnati, Finley charged, were "a great and manifest drawback on the prosperity of this city, as they make it difficult for the labouring white people to obtain employment." Together, according to Finley, white Cincinnati residents and the American Colonization Society would facilitate the deportation of African Americans from the city.[40]

In 1829, the city's proclamation dovetailed with increasing calls for the removal of Black people by white colonization supporters, many of whom were members of the Cincinnati Colonization Society. The Black community reacted to the pronouncement with dread. Some African Americans, one reporter noted, "had resided here for a considerable time and were comfortably situated—they became unsettled and deprived of employment by this act of banishment and proscription, and much suffering and distress ensued." Fearing violent reprisals from white people, some Black residents bandied around proposals to relocate to Canada. Led by Black activist James C. Brown, a delegation of African Americans would "obtain liberty to settle . . . and purchase a large tract of land" outside the United States in the British province of Upper Canada.[41]

Time was running out. Seeing little response from African Americans to the city proclamation, white mobs roiled in mid-August. More than three hundred people, many of them poor Irish immigrants, torched Black businesses and homes, assaulting and killing people as they stormed their way through the Fourth Ward. African Americans understood that the mob's terror was intended to push them out of the state permanently. As one man wrote of the race riots, white Ohioans were "determined to drive them [free Black people], not only from their homes and city, but from the State." In the end, "so great had been the loss of property" and "so horrid and fearful had been the scene" that more than half the African American community left Cincinnati permanently, not wanting to live in "constant fear of the mob which had so abused and terrified them." Some resettled in outlying towns while others journeyed all the way to present-day Ontario, founding a free Black colony named after the British abolitionist William Wilberforce.[42]

All was not to remain quiet on the northwestern front. In 1836, another cycle of mob violence swept through Cincinnati, this time driven not by a growing Black population but by abolitionists. Just after the 1829 riots, a seminarian named Lyman Beecher presided over a weeklong debate over slavery and abolition at the Lane Theological Seminary, located just outside Cincinnati. What the white faculty and students concluded reshaped the contours of the abolitionist movement across the United States in the antebellum era. The shocking brutality of the 1829 riots made two things clear: all Christians had to support immediate abolition *and* African colonization was fundamentally problematic. These ideas were supported by another abolitionist new to Cincinnati: the failed Alabama cotton planter and wealthy jurist James Gillespie Birney. After freeing his enslaved people, soundly rejecting African colonization, and declaring himself an abolitionist, Birney set up shop in Cincinnati in 1836, publishing a newspaper called the *Cincinnati Weekly and Abolitionist.*[43]

It did not take long for Birney to attract the ire of Kentucky slaveholders and Cincinnati merchants. Within weeks, a white mob again stormed through Cincinnati's streets, targeting Black residents and known abolitionists. Beatings, killings, and burned buildings ensued, stopping only when the governor declared martial law. But the peace did not last. In July, white people violently attacked Black people attending Independence Day celebrations. Forty white men targeted and destroyed Birney's printing press, offering a hundred-dollar bounty for the abolitionist's capture. The Ohio Anti-Slavery Society put Birney back on his feet, loaning him two thousand dollars to continue publishing his paper. In response, anti-abolitionist white people colluded with the city mayor to shut Birney's paper—and all other abolitionist publications—down. Birney had already built a new press, but a white mob destroyed it before wreaking havoc on African American neighborhoods. The riots and attacks on Black individuals and property continued through the late summer, uninterrupted by city officials, until local organizers succeeded in stamping out the violence with persistent night patrols. No arrests were made, but national outrage was swift and strong. It helped galvanize a new generation of Black activists in Ohio who petitioned the legislature to repeal the state's anti-Black laws in 1849. And the violence inspired a young eyewitness—Beecher's daughter, Harriet Beecher Stowe—to write a best-selling indictment of slavery, *Uncle Tom's Cabin*.[44]

Cincinnati remained a magnet for African Americans, including two men formerly enslaved at Monticello: Israel Gillette and Joseph Fossett. Both men would make the city their home in the 1840s. Gillette, who had purchased his freedom in Virginia for five hundred dollars, painted a rosier picture of the city. "When I came to Ohio I considered myself wholly free, and not till then," he declared. For Gillette, the divide between slave states and free states was a stark one. In Ohio, he was able to remarry his wife "in conformity to the laws of this State" as a free, law-abiding man. Gillette also became literate. "Since I have been in Ohio I have learned to read and write," he boasted, though he conceded that "my duties as a laborer would not permit me to acquire much of an education." Along the banks of the Ohio River, Gillette was a wage earner for the first time in his life. "I was employed as a waiter in a private house," Gillette recalled, initially earning ten dollars a month. But after "I went on board a steam boat, I got higher wages still," sometimes in excess of fifty dollars per month. After fourteen years of waiting tables aboard ships plying the river, Gillette invested his savings in a land purchase, a farm just outside Chillicothe.[45]

When Joseph Fossett arrived in Cincinnati in 1837, only half his family was with him. His wife and four of his children crossed the Ohio River at his side, but four other children remained in bondage in Virginia. Though Fossett established a firm foothold in Cincinnati—buying a city lot for five hundred dollars and setting up a blacksmithing business—he spent the next six years trying to free his children from slavery. The white owner of Fossett's son Peter reneged on his promise to liberate him—the enslaver had "become very fond of me, and would not arrange any terms by which I could gain my freedom." But with his parents in Ohio, Peter Fossett "wanted to be with them and be free, so I resolved to get free or die in the attempt." His first attempt failed, and after his second, he was "caught, handcuffed, and taken back and carried to Richmond and put in jail." For the second time in his life—the first being at the Monticello dispersal sale of 1827—"I was put up on the auction block and sold like a horse." Eventually, Peter Fossett found his way to Cincinnati after his father, family members, and others pooled their resources to purchase his freedom.[46]

Madison Hemings arrived in southern Ohio just as the 1836 riots fizzled out, but the raw wound of racial violence remained open and on display. The white mobs and persistent threats of violence may have influenced Hemings's decision to live east of Cincinnati, in an area where many free Black people from central Virginia had already settled. The state had also recently added to its catalogue of anti-Black legislation. Fearing that the fallout from the Nat Turner revolt in 1831 would have "a tendency to drive free people of color . . . to seek an asylum in the free states," Ohio lawmakers passed a law that prohibited African Americans from seeking poor relief and paying property taxes to support public schools. Both bills were explicitly designed to prevent Black people's "further migration to this State."[47]

There is no evidence that Madison Hemings complied with these or any other anti-Black laws. The archival record does not indicate that he presented his manumission papers, registered as a free Black man, or located two freeholders to post the required five-hundred-dollar surety bond. Indeed, unlike in Virginia, where Hemings submitted to the humiliation of being measured and questioned at the Charlottesville courthouse at three-year intervals, he remained—in legal terms at least—mostly invisible in Ohio. Though he and his growing family appeared on the federal census between 1840 and 1870—always described as "colored" or "mulatto"—Hemings apparently resisted being surveilled, controlled, and excluded by white Ohioans.[48]

Even after Hemings and his family settled in Ohio, he left no legal trace in the public record. Between 1836 and 1856, he did not serve as a bondsman, witness a will, sign a deed, purchase property, or practice any of the "legal consciousness" that he had exhibited in Charlottesville. He may have decided that because state citizenship, even in the "free" jurisdiction of Ohio, was linked to whiteness, that legal status held little meaning to him as a person of color. Hemings chose to claim a different kind of inclusion and belonging that was not predicated on white recognition. In his memoir, he asserted a citizenship that hinged on his own success and achievements, not on how white officials or jurists saw him. He portrayed himself as a master craftsman and as a husband, father, and brother who was enmeshed in the African American community in southern Ohio.[49]

Madison Hemings's mastery of his craft was a testament to his success as a Black American. After settling in Pike County, where he and his family "lived for four or five years," Hemings labored on numerous building projects for a series of white men in Waverly, transforming the "building on the corner of Market and Water Streets from a store to a hotel for the late Judge Jacob Row." Until 2014, that building, known as Emmitt House, survived, and its staircases, doors, and other fine woodwork displayed Hemings's fine craftmanship. Emmitt House collapsed in a fire, but town officials later discovered that the Park Hotel—which still stands today—was yet another building to which Hemings had turned his remarkable hand. He also performed the "carpenter work for the brick building . . . in which the Pike County Republican is printed." It was no accident that when Hemings related his life story to that newspaper, he did so in a space that he had built.[50]

Still, while he worked in Waverly, neither Hemings nor his family could live there. Waverly was a "sundown town"—a municipality whose residents favored racial segregation and intimidation. As one white resident recalled, in the fall of 1829, when the "town was laid out," a free African American "settled here, with the intention of making it his home, but the prejudice against his race was so strong among the other people that he concluded not to remain." Another white settler in Waverly (and the owner of the Emmitt House), James Emmitt, added a name and a racist caricature to the story. "There was a yellow n——r named Love, living on the outskirts of town," who was "a low-minded, impudent, vicious fellow, with the cheek of a mule." Love's "insulting" behavior toward local white people became so "objectionable" that "a lot of the better class of citizens got together one night, made a descent upon his cabin, drove him out, and stoned him a long way in his flight back to Sharonville." But the white people were not to blame for nearly stoning the man to death, according to Emmitt. It was Love's fault. "Our first acquaintance" with African Americans in Waverly, Emmitt blustered, was "with rather rough, objectionable members of that race," and "many things occurred to intensify the prejudice" of white Ohioans toward African Americans.[51]

Beatings, a barrage of stones, vicious threats—these were why Madison Hemings did not live in Waverly. They also offer a plausible reason for his relative invisibility in the legal record for so many decades. Indeed, the racial violence that unfolded in Waverly, and in many other small Ohio towns, pointed to the belief popular among white people that a multiracial society was an impossibility. "The existence in any community of a people forming a distinct and degraded caste, who are forever excluded by the fiat of society and the laws of the land," must "be fraught with unmixed evil," Ohio lawmakers declared, their warning underscoring the long-standing idea—harkening back to Jefferson's rough draft of the Declaration of Independence—that people of African descent could not be recognized as Americans.[52]

But neither was the Hemings family safe in rural Ohio. In the 1830s and 1840s, even in an area surrounded by African American property owners, many of whom originally hailed from slave states, the threat of white violence loomed large. "A lot of VA Negroes settled up on Pee-Pee Creek," Emmitt noted, but their presence "enraged their white neighbors" who "made almost constant war" on these African Americans. The leader of these terrifying exploits was a man named Tim Downing. He and his "gang" burned the hay and wheat cultivated by farmers of color, harassed their livestock, and did "everything possible to make life absolutely miserable." Resentful white settlers might also report their unregistered African American neighbors to state officials, hoping to compel their banishment from the state.[53]

But the "brunt of their hatred" was saved for the most prosperous of the Pee Pee farmers of color. One night, Downing and his followers shouldered their guns to do a "little killing and burning," avowing to clear out the "whole nest" of African Americans. Targeting the wealthiest Black farmer, Downing trained his rifle on the man's cabin and fired. What Downing did not anticipate was that the man would fire back, hitting Downing's brother in the leg. The bullet struck an artery, and the brother soon bled to death. Downing was determined to arm himself with the law, but a jury acquitted the alleged African American shooter. Furious, Downing lay in wait for the farmer's son, opening fire and striking him "in the head, fracturing his skull and allowing a portion of his brain to ooze out." When the young man recovered, the terrorized family moved away.[54]

Madison Hemings and his wife and children may have been motivated by the same fear. He lived in Pee Pee Township, in Pike County, for a few years, in proximity to four African American households. Hemings and his family then moved, possibly because of the violent reprisals by white people, and settled in the adjacent Pebble Township, an area of small farmers who were predominantly African American or German. And when he finally did purchase property, in 1856, Hemings did so in another jurisdiction altogether—Ross County.[55]

Despite threats of racial violence, Hemings clung fiercely to his African American identity, the only child of Thomas Jefferson and Sally Hemings to do so. He strove for inclusion and belonging that was recognized and respected by the Black community around him. Ray Malone, a white descendant of a neighbor of Madison Hemings's, recalled that he was "considered an honorable person" by Chillicothe African Americans, and that it was widely accepted that he was Jefferson's son. A descendant, Shay Banks-Young, described Hemings as having a "wonderful reputation as a good man." Beyond that, Hemings's determination to retain his surname and his African American identity earned the respect of his neighbors— and subsequent generations of family members. "A lot of us wouldn't even have our history of the Hemings life if it wasn't for him," Banks-Young declared. He was the "only one who has the name" and "shared out loud his history." The other siblings—Harriet, Beverly, and Eston—"either went white and passed through" or the "name was changed." Madison Hemings's perseverance in Ohio, despite violence and exclusion, "validates . . . all of those other oral histories," Banks-Young emphasized.[56]

Though Hemings remained firmly ensconced in the local African American community, he stayed out of state officials' sight. It was not until 1856 that Madison Hemings's name appeared in Ohio records—the same year that the antislavery Republican Party first showed up on the presidential ballot. Hemings purchased a farm of twenty-five acres for $150, becoming an Ohio landowner for the first time. He moved his still growing family—nine children, including a newborn daughter, Ellen Wayles—to the new farm. The purchase may have been an investment, as Hemings sold it three years later at a $100 profit. Perhaps uncoincidentally, it was not until the end of the Civil War and the passage of the Thirteenth Amendment in 1865 that Hemings finally bought a large piece of property to farm: sixty-six acres in Ross County for $660. He became increasingly prosperous during the 1860s, claiming real estate worth $1,500 and $300 of personal property in 1870.[57]

Still, Madison Hemings's identity remained rooted in his family and in fine woodwork until his death in 1877. His estate inventory indicated few personal goods: a bedstead and bedding, five chairs, two kettles, and a large cupboard. As a record of his livelihood, it listed a black mare, seven hogs, a harness and plaices, a large harrow plow, a wagon, and piles of lumber. More revealing was an item valued at two dollars—"woodwork of 2 shovel plows." Even though he was deemed a "farmer" on the federal census, Hemings was making his own farming implements, and perhaps those of his neighbors as well. For this he owned a slew of tools: chisels, augers, a hatchet, bench and molding planes, a square level, saws, and a grindstone.[58]

Madison Hemings's estate revealed much about his world—who he was, and what he cherished. But in the last decade of his life, he took further steps to shed light on his identity. The year 1870 appears to have been a turning point. In that year Congress passed the Fifteenth Amendment, part of a triad of Reconstruction Amendments aimed at dismantling race-based chattel slavery and African American inequality in the United States. Perhaps most important for Madison Hemings, this federal legislation meant an end to states' authority to determine citizenship and also granted African American men the right to vote.[59]

Despite the presence of de jure segregation in postbellum Ohio, Black citizenship seems to have had a profound effect on Madison Hemings. Finally recognized as an American, he decided that he could tell his story. In 1870, he revealed to federal census taker William Weaver that Thomas Jefferson was his father, thereby allowing details of his blood connection to Jefferson to be inscribed in the public record. Astonished, Weaver scribbled excitedly in the margins of his notebook: "This man is the son of Thomas Jefferson!" Three years later, Hemings revealed his identity even more publicly when he dictated a memoir to S. F. Wetmore, which was published in the columns of the *Pike County Republican*.[60]

Yet the 1873 memoir was much more than personal history. For Hemings, revealing his own story also meant revealing his *family's* story— the basis of his claim to inclusion and belonging in the United States, not just as a free man but also as a citizen. Unlike so many Black activists in the Civil War era, Hemings did not invoke his father's famous second paragraph of the Declaration of Independence; he did not cite "all men are created equal" as grounds for establishing equal protections before the law, or voting rights for African Americans. Even the American Revolution received barely a mention. For Hemings, the founding era was important as another moment of upheaval for the enslaved Hemings family—through inheritance, Madison Hemings's ancestors passed through several owners in the 1770s, from slave trader John Wayles to his daughter Martha and finally to her husband, Thomas Jefferson, "who in the course of time became famous."[61]

Rather than point to abstract principles, Madison Hemings refuted racist prescriptions with his own lived experience. He highlighted his family's story to demonstrate that Black people were not "separate," they were African *Americans.* Hemings made this point eloquently, showing how race mixing through three centuries of his family obfuscated any clear racial or national distinctions—white and Black, African and American. The only time he referenced a separate national identity was when he described his great-grandmother, "a fullblooded African, and possibly a native of that country," implying that every other mixed-race member of his family born in North America could not be easily shoehorned into the same category. If anyone intentionally blurred the lines, it was white men— from the "captain of an English trading vessel" to John Wayles to Thomas Jefferson—each of whom made "concubines" of enslaved Hemings women.[62]

Madison Hemings's memoir suggested that the binaries that Jefferson had created in 1776 were false ones—they rang hollow when confronted with the reality of race in America. Born in Virginia and the son of a former president, Hemings claimed the United States as his own, comporting with both legal requirements for citizenship—*jus soli* (right of the soil) and *jus sanguinis* (right of blood). And when describing the American Revolution, he defined the event as "our revolutionary troubles," the pronoun "our" an assertion of his role in the nation and its history. He also used the memoir to reveal all that enslavement and racism had cast into shadow: his lineage, his personhood, his family, and his independence. But perhaps most powerfully, Madison Hemings's memoir enabled him to identify himself in a way his father had refused to imagine a century earlier: as an independent and equal African American man, and as a citizen of the United States.[63]

SIX

J. W. Jefferson

Race, History, and the Civil War, 1852–1890

IN 1888, THE PROPRIETOR OF J.W. Jefferson and Company sat down in his offices at 274 Front Street, in Memphis, and wrote a letter to the newly elected U.S. president, Benjamin Harrison. Hoping to brandish his Republican credentials, Jefferson told the president a story. "My earliest remembrances as a 'few years old boy' in 1840," he mused, were "of accompanying my farther to the Polls & he voting the Whig ticket" for General William Henry Harrison. Later, in 1861, when "our opponents" fired "shot on our flag & rebeled against the Grandest fabric ever bequeathed to man," Jefferson had jumped into action, serving in the 8th Wisconsin Volunteer Infantry first as a major, then as a colonel, in the western theater of the Civil War. Jefferson relied on his father's voting record and his own wartime service to emphasize his fervent commitment to "union," something he knew Harrison's great-grandfather—the Declaration of Independence signer Benjamin Harrison V—"assisted in giving us."[1]

J. W. Jefferson could easily have drawn upon his own storied lineage and connections to the Declaration, but he did not. He chose not to tell Harrison that he was a grandson of Sally Hemings and Thomas Jefferson. Likewise, he opted not to convey any information that would call into question his identity as a white man, or lay bare the fact that he was the son of a formerly enslaved man. Instead, Jefferson bent the truth. Born in 1835 to Eston Hemings, the youngest son of the third president and his "concubine" Sally Hemings, Jefferson was first known as John Wayles Hemings. As an infant, he spent only a few years in Virginia before his parents struck out for Ohio. In 1852, the Hemings family moved again, this time to Wisconsin, where the Hemingses would become Jeffersons, and their African American identity would be traded for a white one. John Wayles Hemings became John Wayles Jefferson, a white boy of seventeen. Initially

Alexander Marquis, *Portrait of Colonel John W. Jefferson*, 1874, oil on canvas. (Museum of Wisconsin Art Collection.)

a successful hotelkeeper, he joined the Union Army as a twenty-six-year-old white man in 1861. After the war, he moved to Memphis, establishing himself as a plantation owner and cotton broker. At this point he altered his name again, this time becoming J. W. Jefferson, perhaps to distance himself even farther from his mixed-race heritage.[2]

When he addressed his letter to Harrison, in 1888, Jefferson had been known as a white man for thirty-six years. And yet the history that he created for himself in those pages—embellishing his antebellum voting record and party loyalty—suggested how tenuous his claim to whiteness remained. Indeed, Jefferson was always at risk of being recognized as a Black man and a Hemings family member. This was exactly what happened during the Civil War, when he found himself face to face with an old acquaintance from Chillicothe. A white Ohioan "saw and talked" with Jefferson, "who was then wearing the silver leaves of a lieutenant colonel, and in command of a fine regiment of white men from a north-western state." The irony of the son of a formerly enslaved man serving as a white officer in the U.S. Army was not lost on the Ohioan. But Jefferson "begged" him "not to tell the fact that he had colored blood in his veins," since his true racial identity was unsuspected by his commanding officers.[3]

Jefferson may have extracted an oath of silence during this chance encounter, but it was clear that the man from Chillicothe was unwilling to let the matter slide. In fact, he seemed to have dug into Jefferson's past in Wisconsin. "I have lately learned," the man disclosed, that Eston Hemings's eldest son was "now fairly wealthy, and is proprietor and landlord of a large and popular hotel in a certain north-west city." The landlord of the hotel bore a family name, he continued, that was "not Hemings." In a flash, the Ohioan's powers of recognition threatened to tear apart Jefferson's newfound identity and expose his secret. Although nothing more seems to have come of the Ohioan's disclosure, the continued fragility of Jefferson's white identity for decades after he "passed" may have been a reason he never married or had children. The danger of being exposed as a Black man was both proximate and real.[4]

For J. W. Jefferson, the best means of strengthening a credible identity as a white person and U.S. citizen was through the creation of a public personal history, a strategy employed (not for the first time) in his letter to Harrison. During the Civil War, Jefferson undertook a conscious—and risky—self-fashioning project intended to underscore his visibility as a white man. He became something of a war correspondent, his letters to family members published in Wisconsin newspaper columns. Readers, he hoped, would not question the racial identity of a Union officer wounded in action in the war's western theater, or doubt the credibility of a man who ascended through the army's ranks. The Civil War was both an opportunity and a crucible: "manly" wartime service combined with a highly visible personal history would erase any doubts that Jefferson was a white American citizen.[5]

Before Reconstruction, becoming a white person was the surest means to claim legal settlement across what is now the Midwest. Even in Wisconsin, a state that did not restrict free Black immigration and settlement, white officials used the explicit exclusion of Black men from voting rights to discourage African American settlement before the Civil War— only about 1,000 free Black people lived in a state of 305,000 people when Jefferson and his family arrived there in 1852. According to the 1848 state constitution, suffrage was limited to white male settlers, including some unnaturalized immigrants and Native Americans. Wisconsin lawmakers also probably relied on the anti-Black laws of adjacent states, including Iowa and Illinois, to further deter African American immigration. And in 1863, white Wisconsin residents petitioned the legislature to outlaw Black immigration altogether. In the Civil War era, migration, settlement, and suffrage were rights limited to white people alone.

And as Jefferson probably knew, legal settlement and whiteness formed the basis for claims to state citizenship. Only as a white man was Jefferson able to amass a real estate empire as a hotelkeeper in Madison, serve as an officer in the Civil War, establish himself as a cotton factor in Memphis, and become a powerful political figure: a loyal Whig and Republican who wrote personal letters to a sitting U.S. president. In Madison and later in Memphis, Jefferson could cast his vote freely, cross state borders, and buy and sell property at will. In short, before the establishment of birthright citizenship in the Fourteenth Amendment in 1868, citizenship remained highly localized, both defined and policed at the state level. Thus the only way for J. W. Jefferson to be legally categorized as a settler and citizen across multiple jurisdictions—Ohio, Wisconsin, Tennessee— before the Reconstruction era was to become a white man.

But adopting a white identity to claim inclusion and equal rights resulted in another kind of exclusion for Jefferson, this time from his own African American family. Over the course of several decades, Jefferson erased his African American identity and familial connections. He collapsed his first two names into initials to emphasize the Jefferson surname, thereby evoking the memory of a white man and former president. John

Wayles Hemings, a Black grandson of Sally Hemings, no longer existed. J. W. Jefferson, a white man with a white past, had taken his place.

Eston Hemings's day of emancipation, like his brother Madison's, was marked by humiliation. In 1832, when Eston was twenty-three years old, he strode into the courthouse in Charlottesville. Three other free Black men lined up next to him, including Burwell Colbert, another African American man whom Jefferson had freed in his will. When it was Hemings's turn, the clerk took thorough stock of his appearance, rather as a slave trader would do to an enslaved person on an auction block. He whipped out a measuring stick, ascertaining that Hemings was six feet, one inch tall. He examined Hemings's legs and arms, checking for "deformities." Then the clerk turned his attention to the complexion of Jefferson's "bright mulatto" son. "No scars or marks," the clerk's report concluded. When the process was complete, the sum of Eston Hemings's identity as a free man—at least according to the state of Virginia—was nothing more than his name, height, and skin color.[6]

In an attempt to counter and resist this state surveillance, Eston, like his brother, began creating his own legal record in Charlottesville. More than anything else, this meant buying and selling real estate. In 1830 he bought his first piece of property with his brother—a house for the Hemings family. Two years later, Eston and his new wife, Julia Ann Isaacs, received a portion of a lot in Charlottesville valued at nine hundred dollars from his mother-in-law, also a free woman of color. Hemings served as a bondsman at least twice, first for the estate of Critta Bowles (whose great-niece was later taken to Arkansas by Lewis Randolph) and later for the marriage of a family member, Agnes Isaacs. But in 1837, six months after Eston Hemings buried his father-in-law and five years after he officially gained his freedom, he and his wife decided to leave Virginia. The move was probably prompted by the increasing hostility of white people to free Black people in the wake of the Nat Turner revolt, as well as by the proposal to deport free Black Virginians to Africa. Although the couple and their two young children, John Wayles and Anna, were bound for the free state of Ohio, they continued to buy and sell property and visit mixed-race family members in Virginia until at least 1849.[7]

After they settled in the town of Chillicothe, it was not long before everyone, white and Black, knew who Eston Hemings was and what he looked like. Eston, like his brother Madison, defied Ohio law, choosing not to register as a free person of color with state officials. But he lost no time in establishing himself as a popular and recognizable musician, not a carpenter, as he had been in Virginia. A number of Ohio newspapers remarked on his appearance. Hemings was a "fine looking man, very slightly colored," claimed a reporter for the *Chillicothe Leader.* "Very erect and dignified," later recalled a columnist for the *Daily Scioto Gazette,* his hair "nearly" straight and with a "tint of auburn," while on his face an "indistinct suggestion of freckles" could be seen. With his "quiet, unobtrusive, polite, and decidedly intelligent" demeanor, Hemings "attracted everybody's attention." As a "master of the violin, and an accomplished 'caller' of dances," he was in great demand at the town's "'swell' entertainments." Hemings often played as part of a trio with a clarinetist and a bass violinist, and when they "cut loose," as the *Chillicothe Leader* termed it, "there was only one thing to do—dance." Among the tunes the trio struck up was "Money Musk," a Scottish fiddle tune so well loved by Thomas Jefferson that he wrote down its music by hand.[8]

By 1850, Eston Hemings had become the picture of Black respectability and success—his three teenage children had each "attended school within the year" and he valued his real estate holdings at two thousand dollars. But "notwithstanding all his accomplishments and deserts," Hemings continued to encounter insurmountable racial barriers in Chillicothe. "The fact remained that he had a visible admixture of negro blood in his veins," the *Scioto Gazette* observed, and in antebellum Ohio, skin color created "a great gulf, an impassable gulf" between the races. As Hemings's descendant Julia Westerinen observed, "It must have been really humiliating for him to play a master fiddle" and "have a beautiful piece of property but never be good enough to fit into the white community." He always would have been "just a cut below the lowest of the whites," Westerinen concluded.[9]

But it was not just racial exclusion that pushed Eston Hemings to leave Ohio in 1852; it was probably also the threat of violence and reenslavement. The passage of the Fugitive Slave Act as part of the Compromise of 1850 engineered by Kentuckian Henry Clay had magnified those threats exponentially. The new law required Black fugitives—even in free states—to be captured and returned to their owners, and it charged the federal government with ensuring that enslavers' lost human property was found, returned, and prosecuted. In short, the act eliminated the free states as havens of freedom and safety in the United States for African Americans, transforming slavery from a sectional institution into a national one that was also policed and protected by the federal government. From their position in southern Ohio, so proximate to the slave states of Virginia and Kentucky, the Hemings' lives and family integrity were even less secure. Emboldened by the 1850 law, slave catchers prowled the northern side of the Ohio River, their eyes peeled not just for Black fugitives but also for vulnerable free African Americans, including children, whom they could then sell into slavery for profit. Eston Hemings may have viewed his family's potential kidnapping and enslavement as too great a risk.[10]

By 1852, Eston and Julia Ann Hemings had sold their property in Chillicothe, ready to move farther west. Madison Hemings said only this about his brother's departure: "In the fall of 1852 he removed to Wisconsin, where he died a year or two afterwards." What Madison did not say was that this move was different from the family's other moves—that after it he was unlikely to see or hear from his brother again. Eston did not actually pass away until 1856, but Madison's identification of Wisconsin as the place "where he died" is significant, for it was there that Eston and his family abandoned their African American identity, adopting a white one in its stead. In doing so, they also left their family members behind, underscoring the way racial passing equated with social death in African American communities.[11]

Julia Westerinen imagined that her ancestor made the "heart-wrenching decision to leave everything," to "uproot himself and disappear forever" based upon his children's uncertain—and unsafe—future in Ohio. She suggested that Eston Hemings "looked at his children, saw that they were intelligent, they were being educated, they should have the opportunities that white people did." Yet Westerinen believed that Hemings would have suffered, since he could "never visit again" and "never communicate in any way" with his African American family. Whether his choice was "the correct decision or not," Westerinen added, "I don't know." Another descendant, Mary Jefferson, thought that Hemings faced a "hard decision" to "shut out part of his heritage and make that executive choice" of changing "his last name and add 'Jefferson' to it and register as white." But regardless of how Eston came to his decision in Chillicothe in 1852, what had become clear was that his identity as a free person would always be secondary—at least in the white community—to his "visible admixture of negro blood."[12]

In 1852, John Wayles Hemings's life as a young Black man ended. He was seventeen years old. Wisconsin may have been a free state, but like Ohio it was rife with anti-Black sentiment. From the 1820s until the 1840s, during a lead mining boom, it even contained enslaved people. Following a successful bid for statehood in 1846, Wisconsin legislators feared that giving free African American men the vote would "cause our state to be overrun with runaway slaves from the South." The lawmakers' solution: a state constitution explicitly limiting suffrage to white people, a distinction that would remain on the books until 1866. But in 1854, a landmark decision in the Wisconsin Supreme Court may have let African Americans breathe a little easier. Revolving around an escaped Missouri enslaved man named Joshua Glover and two abolitionists jailed for leading him to safety in Canada, the case resulted in an unexpected outcome: the high court ruled that the Fugitive Slave Act was "unconstitutional and void," an opinion that hinged upon the justices' belief that appointed fugitive slave commissioners "cannot be endowed with judicial powers." John Wayles Hemings—now John Wayles Jefferson—and his family had settled in the only state to refuse to comply with the federal fugitive slave mandate.[13]

By 1855, Eston Hemings Jefferson was working as a cabinetmaker in Madison. After his death a year later, his eldest son, who had been dabbling in real estate, bought a hotel. But it was not just any establishment: the American House was the oldest hotel in the city. Valued at $1,400, it became a new home to John Wayles and several family members, as well as a number of European-born servants. His mother, Julia Ann, lived there, as did twenty-one-year old Beverly Jefferson, the hotel barkeep. John Wayles supervised nearly twenty staff members, including a Bavarian clerk and bellboy, several illiterate Norwegian servants, an English bookkeeper, an American stage agent and driver, and a slew of Germans who filled roles as laborers, hostlers, barbers, and porters. It was clear that John Wayles Jefferson had a knack for business—his personal estate was already valued at some $14,500.[14]

But hotelkeeping did not just demonstrate Jefferson's business acumen—it also became the starting point for his self-fashioning project,

his quest to cement his new identity as a white man. Proof that hotel patrons accepted his racial identity began appearing in local newspaper columns of the day. An editorialist for the *Wisconsin Patriot* noted that Jefferson was as "generous a host as the West has ever known," who "makes
every honest man feel right at home." Reviews like this one pointed to Jefferson as a manly white citizen of prominence, the owner of a respectable
establishment in Madison. They also represented Jefferson's first efforts
to curry favor with the local press, part of his quest to use their columns
to showcase his wealth and status. Stories like the one that appeared in the
Wisconsin Patriot in 1860 marked the beginning of Jefferson's efforts to
make his personal history public. And the same Wisconsin papers that
covered his early years as a hotelkeeper—the *Patriot,* the *State-Journal,* the
Weekly Argus—would also later publish Jefferson's Civil War correspondence. In short, these periodicals would become the vehicle for Jefferson's
white identity.[15]

In 1861, Jefferson put his hotelkeeping on pause, enlisting in the
Union Army as a major in the 8th Wisconsin Volunteer Infantry. "An en-
ergetic and successful man of business," the *State Journal* opined, was
entering "upon the discharge of his military duties with patriotic ardor,
and so far with great success." For the next three years, Jefferson would
affirm this "patriotic ardor" in a bloody civil war. Ridden with malaria and
fending off starvation, Jefferson and his regiment would fight skirmishes
and battles along the Mississippi River, in the heart of the western theater.
It was the first occasion in more than two decades that Jefferson had set
foot in the South. And he did so, for the first time, as a white man.[16]

Jefferson was not the only Hemings descendant to fight for the Union as
a white person. His brother Beverly enlisted in the war early, becoming a
private in the 1st Volunteer Infantry in Wisconsin. A mere three months
after leaving Madison, Beverly Jefferson saw action at the Battle of Falling Waters and helped defeat enemy forces, which included Thomas J.
"Stonewall" Jackson's Confederate brigade. Jefferson's African American
cousins—Madison Hemings's children—in Ohio also joined the war as
white men in 1864, a year after the Emancipation Proclamation was enacted. William Beverly Hemings left southern Ohio for Georgia as part of
the 73rd Ohio Volunteer Infantry. Despite identifying as a Black man at
home, he joined a white regiment that had already seen action at the Sec-

ond Battle of Bull Run, Gettysburg, and Chattanooga. Described as having a "dark" and "florid" skin color, William marched south through the war-torn post-Emancipation South and later participated in the Grand Review of the Armies in Washington, D.C., at the end of the war. Meanwhile, his brother Thomas Eston Hemings went to the South as a private in the 175th Ohio Infantry and never left. Also noted as having a "dark" complexion when enlisting in a white regiment, Thomas Eston was captured by enemy forces after only three months, and later died in a Confederate prison.[17]

In September 1861, Major Jefferson and the 8th Wisconsin rode the Illinois Central Railroad for 350 miles, bound for Saint Louis. There the men marched through town to Benton Barracks, the same Union Army post where dozens of African American men owned by Jefferson's white relatives would later muster into the United States Colored Troops (USCT). In the 1840s and 1850s, Thomas Jefferson's white descendants—members of the extended Carter-Bankhead family—had left Virginia and settled on the banks of the Mississippi River, northeast of Saint Louis. They owned over one hundred people as well as fifteen hundred acres in the prime corn, wheat, and tobacco region known as Little Dixie. During the Civil War, dozens of enslaved men owned by the Carters and Bankheads fled to Union Army recruiting stations in Missouri, joining USCT regiments in 1864 and 1865. These African American men were among the eight thousand enslaved people who fled to Union lines in Missouri even though the terms of the Emancipation Proclamation did not apply in the "loyal" slave state.[18]

Jefferson and the 8th Wisconsin would not be at Benton Barracks for long—they were soon back in railway cars, this time aboard the Iron Mountain Railroad. After a thirty-five-mile rail journey and a five-mile march, the men caught their first glimpse of Confederate destruction. The notorious Confederate general Jeff Thompson and his troops had burned Big River Bridge, forcing the Wisconsin regiment to wade waist-deep across half a mile of swampy water. From Pine Knob, where the Union forces made camp, the 8th Wisconsin was joined by several other regiments from Indiana, Illinois, and Missouri under the command of Colonel William Carlin and marched toward Fredericktown, where Thompson was reportedly encamped with four thousand men. Fredericktown was to be the first place that the 8th Wisconsin saw battle, and it was also where Jefferson wrote his first wartime account, sending it to the editors of a Wisconsin newspaper.[19]

According to the editors, Major Jefferson's "private letter" was "fresh and vivid," quite different from the "facts" already "anticipated by other correspondents." Jefferson disclosed that the first person to warn the Union forces of General Thompson's position was "a negro boy." The troops ridiculed the youth at first, but upon closer examination, he was "proved true." Soon the "sharp sputter of musketry was heard," unleashing "excitement and fright" in the town. Women and children were "running to and fro, seeking cellars and other places of concealment." The wounded streamed in—"some shot in the head, some in the leg, some with an arm off." Jefferson was soon on the battlefield, and "it presented a horrible picture." Dead and wounded were strewn in every direction. One "rebel was shot through the heart, while astride a rail fence," one hand still grasping his old rifle. Not far from him lay Colonel Adin Lowe, whose horse was shot from under him minutes before—"he was pierced through the head by a Minnie ball." The violence did not end on the battlefield. Enraged at the "secession citizens of the place" who appeared to have aided Thompson's forces, the Union men burned and ransacked their houses. And marching out of town, the major and his men found "dead rebel bodies in the road, one of which the hogs had been at." They buried them in a cornfield. Jefferson decreed that the Battle of Fredericktown was the "best test as to the strength, ability, &c., of the opposing forces as has yet been fought" as well as "one of the most brilliant and complete victories we have had during this war." Even in this first dispatch, he was honing his skills as a wartime chronicler.[20]

Jefferson also used his letters to highlight—and embellish—the stark contrast between Union and Confederate sympathizers in southeastern Missouri. In November, having marched over two hundred miles since leaving Wisconsin, the men were in Greenville, an uninhabited town. "Miserable, old, dilapidated, mud plastered, moss-covered log cabins" characterized Greenville, all of them "built without the least regard to architectural taste." Jefferson could not help but draw comparisons to Wisconsin. The courthouse and jail—where the regiment would imprison the eleven Confederates they captured at Fredericktown—were only "about as large as three shanties near the depot in Madison." And the men and women who lived in the "swampy" country, were no better, Jefferson concluded. They "are the very lowest, poorest, and most ignorant kind, living in mud-daubed cabins, tilling a few acres of land," or "in many instances not any." Implicitly, he suggested that "they live in such a way"—devoid of any impulse toward progress or wealth—because of slavery. Jefferson recalled seeing a secessionist "living in an old fashioned brick house, which he commenced 20 years ago and had not finished." In all that time, the man had not even bothered to dig a well, and his African American enslaved man, Reuben, was forced to walk two miles to fill a barrel of water, hauling it with only the help of two sturdy calves.[21]

This disconcerting scene was far different from that of a Missouri judge, "an intelligent, good Union man" and recently released prisoner of war whom the 8th Wisconsin escorted back home. The judge's anxious wife had bought a "beautiful bright colored Union flag" that she flung into the breeze. "Like an electric spark," the major related, "the enthusiasm flew along the line, and cheer after cheer was given . . . until the whole surrounding country resounded with the outbursts of patriotic ardor." This, he insisted, was the "first time that we had seen the stars and stripes unfolded by a private citizen" since they left St. Louis. But this show of patriotism and attachment to the Union was an isolated incident. Most of Missouri, he revealed, was "Union forsaken country." Still, this border South—backward, poor, and provincial—was to be a far cry from the wealthy cotton South that Jefferson would see and laud in the coming years.[22]

In other letters home, Jefferson was careful to remind his readers of his own—and his regiment's—patriotism not just through gallantry on the battlefield but also during the tedium of war. In March 1862, the major was stationed in the swamp, where he and his men had been for a week. Supplied with only two days of rations, the regiment discovered that the railroad bed was in such bad shape that they would have to leave their horses behind. They repaired twelve miles of railroad track that had been abandoned for nearly a year, ever since the "rebels burnt the bridges &c." Their task barely completed, the 8th Wisconsin was ordered south to reinforce General John Pope's efforts to open up the Mississippi River.[23]

Pope intended to attack a Confederate weak point in New Madrid, Missouri. "We have a large body of troops here, as well as the rebels," Jefferson observed, and "no doubt we will have quite a battle." He noted that the Confederate forces had gunboats, while the Union Navy had none, its vessels waylaid in a siege at Island No. 10. To repel the enemy, the regiment manned rifle pits along the riverbank. Under General Joseph Plummer, the 8th Wisconsin pushed twenty miles south of New Madrid, to a place that was "deserted—nothing left here but negroes." Jefferson and his men, who carried nothing with them but their haversacks, camped in the woods along the Mississippi River, just "out of range" of the guns. He could see the Confederates' battery on the Tennessee side, their flag waving above the riverbank. "They shell us to endeavor to find out where we are encamped," Jefferson wrote just moments before a shell exploded fifty yards away. "We are down for certain in Secesh," he lamented, where "things look more like war than any time since I have been in the service." At the end of his letter, the major added that the weather was so hot, the men's faces were "all pealed up." That Jefferson—like the rest of the regiment—was white enough to get sunburned is a subtle but important reminder that these letters served among other things to confirm his racial identity. Less than a month later, the 8th Wisconsin would again see action. Crossing the river at midnight on transport boats, the regiment aided in the capture of nearly six thousand Confederates trying to flee Island No. 10. The arrival of a Union Navy flotilla and the ironclad ships *Carondelet* and *Pittsburgh* helped overwhelm the Confederate forces, who surrendered the island in early April, thus leaving the Mississippi open all the way to Fort Pillow, Tennessee.[24]

In late April or early May the 8th Wisconsin soon headed north, the men crammed aboard steamers bound for Cairo. From Illinois they sailed southeast on the Tennessee River—a move that would have been impossible earlier that year. A few months before that, under General Ulysses S. Grant, Union forces had clinched an important victory, wrenching Fort Donelson and Fort Henry from Confederate control. This was a strategic win for Grant's forces—control of the Cumberland and Tennessee rivers would allow Union troops to push deep into the Confederacy's interior, leaving cities and supply stations like Memphis and Nashville vulnerable to attack. As a result, Major Jefferson and the Wisconsin regiment were able to steam hundreds of miles into enemy territory, disembarking in Mississippi.[25]

Near Farmington, while guarding an outpost in advance of the Union line, Jefferson and his men were attacked, the Confederate artillery forcing the regiment to fall back. Confederate troops hoped to capture a Union battery, but within "forty yards of their prize," the 8th Wisconsin's brigade "arose *en masse,* and opened a deadly volley of musketry" into the enemy's ranks, which suddenly checked their advance, causing them "to turn and flee in wild disorder from the field." Lieutenant Colonel George W. Robbins and Major Jefferson led their "men on through the thickest of the fight, the shells were bursting all around them." The major "had a narrow escape from being killed, a cannon ball passed near his head."[26]

Jefferson may not have penned a letter about this battle, but it made its way into the Wisconsin newspapers anyway. And instead of the major writing about his own bravery in combat, the press increasingly did it for him, noting that he "displayed the greatest coolness and bravery." Jefferson was no longer the only person drawing attention to his actions on the battlefield. But though he escaped death at Farmington, another enemy— disease—posed a grave threat to his life. After contracting typhoid and dysentery, he became so ill that he could barely walk from his tent to a waiting ambulance. The surgeon who examined him ordered Jefferson home to Wisconsin. As if on cue, local newspapers celebrated the homecoming of the "gallant Major Jefferson," and even reported on the status of his convalescence.[27]

Jefferson was away from his regiment for three months. But by the end of August 1862, when the 8th Wisconsin was ordered to march sixty miles from its summer quarters in Mississippi to Tuscumbia, Alabama, he was again among its number. After briefly serving in the town as provost marshal, Jefferson, along with four companies of the regiment, commandeered a railroad heading east. There was much "delay" on the train that was "occasioned by the stubbornness of the drunken 'secesh' conductor." The major soon stepped in to speed up the journey, arresting the conductor. The Wisconsin soldiers took control of the locomotive, managing to drive it thirty miles down the track, to the depot at Courtland. Just south of the Tennessee River, in the midst of cotton country, J. W. Jefferson once again found himself within a few miles of a white Jefferson descendant: great-grandson William Stuart Bankhead. A captain in the 16th Alabama Infantry, Bankhead had not remained on active duty for long. Suffering from rheumatism in his leg, Bankhead resigned his commission in 1861 when his regiment passed through Courtland on its way to Corinth. Ironically, this was where Major Jefferson and the 8th Wisconsin were headed nearly a year later. A town in the northeastern corner of Mississippi, Corinth was an important Confederate rail junction. The lines that ran through it connected the Atlantic coast to the Gulf of Mexico and the Mississippi River.[28]

The battle that the 8th regiment would fight at Corinth in October 1862 was not the first firefight that had engulfed the town that year. In May, just a month after the Union victory at Shiloh, Union troops under the command of Major General Henry Halleck captured the town after a monthlong siege against Confederate forces under General P. G. T. Beauregard. Less than six months later, the junction of the Mobile & Ohio Railroad and the Memphis & Charleston Railroad was again a battle site. Confederate forces numbering twenty-two thousand men converged on Corinth, aiming to wrest the town from Union control and push farther north, into Tennessee. Major Jefferson and the 8th Wisconsin, part of a Union force of twenty-three thousand men under the command of General William Rosecrans, first saw action at Iuka, just west of Corinth. At Iuka, "a desperate battle ensued, continuing three hours, without cessation, until the darkness of night closed the contest." Though brief, it was "one of the severest engagements of the war," with men fighting "sword to sword and bayonet to bayonet."[29]

A few days later, at Corinth, the 8th Wisconsin was ordered back into action and for three hours was "under terrific fire" from forces commanded by Major General Sterling Price. At the end of the day, seventeen Wisconsin men lay dead on the battlefield, with eighty-one wounded and eighteen missing. The next morning, Price's forces attacked the regiment's flanks but were repelled and later forced into a full retreat. The regiment followed in hot pursuit for nearly forty miles, capturing several prisoners and forcing Price's troops to abandon their supplies, "strewn for miles on the trail of his retreat." Just as at Farmington, Jefferson narrowly avoided death. He was "borne from the field" after being thrown from his horse by a spent bullet. He was, declared the *Milwaukee Daily Sentinel,* wounded "slight in the shoulder." Though Jefferson offered no eyewitness account of the fierce battle, the Wisconsin press was again quick to call attention to the major's "great coolness and bravery under fire."[30]

It was soon Christmas, and the 8th Wisconsin spent the holiday at a fort made of cotton bales in Tennessee. To celebrate the occasion, the soldiers hoisted an enormous Union flag over their makeshift home. For the next several months, the regiment would crisscross northern Mississippi, marching between Corinth and the outskirts of Memphis. At times they slept outside without tents, exposed to the cold frosts. In places like Bolivar, Germantown, and Jackson, the men settled into the tedium of noncombat tasks—repairing bridges, building fortifications, and performing guard duty. The autumn victories at Iuka and Corinth had paved the way for a Union push farther south in the spring of 1863. With northern Mississippi secured, the Federals planned to redirect their attention to the southernmost stretch of the Mississippi River, at Vicksburg.[31]

In March the 8th Wisconsin was in Memphis to board a steamer, the *Empress,* that would carry them downriver to Arkansas and then Louisiana, where they would take part in the Vicksburg campaign. In all, the men would travel nearly 400 miles on the Mississippi and Yazoo rivers. It was here that Jefferson and the 8th Wisconsin got their first real glimpse of the wealth of the cotton South—they even camped on a number of plantations. Their route was circuitous and exhausting. As Jefferson, recently promoted to lieutenant colonel, described it, "We marched around Vicksburg on the Louisiana side 90 miles," then crossed the Mississippi River and marched another 170 miles "in a roundabout way." In the spring of 1863, General Grant's initial plan had been to attack Vicksburg from the west, but when this effort failed, he pushed his troops through Mississippi, toward Jackson.[32]

The 8th Wisconsin fought their first battle of the Vicksburg campaign—a skirmish at Fourteen Mile Creek—in southeastern Mississippi. They chased the Confederates, first to Mississippi Springs, then to Jackson. "We had a hard skirmish but whipped them," Jefferson boasted. In Jackson, Major General William Tecumseh Sherman appointed the new lieutenant colonel Jefferson provost marshal, charging him with prisoners of war and the destruction of $5 million of Confederate property, including supplies, cotton, factories, and railroads. But the 8th Wisconsin lingered for only two days, headquartered in the statehouse, before they again took to the road. The whole of May, it seemed to Jefferson, "I have been continually on the March and fighting the rebels." In a letter addressed to his brother Beverly and published in the *Wisconsin Patriot,* he explained that "I cannot write much, as I have no time or spirits." His tone was grim, wearied, aware of the awful and monumental task that awaited him.[33]

In just a few short days, the 8th Wisconsin was "in the rear of Vicksburg, and in sight of the city." Vicksburg's geographical position, high on a bluff overlooking the Mississippi River, made the city a Confederate stronghold that had long been impervious to attack from Union gunboats. It was a nexus of supplies—cattle, corn, and hogs arrived via the Red, Arkansas, and White rivers and it was also a railroad entrepôt connecting the eastern and western corners of the Confederacy. For President Abraham Lincoln, capturing Vicksburg for the Union was a necessity. But General Grant knew that the task would not be easy. "Vicksburg is so strong and so well fortified" that "it must be taken by a regular siege or by starving out the Garrison," Grant observed.[34]

The 8th Wisconsin took part in the offensive, fighting for four days straight. The horror of scrambling uphill through ravines to stage the offensive was indescribable; Jefferson noted simply that the Confederates' "entrenchments and breastworks are awful to attack." Continually striking at the well-engineered fortifications meant that "we are losing a great many men"— Jefferson predicted that "there will be an awful slaughter tomorrow." Though he believed that "Vicksburg will be ours" it nevertheless "had cost and will cost many thousand lives." The soldiers in the 8th Wisconsin soon witnessed a scene that seemed to epitomize the whole war: a man from a Confederate Missouri regiment fired "about a dozen rounds" into the ranks of a Union Missouri regiment, only to realize that "his brother has been shooting at him all day long."[35]

On May 22, the 8th Wisconsin fought in the "grand assault," successfully gaining the outer slope of the enemy's "works," but not without sustaining a severe loss. Five men were killed, and twenty lay wounded, including Jefferson, who was shot in the hand. After the battle, the Wisconsin regiment was "highly complimented" by General Sherman for the "gallant conduct it displayed on the occasion." But with two assaults repulsed by the Confederates, the siege dragged on until July 4, when Confederate general John C. Pemberton finally surrendered to save his starving men. "I have just returned from the city and actually saw the heads, hides and entrails of mules which the rebels have been subsisting on for days," wrote Jefferson of the horrifying scene he encountered. It was this Union victory on Independence Day—which cut the Confederacy in half and placed the Mississippi River under Union control—that served as an important expression of patriotism for Jefferson, one in which he played a crucial role as a white Union officer. Congress, he declared, should be petitioned to "add 24 hours to the 4th of July" because "hereafter we cannot possibly get celebrating" into a single day. Underscoring the important

connection between American independence and this seminal Union triumph also highlighted Jefferson's own links to the Declaration of Independence and to the man who wrote it.[36]

The Vicksburg campaign left a deep impression on Jefferson for
another reason—it introduced him to the Deep South's empire of cotton.
The plantations carved along the Mississippi and Red rivers that he saw
in 1863 and 1864 represented a very different South from the one he had
encountered—and heavily criticized—in Missouri and Arkansas. A fellow
member of the 8th Wisconsin, Sergeant Major George W. Driggs, recorded
many of the scenes that he and the rest of the regiment observed during
their southward journey. Outside Vicksburg, "large and magnificent plantations greet the eye," Driggs wrote, with "each having the appearance of
being a small village in itself." The cotton plantations and opulent dwell-
ings of the white planters "presented a scene to a stranger's eye, so unusual
to a Northerner." The vastness of the plantations made a strong impression on the Wisconsin men. "I saw one plantation which was ten miles long
and five miles wide," Driggs boasted, and on a particular day the regiment
crossed but a single immense estate. "Such a vast extent of territory, and
such extensive corn and cotton fields, I never expected to see," Driggs
marveled. "As far as the eye can reach," he continued, "the waving corn,
nearly three feet high, and vast fields of cotton meet you at every hand."[37]

Yet for Jefferson, the most beautiful cotton country lay in central
Louisiana. "The country about Alexandria was the most beautiful" the
regiment had yet seen, and they had "no conception of the wealth which
exists there, or did exist there before the war." The 8th Wisconsin found
that some of the plantations had been abandoned by white proprietors,
the land still farmed by African Americans. Other planters burned their
mansions rather than have them occupied by Federal troops. At Great
Junction, Mississippi, the 8th Wisconsin made camp at the "largest plantation we have seen in our travels through rebeldom," at some 3,500 acres.
The Wisconsin men took charge of the two gristmills they found there,
grinding corn "for the benefit of the blacks here in the army," who were
ordered to subsist only on burnt rye, cornmeal, and bacon. But while
Driggs saw devastation, Jefferson saw opportunity. In only a few years'
time, he would be the owner of cotton plantations like these, fanning out
along the Mississippi River in the shadow of Memphis.[38]

For all the praise that Driggs heaped on the plantation South, he hardly noted anything about African Americans, and what he did say was laced with racism. Near Lake Saint Joseph, where the plantations were "of the better class" and "men of wealth, of education, refinement and taste once lived," Driggs and the 8th Wisconsin observed six abandoned estates engulfed in flames. The African Americans left behind were "old and decrepid, and worthless as slaves," Driggs noted, suggesting how easily he conflated Black people with human property. Though he did not often mention it, Driggs was confronted with slavery on an almost daily basis—thousands of enslaved people hoping to escape bondage followed the 8th Wisconsin as it traveled throughout the South. Outside Farmington, in early 1862, the regiment was followed by about two thousand African Americans, Driggs recalled. In northern Alabama in August of that year, the 8th Wisconsin witnessed about three hundred African Americans congregating at a depot of the Memphis & Charleston Railroad, all of them hoping to be transported north alongside bales of cotton. But these encounters with Black men and women did little to inspire feelings of empathy among the Wisconsin regiment. The presence of African Americans often had the opposite effect, summoning the white soldiers' racism instead. "Most of them are a worthless, indolent set of beings, too lazy to cook their own meals," Driggs declared. Unable to view African Americans as anything but chattel, he insisted that "they are fast depreciating in value, and thus show their utter worthlessness."[39]

Racism toward African Americans during the campaign must have been a constant reminder to Jefferson of the threat he faced should his African American lineage be exposed. But he was not silent on the issue—he tried to counter racist depictions of African Americans in his own letters and reports. Tellingly, Jefferson never spoke of African Americans as anything but individuals—he was always careful to proffer names in his chronicles. And critically, Jefferson also often inserted dialogue into his own prose to give voice to the free and enslaved African Americans he encountered. He offered an extended account of his superior officer's "colored body servant," John, who was "one of those shrewd, smart servants, that will always make you laugh to see him grin." Outside Pilot Knob, in Missouri, Jefferson narrated John's encounter with a "sesh gent.":

John was near the depot when a southern "sesh gent" rode up to him and dismounted with a roll of three blankets on his arm and bridle rein in his hand, he passed them to John saying, "here n[—]r, hold them." "go to h—l sir," replied John, assuming an air of dignity. "O, ah," returned the gent., "excuse me, be kind enough to hold these, sir." "Allright, sir" retorted John, taking the rein and hitching it, holding on to the blankets. The gentleman went into the building about his business, and John disappeared with the blankets. We did not hear of the above until the other night, when all were about retiring, John came into the tent with a roll of three nice blankets; a medical officer being present and believing that they belonged to the medical department, interrogated John as to what he was doing with those blankets. "Holding them sir," replied John. "I see you are," replied our friend, "but what do you mean by that?" John related the above which took place at the Knob, and completed his story by saying, "I have been holding them ever since." Of course we all laughed heartily at John's shrewd way of getting even with his "secesh gent.," who, he claimed, had insulted him.[40]

Jefferson's account was a subtle rejoinder to his counterparts' racism in myriad ways. His description of John as "smart" and "shrewd" was a departure from the way the Wisconsin men usually defined African Americans. Relating the full story restored John's agency and personhood, a stark contrast with Driggs's generalization of Black men and women as "a pitiable class." And of course, it was also a double act of resistance. Jefferson related John's challenge to the racist assumptions of the "sesh gent" and the Union medical officer just as he used John's story to defy the way African Americans were depicted by his peers in wartime accounts. And he did all of this while preserving—but also risking—his white identity.

But a greater threat to Jefferson's precarious white identity emerged during the Red River Campaign of 1864. Soon after the siege at Vicksburg, he and his men found themselves shunted into yet another Union campaign, this one a multipronged attack on Confederate territory in southwest Arkansas and northwest Louisiana. The Union goal was threefold: to capture the Confederacy's Trans-Mississippi Department headquartered at Shreveport, to cripple Confederate forces west of the Mississippi River, and to prevent collaboration between enemy troops and the French-backed Emperor Maximilian I of Mexico. Federal forces also received orders to seize valuable cotton stores and scuttle the grand cotton plantations that attracted the attention of Driggs and Jefferson—all in the hopes of destroying the economic engine of the Confederacy. In May 1864, the Wisconsin regiment, under the command of Union general A. J. Smith as part of a force of twenty thousand men and sixteen ironclad ships, headed for Shreveport. But early victories at places like Harrison's Hill, just north of Alexandria, where Union forces surprised and captured nearly three hundred Confederate troops, were not a harbinger of what was to come. At Alexandria, the Union fleet was grounded by low water, freed only after the 23rd and 29th Wisconsin Infantry, along with formerly enslaved African Americans, built a series of dams to raise the water level. At a skirmish near Columbia, the 8th Wisconsin sustained several casualties: three dead and sixteen wounded. Jefferson only "narrowly escaped, his horse being shot under him twice."[41]

As part of a campaign that was amounting to a dismal Union failure, the 8th Wisconsin's morale was low. Although the regiment was promised furloughs, the "exigencies of the service would not admit of its coming home at the present time," so the men fought on in Louisiana. The colonel tried to resign after Vicksburg, but rather than accepting his claim, the army simply furloughed him, ordering Lieutenant Colonel Jefferson to act in his stead. By June 1864, Jefferson had had enough, and tendered his resignation. His reasons were many. First, though the regiment had grown to 270 men, the army had yet to fill vacant officer posts. Second, because he had "succeeded in having my men re-enlist for a new term of service," making the 8th Wisconsin "a veteran organization," they were due a furlough. And at the end of that time, Jefferson pointed out, he would have less than one month to complete his three years of military service. He argued that it would "be of no benefit to Govt. for me to again return with my com'd South." Besides, "my own business affairs which I have desirously sacrificed, so as to allow me to serve my Govt. for nearly three years, now demand of me—at least for a while—that I should not enter into a new term of service." Jefferson held out hope that the regiment would be reorganized after the furlough, allowing him to be mustered out.[42]

But the army would not have it. Jefferson's resignation was "not accepted, in order that he be held amenable to the military authorities." For July and August, he remained in Memphis, under arrest. Cheekily, Jefferson contended that "since the order . . . is not very explicit, and does not confine me to my quarters," perhaps he could "have the freedom of the city." But he probably had no chance to wander through Memphis. Although ordered to join his regiment, Jefferson protested that he was "unwell," his illness forcing him to remain "in my convalescent camp." Yet the next morning, he received an order to proceed to Holly Springs, Mississippi, to rejoin the 8th Wisconsin. He apparently followed these orders, for in September he and his regiment were working to deflect an attack from 250 guerrillas at Red River Bridge, near Springfield, Louisiana. By October, however, the army had changed course once again—this time directing him to "proceed without delay" to Wisconsin, where he would "muster out of service." In October 1864, Lieutenant Colonel Jefferson boarded a steamer up the Mississippi to Cairo, then traveled to Wisconsin by rail—following much the same route north as he had south in 1861.[43]

In 1850, the son of a Scottish gentleman arrived in Milwaukee. Probably educated at the Royal Scottish Academy in Edinburgh, Alexander Marquis quickly set up shop as a portrait painter and art teacher. For the next thirty years, Marquis endured grinding poverty but remained committed to his art—he painted some three hundred portraits of prominent Wisconsinites. A follower of the Scottish painter Sir Henry Raeburn, Marquis attempted to emulate his style. Yet this did little to augment his popularity— critics deemed Marquis "not an especially gifted painter." Still, in 1874, a resident of Madison hired Marquis to paint his portrait. The man insisted that he be painted in uniform as a Union army officer. Marquis depicted the uniformed man with a pale face, aquiline nose, and wavy reddish-brown hair and beard.[44]

Detractors immediately found fault with the painting. Marquis had neglected the figure's right sleeve, one critic noted, leaving it a different color from the rest of the military uniform. Someone else pointed out that Marquis had failed to get the subject's beard straight. If Marquis had been aiming for a painting that looked like a photograph, he had failed, most agreed. A few years later, in 1880, Marquis admitted defeat in Milwaukee, moving west to try his luck in another western town: Denver. But there is no record that the subject of Marquis's 1874 portrait was at all displeased with the painting. In fact, it did everything that J. W. Jefferson hoped it would—it reasserted his core identity as a white Civil War officer. Regardless of its quality, Marquis's portrait represented the culmination of Jefferson's self-fashioning project.[45]

Although Jefferson's portrait was painted in Wisconsin, he no longer lived there. Lured to the cotton South and the "magnificent" plantations he and his regiment had seen during the Vicksburg and Red River campaigns, Jefferson took up residence in Memphis after the war. Buying up several indebted Arkansas cotton plantations along the Mississippi River, Jefferson became both a cotton planter and a broker. He and several business partners invested in at least two plantations, Fain and Whitmore. In the 1880s, J. A. Hayes, a Confederate war veteran from South Carolina, went to work on one of Jefferson's plantations. In Mississippi County, Hayes "opened up about 200 acres of land, and has now under the plow 1,000 acres, employing about 125 hands to assist him in keeping the farm in good condition." So productive was the plantation, that Hayes's yield on Jefferson's land was "three-quarters to one bale of cotton to the acre." Reaping incredible wealth from his holdings, Jefferson shipped cotton across the United States and to Europe. And in 1874, when the Memphis Cotton Exchange was incorporated, J.W. Jefferson & Company became a charter member. This left no question as to Memphis's postwar economic purpose—a grand brick building marked by "four slate covered domes" on its roof, each "ornamented with the design of an open cotton boll in galvanized iron." Like other Memphis cotton merchants, J. W. Jefferson anchored his business on Front Street. No one questioned that he was anything other than an entrepreneur, staunch Republican supporter, and Civil War veteran. In Memphis, Jefferson was "regarded by all as a gentleman to be esteemed" who was "well known throughout the south, his adopted home." In a sense, J. W. Jefferson had succeeded in becoming just like every other white man.[46]

Epilogue

IN 1888, A WOMAN CHOSE TO HAVE her photograph taken. Seated, wearing a lace-collared dress and heavy pearl necklace, the woman looks unflinchingly at the camera. It is a determined gaze, uninhibited and unafraid. She has light-colored eyes and wavy white hair parted and tucked into a bun at the nape of the neck, with a few strands pulled loose at the ears. Hers is a stern and heavy brow, slightly furled. Under it, black-rimmed spectacles cling to the bridge of an elegant nose. The woman appears to be an elderly white woman, but she is in fact Black. Her name is Ellen Wayles Hemings Roberts, and she was among the first in her family to be photographed. Of her mother, Mary McCoy Hemings, grandmother, Sally Hemings, and great-grandmother, Elizabeth Hemings, no portraits were made—only descriptions and lists left by white enslavers and state bureaucrats remain. Ellen Roberts's photograph was the first true image to show the world not just what she looked like but also who she *was*.[1]

Born just a few years before the outbreak of the Civil War, in 1856, Ellen was the youngest daughter and one of the nine children of Madison and Mary Hemings. She was also a granddaughter of Sally Hemings and Thomas Jefferson, though she was more than half a century younger than Jefferson's first white grandchild, Ann Cary Randolph, who was born in 1791. In contrast, Ellen Wayles Hemings Roberts—who shared the given names of her white cousin Ellen Wayles Randolph Coolidge—lived well into the twentieth century, dying at the beginning of World War II. Ellen was born a free person in a free state, and she witnessed the death of U.S. slavery in 1865, but, like her father, she lived in what remained a deeply racist, violent, and exclusionary society: postbellum Ohio.[2]

Ellen's situation in Ohio may have come to a head after she married Andrew Jackson (A. J.) Roberts, an Oberlin graduate and schoolteacher, in 1878. The problem—at least for white observers of the era—is imme-

Roberts family portrait, ca. 1910s: Ellen Wayles Hemings Roberts (*bottom right*) and
Andrew Jackson Roberts; (*top, left to right*) their three children: Myrtle E. Roberts,
William G. Roberts, and Frederick M. Roberts. (Collection #168, Roberts Family
Papers, African American Museum at Oakland, Oakland Public Library, Oakland,
California.)

diately apparent from family photographs. A.J. was a "tall, thin man, very
dark-complected" who looked "Nubian black." Ellen, on the other hand,
was so light-skinned that she appeared white. In southern Ohio, their
union may have been perceived as an interracial marriage. Though Ohio
was long viewed as an abolitionist stronghold, especially in the 1840s and
1850s, racial violence and exclusionary practices continued well into the
Reconstruction era. Most of Ohio's anti-Black laws were repealed in 1849,
but additional exclusionary legislation was enacted in the 1860s and 1870s.
In 1861, lawmakers made it illegal for a "person of pure white blood" to
marry any individual with a "distinct and visible admixture of African
blood, and any negro." In 1864 and 1878, the state legislature passed laws
requiring the Board of Education to establish "separate schools for colored children." Racial violence also escalated, with at least ten lynchings

recorded between 1876 and 1916. In 1884, the Roberts couple opted to leave Ohio, three years before all anti-Black laws were repealed.[3]

Like her uncle Eston Hemings, Ellen Roberts moved farther west. But unlike him, she did so in order to retain her African American person-hood. Out in Los Angeles, the Robertses were not ostracized because they had what appeared to be a racially mixed marriage but instead were cele-brated as some of "California's most progressive pioneer citizens." As her descendent Patricia Roberts declared, the couple was "one of the first founding families of Los Angeles." In a city that contained a small African American population but was home to substantial numbers of people of Hispanic and Asian descent, Ellen and A. J. Roberts carved out a life for themselves where the color line was never just Black and white. A. J. Roberts started a hauling company, transporting goods in horse-drawn wagons, an enterprise that soon blossomed into the Los Angeles Van, Truck, and Storage Company. Later, he opened Los Angeles' first Black-owned mortuary.[4]

But it was his and Ellen's son Frederick Madison Roberts who ex-plicitly took up the cause of Black inclusion and equality. A graduate of Colorado College and later a tax assessor, newspaper editor, and some-time Nevada gold prospector, Frederick Roberts initially appeared des-tined to fill his father's shoes, studying mortician science in Chicago. But his political ambitions soon became apparent. As the owner and editor of the *New Age* newspaper, Frederick Roberts made a name for himself in editorials that encouraged Black migration and the growth of Black busi-nesses, lauding California as the "promised land" for African Americans. "Individually and collectively," he wrote in 1915, "we [African Americans] are doing better than any equal number of a class of people in the country." Indeed, Roberts thought that Black Americans in California should rec-ognize that they were "living in the best part of the world and that his Race in this section is behind no one else."[5]

But racial prejudice was omnipresent in Southern California. White people condemned the rising African American population in Los Ange-les, which hovered around eight thousand persons in 1910. In 1912, A. J. Davis, a white Los Angeles resident who hailed from the South, entreated lawmakers to "draw the color line before it is too late." African Americans, Davis wrote, were "invading every possible avenue they can, they crowd into our street cars and . . . infest our amusement places and are a nuisance on our streets." Without racial segregation, white people would "lower themselves to their equal." The best solution was to "arrest this rapidly growing condition of contamination and stop the evil." One Black woman, Louise McDonald, felt racism acutely in Los Angeles. "Civil privileges are here unknown," she declared in 1912. In fact, "we suffer almost anything (except lynching) right here in the beautiful land of sunshine."[6]

Increasingly, Frederick Roberts, who was a member of the National Association for the Advancement of Colored People and the National Urban League, used the *New Age* to call out and condemn racism in Los Angeles. In 1913 he drew attention to the "growing discrimination" exhibited by the police, mayor, and city council. "Insulting signs and other more direct methods of denying equal privilege" were on the rise. In an effort to "brand Race patrons as undesirable," white people increasingly tried to police and control public areas. In 1913, Roberts proposed boycotts and protests against Anheuser Busch for its "Race ridiculing posters" and advertisements, plastered across the city. And in 1915, he criticized the production of D. W. Griffith's *The Clansman* (later renamed *Birth of a Nation*) and joined a broader effort to ban the film, which he thought would destroy "the best feeling . . . in the West," from movie theaters across Los Angeles. Setting the *New Age* apart from its racist rival, the *Los Angeles Times,* Roberts sought to make his paper into a bastion of Black civil rights.[7]

But Roberts was not content to simply highlight racial prejudice in Los Angeles. During the Mexican Revolution (1910–1917), he drew attention to the perceived inequality of Mexico to white European nations, as described by President Woodrow Wilson and a slew of white journalists. The conflict, in their eyes, underscored the "Brutality of the Barbarous Mexicans." Meanwhile, white pundits wrote glowingly of the European nations embroiled in World War I. For white people, Roberts explained, the "Mexican war was savage and uncivilized" while "European war is refined, a titanic struggle of enlightened nations." But in Roberts's eyes, war was always brutal, "be the scene Europe or Mexico." Racism directed toward Mexico was simply an extension of white supremacy in the United States. "Oh, the consistency of the dominant, superior Race!" he lamented. Regardless of race, nations were equal, as were the wars they made upon each other, he argued.[8]

Increasingly, Roberts championed the equality of nations in the world as well as the equality of the races at home. In 1918 he presented himself as

a democrat, running as a Republican for a seat in the California state legislature. Competing against an anti-Black Democrat in a staunchly white
district, Roberts positioned himself not just as an advocate of African
American rights, but also as a U.S. citizen. Against the odds, he won the
election, becoming the "first Black elected to a State office west of the
Mississippi," according to his wife, Pearl Hinds Roberts. Roberts's supporters deemed the triumph "a practical demonstration of pure democracy," because "without the support of a very considerable part of the
White voters," the "election of Mr. Roberts would have been impossible." As a lawmaker, Roberts quickly backed a bill to strengthen Black civil
rights—he proposed making racial discrimination in public places an expensive felony. But his other bills centered on welfare issues that appealed
to both white and Black constituents—better sanitation and schools, as
well as tax relief. Roberts's agenda, wrote one supporter, "gives the lie to
those white Americans who have contended that a Negro American could
think only in terms of black." He was no longer just a "Race man," a critic
of white racism and proponent of Black civil rights. Instead, Roberts, as
this statement made clear, was a talented politician capable of advocating
for the needs and rights of all people, regardless of race.[9]

Facing pressure as the Ku Klux Klan gained power and influence in
Southern California in the 1920s, Roberts hewed close to his democratic
vision. In the wake of the horrific Tulsa race riots of 1921, *Birth of a Nation*
was brought back to the silver screen in Los Angeles. Black intellectuals
and politicians feared that its presence would unleash a violent white mob,
threatening the lives of African Americans. But Roberts did not condemn
the film as anti-Black; rather, he argued, the film was "un-American." The
problem with white racism, he suggested, was not just that it traumatized
and excluded African Americans. It also harmed the nation. As he later
wrote, the "very existence of the principles, upon which our nation was
founded are at stake." By claiming adherence to first principles, Roberts
fashioned himself as not just an advocate of Black rights but a defender of
American ideals.[10]

Nearly half a century earlier, Frederick Roberts's grandfather Madison Hemings had kept largely mum about equal rights. Instead, he emphasized his status as an independent property holder—he had a family, owned
a farm, and was a well-respected and accomplished carpenter and pillar of
the African American community in southern Ohio. Hemings also high-

lighted his mixed-race heritage, which stretched back to the early eighteenth century, to assert his identity as an American, rather than as an African who belonged elsewhere, somewhere beyond the borders of the United States. These two things—independence and family history—formed the basis for Madison Hemings's claim to inclusion and belonging.[11]

Frederick Roberts, on the other hand, believed that African Americans were both independent *and* equal in 1910s California—unlike the other "sections" of the United States. It was only the infiltration of white racism from the South that jeopardized Black people's status in California, threatening to render them excluded and inferior. Initially, his response to the rising tide of anti-Black racism in Los Angeles took the form of protest and boycotts; he also challenged white officials' discriminatory policies in his *New Age* editorials. But later Roberts asserted that all races—and all nations—were equal. Racial hierarchies, he suggested, whether within America or outside it, were artificial constructs, the result of white supremacy. He rooted his claims in the Revolutionary era, invoking the Declaration of Independence—the first member of Madison Hemings's family to do so publicly. In his mind, the Founders had imagined the United States as a multiracial democracy—they had simply failed to live up to this ideal at the time. In the twentieth century, Roberts saw a chance to finally fulfill America's founding promise of equal rights.[12]

This claim, of course, was far different from the one made by Frederick Roberts's white great-grandfather, Thomas Jefferson, in 1776. Family oral history passed on the connection to Jefferson as "a genealogical fact." Indeed, as Frederick's daughter Patricia Roberts declared, "Thomas Jefferson is my great-great grandfather. Period." But Jefferson had envisioned equality differently in the eighteenth century: the United States would be comprised of equal property-holding white citizens, not people of African descent, according to his thinking. And Jefferson's primary concern, like that of many of his peers, was securing equality with European states. Still, in the nineteenth century, Jefferson's white descendants retooled his conception of equality, asserting that it was the continued presence (rather than the "removal") of supposedly inferior, nonwhite peoples that enabled—and preserved—white democracy. Both Meriwether Lewis Randolph and Thomas Jefferson Randolph had argued that they were dependent *and* unequal without race-based chattel slavery; profits from African American "property" augmented and assured their status. Nicholas Trist and Joseph

Coolidge also embraced a new vision of the international system defined by racial hierarchy; white Anglo-Saxon nations were superior and equal, while nonwhite, non-Christian nations were inferior.[13]

Unlike Jefferson or the white descendants discussed in this book, Frederick Roberts interpreted the Declaration of Independence as both universal and transcendent—it was not a treatise limited to the American Revolutionary moment, but rather an articulation of principles that applied to all people, in all times. And its core principle was equality—not of white men, but of all races, regardless of skin color. Roberts's vision of the United States was of a multiracial democracy, a nation rooted in universal rights that offered belonging to all. The American "people" was an elastic and inclusive idea, not an exclusionary one. In that sense, Frederick Roberts's idea of America—not that of Jefferson or his white family members—most closely resembles our own.[14]

Notes

Introduction

1. In the final copy of the Declaration, Congress changed "equal & independent station" to "separate and equal station" in the first paragraph of the text, and "all men are created equal & independent" to "all men are created equal" in the second paragraph. For Jefferson's "original rough draught," see Julian P. Boyd, ed., *The Papers of Thomas Jefferson* (Princeton: Princeton University Press, 1950–), 1:243–47. For the finalized text, see Declaration of Independence, July 4, 1776, Yale Law School, Avalon Project, https://avalon.law.yale.edu/18th_century/declare.asp.

2. See Eliga H. Gould, *Among the Powers of the Earth: The American Revolution and the Making of a New World Empire* (Cambridge: Harvard University Press, 2012); Peter S. Onuf, "A Declaration of Independence for Diplomatic Historians," *Diplomatic History* 22, no. 1 (Winter 1998): 71–83; Robert G. Parkinson, *The Common Cause: Creating Race and Nation in the American Revolution* (Chapel Hill: University of North Carolina Press for the Omohundro Institute, 2016); Maya Jasanoff, *Liberty's Exiles: American Loyalists in the Revolutionary World* (New York: Knopf, 2011); Gould, *Crucible of Peace: The Turbulent History of America's Founding Treaty* (New York: Oxford University Press, forthcoming in 2025).

3. See Fred Anderson, *Crucible of War: The Seven Years' War and the Fate of Empire in British North America, 1754–1766* (New York: Knopf, 2007); Kathleen DuVal, *Independence Lost: Lives on the Edge of the American Revolution* (New York: Random House, 2015); Andrew Jackson O'Shaughnessy, *The Men Who Lost America: British Leadership, the American Revolution, and the Fate of the Empire* (New Haven: Yale University Press, 2013); Maya Jasanoff, *Edge of Empire: Lives, Culture, and Conquest in the East, 1750–1850* (New York: Knopf, 2007).

4. See Peter S. Onuf, "Federalism, Democracy, and Liberty in the New American Nation," in *Exclusionary Empire: English Liberty Overseas, 1600–1900,* ed. Jack P. Greene, 132–59 (New York: Cambridge University Press, 2009); Michal Jan Rozbicki, *Culture and Liberty in the Age of the American Revolution* (Charlottesville: University of Virginia Press, 2011), 31, 57–60; Christopher Hill, *God's Englishman: Oliver Cromwell and the English Revolution* (New York: Harper and Row, 1972), 262–65; Hill, *The World Turned Upside Down: Radical Ideas During the English Revolution* (London: Penguin, 2020), 33; Alexander Keyssar, *The Right to Vote: The Contested History of Democracy in the United States* (New York: Basic, 2009); "Slave Population of the United States," 1790–1850, U.S. Census Bureau, https://www2.census.gov/library/publications/decennial/1850/1850c/1850c-04.pdf.

5. See Peter S. Onuf, *Jefferson's Empire: The Language of American Nationhood* (Charlottesville: University of Virginia Press, 2000), 10, 19, 71; Kariann Akemi Yokota,

Unbecoming British: How Revolutionary America Became a Postcolonial Nation (New York: Oxford University Press, 2014).

6. Thomas Jefferson, *A Summary View of the Rights of British America*, 1774, Yale Law School, Avalon Project, https://avalon.law.yale.edu/18th_century/jeffsumm .asp; Annette Gordon-Reed and Peter S. Onuf, *"The Most Blessed of the Patriarchs": Thomas Jefferson and the Empire of the Imagination* (New York: Liveright, 2016).

7. "Thomas Jefferson to Edward Rutledge, 14 July 1787," *Founders Online*, National Archives, https://founders.archives.gov/documents/Jefferson/01-11-02-0506; Thomas Jefferson, *Notes on the States of Virginia* [1785], Query XIV, "Laws," and Query XVIII, "Manners," Jefferson Papers, Massachusetts Historical Society, https://www.masshist.org/thomasjeffersonpapers/notes/; Onuf, *Jefferson's Empire*, 162–63; Michael A. Blaakman, *Speculation Nation: Land Speculation in the Revolutionary American Republic* (Philadelphia: University of Pennsylvania Press, 2023), 9–17.

8. See Nicholas Guyatt, *Bind Us Apart: How Enlightened Americans Invented Racial Segregation* (New York: Basic, 2016); Parkinson, *Common Cause*, 185–263; Peter S. Onuf, "Every Generation Is an 'Independant Nation': Colonization, Miscegenation, and the Fate of Jefferson's Children," *William and Mary Quarterly* 57, no. 1 (January 2000): 153–70.

9. Thomas Jefferson, *Notes on the States of Virginia* [1785], Query XIV, "Laws"; "Thomas Jefferson to Edward Coles, 25 August 1814," *Founders Online*, National Archives, https://founders.archives.gov/documents/Jefferson/03-07-02-0439.

10. See Onuf, *Jefferson's Empire*, 5; Sam W. Haynes, *Unfinished Revolution: The Early American Republic in a British World* (Charlottesville: University of Virginia Press, 2010); Jay Sexton, *The Monroe Doctrine: Empire and Nation in Nineteenth-Century America* (New York: Farrar, Straus and Giroux, 2011); "Thomas Jefferson to Samuel R. Demaree, 12 January 1813," *Founders Online*, National Archives, https://founders.archives.gov/documents/Jefferson/03-05-02-0474; "From Thomas Jefferson to James Monroe, 11 June 1823," *Founders Online*, National Archives, https://founders.archives.gov/documents/Jefferson/98-01-02-3559.

11. "Proposals to Revise the Virginia Constitution: I. Thomas Jefferson to 'Henry Tompkinson' (Samuel Kercheval), 12 July 1816," *Founders Online*, National Archives, https://founders.archives.gov/documents/Jefferson/03-10-02-0128-0002; "To James Madison from Thomas Jefferson, 6 September 1789," *Founders Online*, National Archives, https://founders.archives.gov/documents/Madison/01-12-02 -0248; Gordon-Reed and Onuf, *Most Blessed of the Patriarchs;* Herbert E. Sloan, *Principle and Interest: Thomas Jefferson and the Problem of Debt* (Charlottesville: University of Virginia Press, 1995).

12. "Proposals to Revise the Virginia Constitution: I. Thomas Jefferson to "Henry Tompkinson (Samuel Kercheval), 12 July 1816."

13. See Alan Taylor, *American Republics: A Continental History of the United States, 1783–1850* (New York: Norton, 2021); Ned Blackhawk, *The Rediscovery of America: Native Peoples and the Unmaking of U.S. History* (New Haven: Yale University Press, 2023), 211–49; John Craig Hammond, "Slavery, Sovereignty, and Empires:

North American Borderlands and the American Civil War, 1660–1860," *Journal of the Civil War Era* 4 (June 2014): 264–98.

14. See Sven Beckert, *Empire of Cotton: A Global History* (New York: Vintage, 2014); Walter Johnson, *River of Dark Dreams: Slavery, Capitalism, and Imperialism in the Mississippi Valley's Cotton Kingdom* (Cambridge: Harvard University Press, 2013); Calvin Schermerhorn, *The Business of Slavery and the Rise of American Capitalism* (New Haven: Yale University Press, 2015); Steven Mintz, *Moralists and Modernizers: America's Pre–Civil War Reformers* (Baltimore: Johns Hopkins University Press, 1995); Kate Masur, *Until Justice Be Done: America's First Civil Rights Movement, from the Revolution to Reconstruction* (New York: Norton, 2021); Brian D. Schoen, *Fragile Fabric of Union: Cotton, Federal Politics, and the Global Origins of the American Civil War* (Baltimore: Johns Hopkins University Press, 2009); Dael Norwood, *Trading Freedom: How Trade with China Defined Early America* (Chicago: University of Chicago Press, 2022).

15. See Blaakman, *Speculation Nation;* Thomas Perkins Abernathy, *Western Lands and the American Revolution* (New York: Appleton-Century, 1937); Joshua D. Rothman, *Flush Times and Fever Dreams: A Story of Capitalism and Slavery in the Age of Jackson* (Athens: University of Georgia Press, 2012); Michael John Witgen, *Seeing Red: Indigenous Land, American Expansion, and the Political Economy of Plunder in North America* (Chapel Hill: University of North Carolina Press for the Omohundro Institute, 2023); Gregory Ablavsky, *Federal Ground: Governing Property and Violence in the First U.S. Territories* (New York: Oxford University Press, 2021).

16. See Kate Masur, "State Sovereignty and Migration Before Reconstruction," *Journal of the Civil War Era* 9, no. 4 (December 2019): 588–611; John Craig Hammond, "'The Most Free of the Free States': Politics, Slavery, Race, and Regional Identity in Early Ohio," *Ohio History* 121 (2014): 35–57; Kevin Kenny, *The Problem of Immigration in a Slaveholding Republic: Policing Mobility in the Nineteenth-Century United States* (New York: Oxford University Press, 2023); Allison Brownwell Tirres, "Ownership Without Citizenship: The Creation of Non-Citizen Property Rights," *Michigan Journal of Race and Law* 19, no. 1 (Fall 2013): 1–52.

17. See Lauren Benton and Lisa Ford, *Rage for Order: The British Empire and the Origins of International Law, 1800–1850* (Cambridge: Harvard University Press, 2018); Michael Verney, *A Great and Rising Nation: Naval Exploration and Global Empire in the Early U.S. Republic* (Chicago: University of Chicago Press, 2022); Nicole Phelps, "One Service, Three Systems, Many Empires: The U.S. Consular Service and the Growth of U.S. Global Power, 1789–1924," in *Crossing Empires: Taking U.S. History into Transimperial Terrain,* ed. Kristin Hoganson and Jay Sexton (Durham, N.C.: Duke University Press, 2020), 135–58; Nicholas Guyatt, *The Hated Cage: An American Tragedy in Britain's Most Terrifying Prison* (New York: Basic, 2021); Jennifer Pitts, *Boundaries of the International: Law and Empire* (Cambridge: Harvard University Press, 2018).

18. On Jefferson's African American descendants, see Lerone Bennett, "Thomas Jefferson's Negro Grandchildren," *Ebony* (November 1954): 78–80; Fawn Brodie, "Jefferson's Unknown Grandchildren: A Study in Historical Silences," *American*

Heritage 27, no. 6 (October 1976): 23–33, 94–99; Annette Gordon-Reed, *The Hemingses of Monticello: An American Family* (New York: Norton, 2008); Lucia Stanton, *Free Some Day: The African American Families of Monticello* (Charlottesville, Va.: Thomas Jefferson Foundation, 2000); Stanton, *"Those Who Labor for My Happiness": Slavery at Thomas Jefferson's Monticello* (Charlottesville: University of Virginia Press, 2012); Catherine Kerrison, *Jefferson's Daughters: Three Sisters, White and Black, in a Young America* (New York: Random House, 2018).

On the genealogies of Jefferson's white descendants, see George Green Shackleford, *Collected Papers to Commemorate Fifty Years of the Monticello Association of the Descendants of Thomas Jefferson,* 2 vols. (Charlottesville, Va.: Monticello Association, 1984), 2:76–88. For biographical treatments, see Robert W. Drexler, *Guilty of Making Peace: A Biography of Nicholas P. Trist* (Lanham, Md.: University Press of America, 1991); Wallace Ohrt, *Defiant Peacemaker: Nicholas Trist in the Mexican War* (College Station: Texas A&M Press, 1997); Dean B. Mahin, *Olive Branch and Sword: The United States and Mexico, 1845–1848* (Jefferson, N.C.: McFarland, 1997); Lisa Francavilla, "Ellen Wayles Randolph Coolidge: Thomas Jefferson's Granddaughter in New England and Beyond," in *Virginia Women: Their Lives and Times,* ed. Cynthia A. Kierner and Sandra G. Treadway (Athens: University of Georgia Press, 2015); Joseph Carroll Vance, "Thomas Jefferson Randolph," Ph.D. diss., University of Virginia, 1957; Grace Benton Nelson, *The Life and Times of Meriwether Lewis Randolph: Grandson of Thomas Jefferson and Arkansas's Last Territorial Secretary* (Arkadelphia, Ark.: Clark County Historical Association, 2014).

19. See for example, Honor Sachs, *The Book of Judith: A Story of Law, Family, and Mixed-Race Ancestry in Slavery and Freedom* (forthcoming); R. Isabela Morales, *Happy Dreams of Liberty: An American Family in Slavery and Freedom* (New York: Oxford University Press, 2022); Adele Perry, *Colonial Relations: The Douglas-Connolly Family and the Nineteenth-Century Imperial World* (New York: Cambridge University Press, 2015); Daniel Livesay, *Children of Uncertain Future: Mixed-Race Jamaicans in Britain and the Atlantic Family, 1733–1833* (Chapel Hill: University of North Carolina Press for the Omohundro Institute, 2018); Anne E. Hyde, *Empires, Nations, Families: A History of the North American West* (Lincoln: University of Nebraska Press, 2011).

20. See Gordon-Reed, *Hemingses of Monticello,* 52–59; Stanton, *"Those Who Labor for My Happiness,"* 58, 64, 94, 169.

21. Susan Kern, *The Jeffersons at Shadwell* (New Haven: Yale University Press, 2010), 210–35; "From Thomas Jefferson to Chastellux, 26 November 1782," *Founders Online,* National Archives, https://founders.archives.gov/documents/Jefferson/01-06-02-0192.

22. Rayford W. Logan, "Memoirs of a Monticello Slave," MS 2041, Special Collections, University of Virginia; Sarah Nicholas Randolph, "Mrs. Thomas Mann Randolph," in *Worthy Women of Our First Century,* ed. O. J. Wister and Agnes Irwin (Philadelphia: Lippincott, 1877), 25–26; Dumas Malone, "Polly Jefferson and Her Father," *Virginia Quarterly Review* 7 (1931): 81–95.

23. Gordon-Reed, *Hemingses of Monticello,* 112–391; Gordon-Reed and Onuf, *"The Most Blessed of the Patriarchs,"* chap. 4; Stanton, *"Those Who Labor for My Hap-*

piness," 64–69, 96, 175–179, 244–248; Madison Hemings, "'Life among the Lowly,' No. 1," *Pike County (Ohio) Republican,* March 13, 1873 (quotations).

24. See Fraser D. Neiman, "Coincidence or Causal Connection? The Relationship Between Thomas Jefferson's Visits to Monticello and Sally Hemings's Conceptions," *William and Mary Quarterly* 57, no. 1 (2000): 198–210; Gordon-Reed, *Hemingses of Monticello,* 403–6.

25. Madison Hemings, "'Life among the Lowly,' No. 1," *Pike County (Ohio) Republican* (March 13, 1873).

26. See Van Gosse, *The First Reconstruction: Black Politics in America from the Revolution to the Civil War* (Chapel Hill: University of North Carolina Press, 2021); Masur, *Until Justice Be Done.*

27. Jay Sexton and Ian Tyrell, eds., *Empire's Twin: U.S. Anti-Imperialism from the Founding Era to the Age of Terror* (Ithaca: Cornell University Press, 2015), 59–75 (quote on 75); Jay Sexton, "The British Empire After A. G. Hopkins's *American Empire,*" *Journal of Imperial and Commonwealth History* 49, no. 3 (2021): 459–80.

Chapter 1. Joseph and Ellen Coolidge

Throughout this chapter, to avoid confusion with contemporary sources, I have used Wade-Giles transliteration for place names in nineteenth-century China, pinyin to refer to the Qing imperial state, and nineteenth-century names for other locations.

1. *Thomas Jefferson's Granddaughter in Queen Victoria's England: The Travel Diary of Ellen Wayles Coolidge, 1838–1839,* ed. Ann Lucas Birle and Lisa A. Francavilla (Charlottesville: University of Virginia Press, 2011), 11–13.

2. See Peter S. Onuf, *Jefferson's Empire: The Language of American Nationhood* (Charlottesville: University of Virginia Press, 2000), 71; Merrill D. Peterson, "Jefferson and Commercial Policy, 1783–1793," *William and Mary Quarterly* 22 (1965): 584–610; John E. Crowley, *The Privileges of Independence: Neomercantilism and the American Revolution* (Baltimore: Johns Hopkins University Press, 1993), 156–63; Doron S. Ben-Atar, *The Origins of Jeffersonian Commercial Policy* (New York: Palgrave Macmillan, 1993); Dael Norwood, *Trading Freedom: How Trade with China Defined Early America* (Chicago: University of Chicago Press, 2022).

3. See Temmu Ruskola, "Canton Is Not Boston: The Invention of American Imperial Sovereignty," *American Quarterly* 57, no. 3 (September 2005): 839–84; Jennifer Pitts, *Boundaries of the International: Law and Empire* (Cambridge: Harvard University Press, 2018); Antony Anghie, *Imperialism, Sovereignty and the Making of International Law* (Cambridge: Cambridge University Press, 2004); Christa Dierksheide, "Becoming Co-Imperialists: Anglo-Americans and the First Opium War," in *Ireland and America: Empire, Revolution, and Sovereignty,* ed. Francis D. Cogliano and Patrick Griffin (Charlottesville: University of Virginia Press, 2021), 285–300.

4. "To Thomas Jefferson from George Ticknor, 27 March 1824," *Founders Online,* National Archives, https://founders.archives.gov/documents/Jefferson/98-01-02 -4148.

5. *Jefferson's Granddaughter*, 13, 339.

6. *Jefferson's Granddaughter*, 50, 315–16.

7. *Jefferson's Granddaughter*, 339.

8. *Jefferson's Granddaughter*, 339–40, 105–6.

9. *Jefferson's Granddaughter*, 37, 231–37.

10. *Jefferson's Granddaughter*, 23, 67–69, 59–60, 83–86; Ellen Wayles Coolidge to Virginia Trist, December 8–11, 1838, Nicholas Philip Trist Papers, Southern Historical Collection, University of North Carolina.

11. *Jefferson's Granddaughter*, 97, 242, 212–17.

12. *Jefferson's Granddaughter*, 167, 104, 123–26, 117–19, 127–31, 136, 129.

13. *Jefferson's Granddaughter*, 76, 81.

14. *Jefferson's Granddaughter*, 324–25, 274.

15. Sarah Coles Stevenson to Emily Coles Rutherford, February 4, April 8, 1839, Sarah Coles Stevenson Papers, Duke University; *Jefferson's Granddaughter*, 35, 256, 178–79.

16. For recent scholarship on America's postcolonial dependence on Britain, see Sam W. Haynes, *Unfinished Revolution: The Early American Republic in a British World* (Charlottesville: University of Virginia Press, 2010); A. G. Hopkins, *American Empire: A Global History* (Princeton: Princeton University Press, 2018); Elisa Tamarkin, *Anglophilia: Deference, Devotion, and Antebellum America* (Chicago: University of Chicago Press, 2007); Kariann Yokota, *Unbecoming British: How Revolutionary America Became a Post-Colonial Nation* (New York: Oxford University Press, 2011).

   On the U.S.–China trade, see Norwood, *Trading Freedom;* Stephen R. Platt, *Imperial Twilight: The Opium War and the End of China's Last Golden Age* (New York: Knopf, 2018); John R. Haddad, *America's First Adventure in China: Trade, Treaties, Opium, and Salvation* (Philadelphia: Temple University Press, 2013).

17. Ellen Wayles Coolidge to Augustine Heard, November 29, 1839 (BM-8-5, Reel 516), Augustine Heard Papers, Baker Library, Harvard Business School.

18. Paul Van Dyke, *The Canton System: Life and Enterprise on the China Coast, 1700–1845* (Hong Kong: Hong Kong University Press, 2005); Jacques M. Downs, *The Golden Ghetto: The American Commercial Community at Canton and the Shaping of American Commercial Policy, 1784–1844* (Bethlehem, Pa.: Lehigh University Press, 1997); Charles Toogood Downing, *The Stranger in China; or, The Fan-qui's visit to the Celestial Empire in 1836–7* (Philadelphia: Lea & Blanchard, 1838), 1:122–23 (quotations).

19. Downing, *Stranger in China,* 1:140.

20. Downing, *Stranger in China,* 1:140; Robert Bennet Forbes to Samuel Russell, October 31, 1839, Russell and Company Papers, series 2, reel 5, Library of Congress.

21. Ellen Wayles Coolidge to Augustine Heard, December 4, 1839, November 29, 1839 (BM-8-5, reel 516), Augustine Heard Papers, Baker Library, Harvard Business School.

22. George Little, *Life on the Ocean; or, Twenty Years at Sea: Being the Personal Adventures of the Author* (Boston: Waite, Pierce, and Company, 1844), 107.

23. Quoted in Tim Sturgis, *Rivalry at Canton: The Control of Russell & Co., 1838–*

1840 and the Founding of Augustine Heard & Co. (London: Warren Press, 2006), 14; Sibing He, "Russell and Company, 1818–1891: America's Trade and Diplomacy in Nineteenth-Century China," Ph.D. diss., University of Miami, 1997, 66–68, 97–101.

24. Edward Delano quoted in Geoffrey C. Ward, *Before the Trumpet: Young Franklin Roosevelt, 1882–1905* (New York: Knopf, 2014), 71; John Murray Forbes, *Letters and Recollections of John Murray Forbes,* ed., Sarah Forbes Hughes (Boston: Houghton Mifflin, 1899), 3:281.

25. Joseph Coolidge to Baring Brothers, January 20, 1840, Baring Brothers Archive, ING, London; Elliot quoted in Robert Bennet Forbes, *Remarks on China and the China Trade* (Boston: Samuel N. Dickinson, 1844), 48; Elliot quoted in Susanna Hoe and Derek Roebuck, *The Taking of Hong Kong: Charles and Clara Elliot in China Waters* (London: Routledge, 1999), 52 .

26. Peter Ward Fay, *The Opium War, 1840–1842* (Chapel Hill: University of North Carolina Press, 1975), 154–62; James Matheson to J. A. Stewart MacKenzie, January 26, 1839, James Matheson Private Letter Book, MS JM C5/3, Cambridge University Archives, Cambridge.

27. Viscount Palmerston to Charles Elliot, June 15, 1838, FO 288/8, ff. 18–19, National Archives, Kew.

28. Speech of Viscount Palmerston, "War with China," House of Commons Debate, April 9, 1840, in *Parliamentary Debates* 53:844–950.

29. Quoted in Richard J. Grace, *Opium and Empire: The Lives and Careers of William Jardine and James Matheson* (Montreal: McGill-Queens University Press, 2014), 125; see Haddad, *America's First Adventure in China,* 125–31; House of Commons Debate, April 8, 1840, in *Parliamentary Debates* 53:820, 818.

30. Alfred Eckes, *Opening America's Market: US Foreign Policy Since 1776* (Chapel Hill: University of North Carolina Press, 1995), 1, 12; "To James Madison from Augustus B. Woodward, 12 June 1809," *Founders Online,* National Archives, https://founders.archives.gov/documents/Madison/03-01-02-0266.

31. See Haddad, *America's First Adventure in China,* 22–25; Li Chen, "Law, Empire, and Historiography of Modern Sino-Western Relations: A Case Study of the *Lady Hughes* Controversy in 1784," *Law and History Review* 27 (2009): 1–53.

32. See Song-Chuan Chen, *Merchants of War and Peace: British Knowledge of China in the Making of the Opium War* (Hong Kong: Hong Kong University Press, 2017).

33. Song-Chuan Chen, "Strangled by the Chinese and Kept 'Alive' by the British: Two Infamous Executions and the Discourse of Chinese Legal Despotism," in *A Global History of Execution and the Criminal Corpse,* ed. Richard Ward, 199–219 (London: Palgrave Macmillan, 2015).

34. Ellen Wayles Coolidge to Augustine Heard, December 2, 1839 (BN-3-2, reel 517), January 31, 1840 (BN-3-5, reel 518), March 3, 1840 (BN-3-5, reel 518), Augustine Heard Papers, Baker Library, Harvard Business School.

35. Thomas Dealtry, "Remarks on the Opium Trade," *Chinese Repository* 5 (November 1836), 297–305 (quote on 300); Speech of William Ewart Gladstone, House of Commons, April 8, 1840, in *Parliamentary Debates* 53:820, 818.

36. John C. Calhoun, "Speech on His Resolutions in Reference to the Case of the *Enterprise,* March 13, 1840," *Speeches of John C. Calhoun, Delivered in the Congress*

of the United States from 1811 to the Present Time (New York: Harper and Brothers, 1843), 388–89; Norwood, *Trading Freedom,* 73–94.

37. Joseph Coolidge to Joshua Bates, June 21, 1840, Baring Brothers Archive, ING, London.

38. Ellen Wayles Coolidge to Augustine Heard, January 2–3, 1840 (BN-3-5, reel 518), Augustine Heard Papers, Baker Library, Harvard Business School; Robert Bennet Forbes to Samuel Russell, October 31, 1839, Russell and Company Papers, series 2, reel 5, Library of Congress.

39. Ellen Wayles Coolidge to Augustine Heard, January 2–3, 1840 (BN-3-5, reel 518); Joseph Coolidge to Augustine Heard, December 13, 1839 (EM-12-2, reel 538), Augustine Heard Papers, Baker Library, Harvard Business School.

40. Joseph Coolidge to Augustine Heard, January 26, 1840 (EM-12-2, reel 538), Augustine Heard Papers, Baker Library, Harvard Business School.

41. Joseph Coolidge to Baring Brothers, January 20, 1840, Baring Brothers Archive, ING, London.

42. Joseph Coolidge to Augustine Heard, January 20, 1840, December 22, 1840 (EM-12-2, reel 538), Augustine Heard Papers, Baker Library, Harvard Business School.

43. Joseph Coolidge to Augustine Heard (BM-10-6, reel 516), November 29, 1839, Augustine Heard Papers, Baker Library, Harvard Business School; Joseph Coolidge to James Matheson, October 9, 1841, November 1, 1841, January 4, 1842, Jardine and Matheson Papers, University of Cambridge.

44. Edward Delano quoted in Ward, *Before the Trumpet,* 74; Robert Bennet Forbes to Samuel Russell, October 31, 1839, series 2, reel 5, Russell and Company Papers, Library of Congress.

45. Joseph Coolidge to Baring Brothers, January 20, 1840, Baring Brothers Archive, ING, London.

46. Ellen Wayles Coolidge to Augustine Heard, April 15, 1840 (BM-3-5, reel 518), Augustine Heard Papers, Baker Library, Harvard Business School; Joseph Coolidge to Augustine Heard, March 3, 1840 (EM-12-2, reel 538), Augustine Heard Papers, Baker Library, Harvard Business School.

47. Augustine Heard to Joseph Coolidge, May 8, 1840 (EM-12-1, reel 538), Augustine Heard Papers, Baker Library, Harvard Business School; Joseph Coolidge to Joseph Bates, June 21, 1840, Baring Brothers Archive, ING, London.

48. Joseph Coolidge to Joshua Bates, June 21, 1840, Baring Brothers Archive, ING, London.

49. Joseph Coolidge to Joshua Bates, June 21, 1840, Baring Brothers Archive, ING, London.

50. *Chinese Repository,* ed. Elijah Coleman Bridgman and Samuel Wells Williams, vol. 10: *January–December 1841* (Canton: Printed for the Proprietors, 1841), 416–19.

51. *Chinese Repository,* 416–19; Joseph Coolidge to Paul S. Forbes, May 25, 1844 (EM-12-4, reel 538), Augustine Heard Papers, Baker Library, Harvard Business School.

52. See Sibing He, "Russell and Company and the Anglo-American Imperialism of Free Trade," in *Narratives of Free Trade: The Commercial Cultures of Early U.S.-China Relations,* ed. Kendall Johnson (Hong Kong: Hong Kong University Press, 2012), 83–98; Haddad, *America's First Adventure in China;* Ruskola, "Canton Is Not Boston."

53. John Murray Forbes et al. to Daniel Webster, April 29, 1843, in *The Papers of Daniel Webster: Diplomatic Papers,* 2 vols., ed. Kenneth Shewmaker (Hanover, N.H.: Trustees of Dartmouth College, 1983), 1:917-21; President Tyler, Message to Congress, 30 December 1842, in James D. Richardson, ed., *A Compilation of Messages and Papers of the Presidents, 1789-1897,* 10 vols. (Washington, D.C.: Government Printing Office, 1897), 4:211-14.

54. See Forbes, *Letters and Recollections of John Murray Forbes,* 1:115; Daniel Webster to Caleb Cushing, May 8, 1843, in *The Papers of Daniel Webster,* 1:922-26; Eileen P. Scully, *Bargaining with the State from Afar: American Citizenship in Treaty Port China, 1844-1942* (New York: Columbia University Press, 2001); Teemu Ruskola, *Legal Orientalism: China, the United States, and Modern Law* (Cambridge: Harvard University Press, 2013).

55. Joseph Coolidge to Augustine Heard, [1844] (EM-12-4, reel 538), Augustine Heard Papers, Baker Library, Harvard Business School.

Chapter 2. Nicholas Trist

In this chapter I examine a war between two "American" nations, the United States and Mexico. To avoid confusion and awkward locutions, I use the term "American" to mean "U.S. American" throughout.

1. Nicholas P. Trist to Virginia Randolph Trist, March 14, 1835, Nicholas P. Trist Papers, Southern Historical Collection, University of North Carolina.

2. See Albert Castel, "The Clerk Who Defied a President: Nicholas Trist's Treaty with Mexico," *Virginia Cavalcade* 34 (1985): 136-43; Robert W. Drexler, *Guilty of Making Peace: A Biography of Nicholas P. Trist* (Lanham, Md.: University Press of America, 1991); Wallace Ohrt, *Defiant Peacemaker: Nicholas Trist in the Mexican War* (College Station: Texas A&M Press, 1997); Dean B. Mahin, *Olive Branch and Sword: The United States and Mexico, 1845-1848* (Jefferson, N.C.: McFarland, 1997).

3. See James L. Lewis, Jr., *The American Union and the Problem of Neighborhood: The United States and the Collapse of the Spanish Empire, 1783-1829* (Chapel Hill: University of North Carolina Press, 1998); Jay Sexton, *Debtor Diplomacy: Finance and American Foreign Relations in the Civil War Era, 1837-1873* (New York: Oxford University Press, 2005); Richard Huzzey, *Freedom Burning: Antislavery and Empire in Victorian Britain* (New York: Cornell University Press, 2012). James Bandinel, Foreign Office, March 30, 1839, ff. 146-202, 236-38, Add MS 43357, British Library.

4. On the question of how to incorporate nonwhite and non-Christian peoples into an international system bound by law in the nineteenth century, see Jennifer Pitts, *Boundaries of the International: Law and Empire* (Cambridge: Harvard University Press, 2018); Lauren Benton and Lisa Ford, *Rage for Order: The British Empire and the Origins of International Law* (Cambridge: Harvard University Press, 2016).

5. See Kevin Waite, *West of Slavery: The Southern Dream of a Transcontinental Empire* (Chapel Hill: University of North Carolina Press, 2021); Matthew Karp, *This Vast Southern Empire: Slaveholders at the Helm of American Foreign Policy* (Cam-

bridge: Harvard University Press, 2016); Matthew Pratt Guterl, *American Mediterranean: Southern Slaveholders in the Age of Emancipation* (Cambridge: Harvard University Press, 2013); Edward Rugemer, *The Problem of Emancipation: The Caribbean Roots of the American Civil War* (Baton Rouge: Louisiana State University Press, 2009).

6. *Baltimore American* (July 8, 1838); *Baltimore Sun* (July 12, 1838).

7. On the *Venus,* see Thomas N. Layton, *The Voyage of the "Frolic": New England Merchants and the Opium Trade* (Stanford: Stanford University Press, 1997), David Murray, *Britain, Spain, and the Abolition of the Cuban Slave Trade* (New York: Cambridge University Press, 2002), 105–6; Dale T. Graden, *Disease, Resistance and Lies: The Demise of the Transatlantic Slave Trade to Brazil and Cuba* (Baton Rouge: Louisiana State University Press, 2014), 18–19; Mahin, *Olive Branch and Sword,* 13.

8. See Stephen Chambers, *No God but Gain: The Untold Story of Cuban Slavery, the Monroe Doctrine, and the Making of the United States* (New York: Verso, 2015), 24, 47–57, 93, 100–101, 121; Gerald Horne, *Race to Revolution: The United States and Cuba During Slavery and Jim Crow* (New York: Monthly Review Press, 2014).

9. See Huzzey, *Freedom Burning;* Keith Hamilton and Patrick Salmon, eds., *Slavery, Diplomacy and Empire: Britain and the Suppression of the Slave Trade, 1807–1975* (Brighton, UK: Academic Press, 2009).

10. Memorandum on the State of the Slave Trade in Cuba, 1846, ff. 365, Add MS 40591, British Library; Commissioners at Havana to Palmerston, January 1, 1841, FO 84/348, National Archives, Kew; D. R. Murray, "Statistics of the Slave Trade to Cuba, 1790–1867," *Journal of Latin American Studies* 3, no. 2 (1971): 131–49.

11. See Jenny S. Martinez, *The Slave Trade and the Origins of International Human Rights Law* (New York: Oxford University Press, 2012); Lauren Benton, "Abolition and Imperial Law, 1790–1820," *Journal of Imperial and Commonwealth History* 39 (2011): 355–74; Leslie Bethell, "The Mixed Commissions for the Suppression of the Transatlantic Slave Trade in the Nineteenth Century," *Journal of African History* 7 (1966): 73–93; Emily Haslam, "International Criminal Law and Legal Memories of Abolition: Intervention, Mixed Commission Courts, and Emancipation," *Journal of the History of International Law* 18 (2016): 420–47.

12. See John W. Barber, *A History of the Amistad Captives: Being a Circumstantial Account of the Capture of the Spanish Schooner Amistad, by the Africans on Board; Their Voyage, and Capture New Long Island, New York; With Biographical Sketches of Each of the Surviving Africans; Also, an Account of the Trials Had on Their Case, Before the District and Circuit Courts of the United States, for the District of Connecticut* (New Haven: E. L. and J. W. Barber, 1840); Marcus Rediker, *The "Amistad" Rebellion: An Atlantic Odyssey of Slavery and Freedom* (New York: Verso, 2012).

13. James Bandinel, Foreign Office, March 30, 1839, ff. 146–202, 236–38, Add MS 433357, British Library.

14. Richard Madden to Lord Glenelg, April 15, 1839, CO 318/146, National Archives, Kew; Lord Palmerston Letterbook, September 6, 1836, ff. 37, Add MS 49967, British Library; Farida Shaikh, "Judicial Diplomacy: British Officials and the Mixed Commission Courts," in Hamilton and Salmon, *Slavery, Diplomacy and Empire,* 42–64.

15. British-American Diplomacy, Treaty of Ghent, 1814, Yale Law School, Avalon Project, Article 10, https://avalon.law.yale.edu/19th_century/ghent.asp; Act of 1820, May 15, 1820, Statute I, Chap. CXIII, section 4, The Abolition of the Slave Trade, Schomburg Center for Research in Black Culture, New York Public Library, http://abolition.nypl.org/content/docs/text/Act_of_1820.pdf.

16. Campbell Dalrymple and James Kennedy to Nicholas Trist, July 1, 1839, ff. 168, FO 84/274; Campbell Dalrymple and James Kennedy to Nicholas Trist, January 8, 1839, ff. 62, FO 84/274; Campbell Dalrymple and James Kennedy to Nicholas Trist, January 10, 1839, ff. 72, FO 84/274, National Archives, Kew.

17. Quoted in Fabian Klose, "Legal Practitioners: Nineteenth-Century International Jurisdiction and the Ambiguous Role of the Members of the Mixed Commissions," in *Crafting the International Order: Practitioners and Practices of International Law Since c. 1800,* ed. Marcus M. Payk and Kim Christian Priemel, 48–65 (New York: Oxford University Press, 2021).

18. Campbell Dalrymple and James Kennedy to Nicholas Trist, January 10, 1839, ff. 72, FO 84/274, National Archives, Kew.

19. Campbell Dalrymple and James Kennedy to Nicholas Trist, January 10, 1839, ff. 72, FO 84/274, National Archives, Kew.

20. Nicholas Trist to Commissioners, 1839, ff. 338, 347, FO 84/274, National Archives, Kew.

21. James Kennedy and Campbell Dalrymple to Lord Palmerston, October 27, 1839, ff. 226–30, FO 84/274, National Archives, Kew.

22. John Forsyth, 1839, "Africans Taken in the Amistad," U.S. 26th Cong., 1st Sess., H. Exec. Doc. 185 (New York: Blair & Rives, 1840), 57–62; James Kennedy and Campbell Dalrymple to Lord Palmerston, October 27, 1839, ff. 226–30, FO 84/274, National Archives, Kew.

23. See Virginia Randolph Trist to Nicholas Trist, May 11, 1835, Trist Papers, Southern Historical Collection, University of North Carolina.

24. Alexander Everett to Domingo Del Monte, February 12, 1842, in *Centon epistolario de Domingo Del Monte,* 7 vols., ed. Domingo Figarola-Caneda, 5:66 (Havana: Imprenta El Siglo XX, 1923–57).

25. See Edward Everett to Forsyth, Washington, D.C., July 21, 1840, RG 59, Consular Dispatches from Cuba, t-20:14, 67, National Archives and Records Administration, Washington, D.C.; Graden, *Disease, Resistance, and Lies,* 30.

26. Edward Everett to Forsyth, Washington, D.C., July 21, 1840,; Graden, *Disease, Resistance, and Lies,* 30.

27. Drexler, *Guilty of Making Peace,* 51–59; Ohrt, *Defiant Peacemaker,* 76–95.

28. See Nicholas Trist to Virginia Randolph Trist, April 18, 1847; Nicholas Trist to Virginia Randolph Trist, April 25, 1847, reel 2, Nicholas Philip Trist Papers, Library of Congress; James K. Polk, *Diary of a President: James K. Polk,* ed. Milo Quaife, 4 vols. (Columbia, Tenn.: James K. Polk Memorial Association, 2005), 3:483.

29. See Hore Browse Trist to Virginia Randolph Trist, July 31, 1847, Trist Papers, Southern Historical Collection, University of North Carolina; Amy S. Greenberg, *A Wicked War: Polk, Clay, Lincoln and the 1846 Invasion of Mexico* (New York: Knopf, 2013), 215–18.

30. Nicholas Trist to [?], n.d., reel 6, Trist Papers, Library of Congress; Greenberg, *Wicked War*, 95.

31. Polk, *Diary of a President*, 2:468.

32. Polk, *Diary of a President*, 1:71; Democratic *Union*, March 16, 1848; Waite, *West of Slavery*.

33. Polk, *Diary of a President*, 1:71; John Crampton to Lord Palmerston, April 2, 1848, ff. 485, Add MS 48547, British Library; Charles Bankhead to Earl of Aberdeen, July 30, 1845, no. 74, f. 24, Add MS 43170, British Library.

34. Ulysses S. Grant, *Personal Memoirs of U.S. Grant,* 2 vols. (New York: Charles L. Webster, 1894), 1:45; quoted in Richard R. Steinberg, "President Polk and California: Additional Documents," *Pacific Historical Review* 10 (1941): 217–19, at 219.

35. Polk, *Diary of a President*, 2:466; Greenberg, *Wicked War*, 175.

36. Greenberg, *Wicked War*, 200–213.

37. *St. Louis Republican* (February 14, 1847); Consul Giffard to Lord Palmerston, March 27, 1847, ff. 49–53, FO 50/214, National Archives, Kew; Consul Giffard to Lord Palmerston, October 20, 1847, ff. 170–172, FO 50/214, National Archives, Kew; Lord Palmerston, Notes from a Meeting with James Buchanan, July 15, 1846, Palmerston Letter Book, ff. 9, Add MS 48547, British Library.

38. Nicholas Trist to Winfield Scott, June 25, 1847; Nicholas Trist to Edward Thornton, July 15, 1847, reel 2, Trist Papers, Library of Congress.

39. Sexton, *Debtor Diplomacy,* 47; Consul Giffard to Lord Palmerston, October 20, 1847, ff. 170–72, FO 50/214, National Archives, Kew.

40. Lord Palmerston, Notes from a Meeting with James Buchanan, July 15, 1846, Palmerston Letter Book, ff. 9, Add MS 48547, British Library.

41. Nicholas Trist to James Buchanan, August 27, 1847, reel 2, Trist Papers, Library of Congress.

42. Nicholas Trist to James Buchanan, August 27, 1847, reel 2, Trist Papers, Library of Congress; Charles Bankhead to Earl of Aberdeen, September 7, 1846, ff. 137–38, Add MS 49968, British Library.

43. *Projet* prepared by James Buchanan for Nicholas Trist, April 15, 1847, in *Diplomatic Correspondence of the United States, Inter-American Affairs, 1831–1860*, ed. William R. Manning, 12 vols. (Washington, D.C.: State Department, 1932–1939), 8:205–6.

44. James Buchanan to Nicholas Trist, July 19, 1847, in *Diplomatic Correspondence of the United States, Inter-American Affairs, 1831–1860*, 8:213–14.; Nicholas Trist to Mexican Commissioners, September 7, 1847, ff. 22–62, FO 50/212, National Archives, Kew.

45. James Buchanan to Nicholas Trist, October 25, 1847, reel 2, Trist Papers, Library of Congress.

46. Consul Giffard to Lord Palmerston, May 31, 1847, ff. 104–6, FO 50/214, National Archives, Kew.

47. Edward Thornton to Lord Palmerston, October 29, 1847, ff. 11, FO 50/212, National Archives, Kew.

48. Nicholas Trist to Mexican Plenipotentiaries, September 7, 1847, ff. 22–62, FO 50/212, National Archives, Kew.

49. Nicholas Trist to Mexican Plenipotentiaries, September 7, 1847, ff. 22–62, FO 50/212, National Archives, Kew.

50. James K. Polk, *Message from the President of the United States, to the Two Houses of Congress, at the Commencement of the First Session of the Thirtieth Congress,* Senate, December 7, 1847 (Washington, D.C.: Wendell and Van Benthuysen, 1847).

51. Roy P. Basler, ed., *Abraham Lincoln: His Speeches and Writings* (New York: Da Capo, 1990), 220–21.

52. Nicholas Trist to James Buchanan, October 25, 1847, Department of State, Dispatches, 1847–1848, National Archives and Records Administration, Washington, D.C.

53. James K. Polk, *Diary of a President,* 3:185–86; Greenberg, *Wicked War,* 221–23.

54. Andrew Jackson Donelson to James Buchanan, February 21, 1847, Papers of James Buchanan, Library of Congress.

55. Edward Thornton to Lord Palmerston, October 29, 1847, ff. 64–69, FO 50/212, National Archives, Kew; Winfield Scott to Santa Anna, August 21, 1847, in *Diplomatic Correspondence of the United States, Inter-American Affairs, 1831–1860,* 8 vols., ed. William R. Manning (Washington, D.C.: Carnegie Endowment for International Peace, 1938), 8:922; Henry Clay, *Speeches of Henry Clay,* ed. Calvin Colton, 2 vols. (New York: A. S. Barnes, 1857), 2:367–69.

56. Virginia Randolph Trist to [?] Tuckerman, August 23, 1863, enclosure in July 8, 1863, Trist Papers, Southern Historical Collection, University of North Carolina.

57. Nicholas Trist to José Manuel de la Peña y Peña, November 24, 1847, ff. 135–36, FO 50/212, National Archives, Kew; Nicholas Trist to Edward Thornton, December 4, 1847, ff. 171–81, FO 50/212, National Archives, Kew.

58. Percy Doyle to Lord Palmerston, October 20, 1847, ff. 187–89, FO 50/212, National Archives, Kew.

59. Nicholas Trist to James Buchanan, December 6, 1847, in *Diplomatic Correspondence,* 7:984–1020.

60. Nicholas Trist to James Buchanan, December 6, 1847, in *Diplomatic Correspondence,* 7:984–1020.

61. Brian DeLay, *War of a Thousand Deserts: Indian Raids and the U.S.-Mexican War* (New Haven: Yale University Press, 2008); Nicholas Trist to James Buchanan, December 6, 1847, in *Diplomatic Correspondence,* 7:984–1020.

62. James K. Polk, Message to Congress, July 6, 1848, reprinted in "President's Message," *Daily Union* (July 7, 1848).

63. Virginia Randolph Trist to Tuckerman, August 23, 1863, enclosure in July 8, 1863, Trist Papers, Southern Historical Collection, University of North Carolina.

64. Virginia Randolph Trist to Tuckerman, August 23, 1863, enclosure in July 8, 1863, Trist Papers, Southern Historical Collection, University of North Carolina.

Chapter 3. Thomas Jefferson Randolph

1. Israel Gillette Jefferson, "'Life Among the Lowly,' No. 3," *Pike County Republican* (December 25, 1873); *Richmond Enquirer* (November 3, 1826); Lucia Stanton, *"Those Who Labor for My Happiness": Slavery at Thomas Jefferson's Monticello* (Charlottesville: University of Virginia Press, 2012), 162, 195–96.

2. Memoir of Peter Fossett in *New York World* (January 30, 1898); Stanton, *"Those Who Labor for My Happiness,"* 195–96.
3. Bill from Monticello Estate Sale: Martha J. Randolph, [after January 18, 1827] ; Bill from Monticello Estate Sale: Cornelia J. Randolph, [after January 18, 1827]; Bill from Monticello Estate Sale: Joseph Coolidge, [after January 18, 1827]; Bill from Monticello Estate Sale: Nicholas P. Trist, [after January 18, 1827]; Bill from Monticello Estate Sale: Thomas J. Randolph, [after January 18, 1827], Jefferson-Kirk Manuscripts Relating to Thomas Jefferson and the Jefferson and Randolph Families, MS 5291, Special Collections, University of Virginia.
4. George Green Shackleford, *Collected Papers to Commemorate Fifty Years of the Monticello Association of the Descendants of Thomas Jefferson,* 2 vols. (Charlottesville: Monticello Association, 1984), 2:76–88; Joseph Carroll Vance, "Thomas Jefferson Randolph," Ph.D. diss., University of Virginia, 1957.
5. Shackleford, *Collected Papers,* 2:76–88; Vance, "Thomas Jefferson Randolph"; Stanton, *"Those Who Labor for My Happiness,"* 195–96; Melvin I. Urofsky, *The Levy Family and Monticello, 1834–1923: Saving Thomas Jefferson's House* (Chapel Hill: University of North Carolina Press, 2002), 36–40.
6. Thomas Jefferson Randolph to Martha Jefferson Randolph, January 2, 1831, Edgehill-Randolph Papers, MS 1397, Special Collections, University of Virginia; Michal Rozbicki, *Culture and Liberty in the Age of the American Revolution* (Charlottesville: University of Virginia Press, 2011), 31.
7. Sarah E. Nicholas to Jane Randolph, January 11, 1847, Edgehill Randolph Papers, Special Collections, University of Virginia; Mary E. Lyons, *Slave Labor on Virginia's Blue Ridge Railroad* (Charleston, S.C.: History Press, 2020), 33–38; Mary E. Lyons, *Blue Ridge Railroad* (Charleston, S.C., MA: History Press, 2015), 37–38, 55–57.
8. Thomas R. Dew, *Review of the Debate in the Virginia Legislature of 1831 and 1832* (Richmond: T. W. White, 1832), 122–24; U.S. Census, 1790; "Slave Population of the United States," 1790–1850, U.S. Census Bureau, https://www2.census.gov /library/publications/decennial/1850/1850c/1850c-04.pdf; Calvin Schermerhorn, *Money over Mastery, Family over Freedom: Slavery in the Antebellum Upper South* (Baltimore: Johns Hopkins University Press, 2011).
9. See Lyons, *Blue Ridge Railroad;* Joshua D. Rothman, *The Ledger and the Chain: How Domestic Slave Traders Shaped America* (New York: Basic, 2021); Calvin Schermerhorn, *The Business of Slavery and the Rise of American Capitalism, 1815–1860* (New Haven: Yale University Press, 2015); Steven Deyle, *Carry Me Back: The Domestic Slave Trade in American Life* (New York: Oxford University Press, 2006); Robert H. Gudmestad, *A Troublesome Commerce: The Transformation of the Interstate Slave Trade* (Baton Rouge: Louisiana University Press, 2004); Michael Tadman, *Speculators and Slaves: Masters, Traders, and Slaves* (Madison: University of Wisconsin Press, 1989).
10. Vance, "Thomas Jefferson Randolph," 240–42.
11. See Stanton, *"Those Who Labor for My Happiness,"* 196–98.
12. Mary J. Randolph to Ellen W. Randolph, January 25, 1827, Ellen Wayles Randolph Coolidge Correspondence, MS 9090, Special Collections, University of Virginia.

13. See Cynthia A. Kierner, *Martha Jefferson Randolph, Daughter of Monticello: Her Life and Times* (Chapel Hill: University of North Carolina Press, 2012), 214–15.

14. Ellen Wayles Coolidge to Nicholas Trist, September 26, 1826, Ellen Wayles Randolph Coolidge Correspondence, Special Collections, MS 9090, University of Virginia; Gaye Wilson, "Monticello Was Among the Prizes in a Lottery for a Ruined Jefferson's Relief," *Colonial Williamsburg Journal* (Winter 2010), available at https://research.colonialwilliamsburg.org/Foundation/journal/Winter10 /jefferson.cfm.

15. Martha Jefferson Randolph to Ellen W. Randolph, [ca. October 22, 1826], Randolph Collection, Virginia Museum of History and Culture; Ellen W. Coolidge's Essay on Thomas Jefferson's Finances, [1826], Ellen Wayles Randolph Coolidge Correspondence, MS 9090, Special Collections, University of Virginia; Joseph Coolidge to Nicholas P. Trist, [October 31, 1826], Nicholas Philip Trist Papers, Library of Congress.

16. Thomas Jefferson Randolph to Martha Jefferson Randolph, December 18, 1826, Edgehill-Randolph Papers, MS 1397, Special Collections, University of Virginia; Mary J. Randolph to Ellen Wayles Coolidge, January 25, 1827, Ellen Wayles Randolph Coolidge Correspondence, MS 9090, Special Collections, University of Virginia.

17. Mary J. Randolph to Ellen Wayles Coolidge, January 25, 1827, Ellen Wayles Randolph Coolidge Correspondence, MS 9090, Special Collections, University of Virginia.

18. Cornelia Randolph to Ellen Wayles Coolidge, April 10, 1827, Ellen Wayles Randolph Coolidge Correspondence, MS 9090, Special Collections, University of Virginia; Kierner, *Martha Jefferson Randolph,* 214–15.

19. Edward Everett to Thomas Jefferson Randolph, January 25, 1827; Thomas Jefferson Randolph to Jane Randolph, May 28, 1827; Thomas Jefferson Randolph to Jane Randolph, April 18, 1828; Bowen and Gray to Thomas Jefferson Randolph, January 19, 1830, September 10, 1830, Edgehill-Randolph Papers, MS 1397, Special Collections, University of Virginia.

20. Martha Jefferson Randolph to Thomas Jefferson Randolph, February 29, 1828, Edgehill-Randolph Papers, MS 1397, Special Collections, University of Virginia; "Nicholas P. Trist to James Madison, 8 May 1832," *Founders Online,* National Archives, https://founders.archives.gov/documents/Madison/99-02-02-2565.

21. Nicholas P. Trist to James Madison, May 8, 1832, Trist Papers, Southern Historical Collection, University of North Carolina; Thomas Jefferson Randolph, Draft of letter, [1827], Edgehill-Randolph Papers, MS 1397, Special Collections, University of Virginia.

22. Cornelia Jefferson Randolph to Ellen Wayles Coolidge, June 29, 1829; Virginia Jefferson Randolph to Ellen Wayles Coolidge, March 28, 1827, Ellen Wayles Randolph Coolidge Correspondence, MS 9090, Special Collections, University of Virginia. Wormely Hughes, along with his uncle John Hemmings (Sally Hemings's half-brother) and John's wife, Priscilla Hemmings, lived at Monticello into the 1830s.

23. Martha Jefferson Randolph to Ellen Wayles Coolidge, August 15, 1831, Ellen

Wayles Randolph Coolidge Correspondence, MS 9090, Special Collections, University of Virginia; Marc Leepson, *Saving Monticello: The Levy Family's Epic Quest to Rescue the House That Jefferson Built* (New York: Free Press, 2001); Melvin I. Urofsky, *Saving Mr. Jefferson's House: The Levy Family and Monticello, 1834–1923* (Charlottesville: Thomas Jefferson Memorial Foundation, 2000).

24. See Vance, "Thomas Jefferson Randolph"; E. Griffith Dodson, *Speakers and Clerks of the Virginia House of Delegates, 1776–1955* (Richmond: Privately Printed, 1956), 63; Edgar Woods, *Albemarle County in Virginia* (Charlottesville: Michie Company, 1901), 317–18; Hamilton W. Pierson, *Jefferson at Monticello: The Private Life of Thomas Jefferson* (New York: Scribner, 1862), 90–91.

25. Peggy Nicholas to Jane Randolph, [1829], Edgehill-Randolph Papers, MS 1397, Special Collections, University of Virginia; Ann Maury Diary, July 5, 1831, Maury Family Papers, MS 6742, Special Collections, University of Virginia.

26. See Patrick H. Breen, *The Land Shall Be Deluged in Blood: A New History of the Nat Turner Revolt* (New York: Oxford University Press, 2016); Vanessa M. Holden, *Surviving Southampton: African American Women and Resistance in Nat Turner's Community* (Champaign: University of Illinois Press, 2021); Eva Sheppard Wolf, *Race and Liberty in the New Nation: Emancipation in Virginia from the Revolution to Nat Turner's Rebellion* (Baton Rouge: Louisiana State University Press, 2009), 211–15.

27. Thomas Jefferson Randolph, *The Speech of Thomas J. Randolph (of Albemarle) in the House of Delegates of Virginia, on the Abolition of Slavery: Delivered Saturday, January 21, 1832* (Richmond: T. W. White, 1832); memoir of Thomas Jefferson Randolph in *Pike County Republican*, December 25, 1873; Christa Dierksheide, *Amelioration and Empire: Slavery in the Plantation Americas, 1770–1840* (Charlottesville: University of Virginia Press, 2014), 63; Eva Sheppard Wolf, *Race and Liberty in the New Nation*, 211–15.

28. Peggy Nicholas to Mrs. Dabney Carr, February 27, 1832, Carr-Cary Papers, MS 1231, Special Collections, University of Virginia; Peggy Nicholas to Jane Randolph, July 1, 1831, Edgehill-Randolph Papers, MS 1397, Special Collections, University of Virginia.

29. Thomas Jefferson Randolph to William Cabell Rives, William Cabell Rives Papers, Library of Congress; Thomas Jefferson Randolph, *Speech of Thomas Jefferson Randolph (of Albemarle) in Committee of the Whole, on the Report . . . on Federal Regulations*, January 11, 1833 (Richmond: T. W. White, 1833).

30. John W. Murdough to John N. Tazewell, January 12, 1833, Tazewell Family Papers, Library of Virginia.

31. Martha Jefferson Randolph to Ellen W. Randolph Coolidge, September 15, 1833, Ellen Wayles Randolph Coolidge Correspondence, MS 9090, Special Collections, University of Virginia.

32. Peggy Nicholas to Jane Randolph, April 4, 1833; Sarah E. Nicholas to Jane Randolph, October 25, 1833; Jane Randolph to Sarah E. Nicholas, June 18, [1833], Edgehill Randolph Papers, MS 1397, Special Collections, University of Virginia; Martha Jefferson Randolph to Ellen W. Randolph Coolidge, September 15, 1833, Ellen Wayles Randolph Coolidge Correspondence, MS 9090, Special Collections, University of Virginia; Kierner, *Martha Jefferson Randolph*, 251–52.

33. Martha Jefferson Randolph to Ellen W. Randolph Coolidge, September 15, 1833, Ellen Wayles Randolph Coolidge Correspondence, MS 9090, Special Collections, University of Virginia.

34. Martha Jefferson Randolph to Ellen W. Randolph Coolidge, September 15, 1833, Ellen Wayles Randolph Coolidge Correspondence, MS 9090, Special Collections, University of Virginia; Stanton, *"Those Who Labor for My Happiness,"* 238-39.

35. Thomas Jefferson Randolph, Draft of a letter [ca. 1872], Edgehill-Randolph Papers, MS 1397, Special Collections, University of Virginia.

36. George Wythe Randolph, [n.d., ca. 1850s], Additional Papers of the Randolph Family of Edgehill, MS 5533-c, Special Collections, University of Virginia; Susan Wyly-Jones, "The 1835 Anti-Abolition Meetings in the South: A New Look at the Controversy over the Abolition Postal Campaign," *Civil War History* 47, no. 4 (December 2001): 289-309.

37. See Andrew J. O'Shaughnessy, *The Illimitable Freedom of the Human Mind: Thomas Jefferson's Idea of a University* (Charlottesville: University of Virginia Press, 2021), 60-64, 79-80; Robert F. Hunter and Edwin L. Dooley, *Claudius Crozet, French Engineer in America, 1790-1864* (Charlottesville: University of Virginia Press, 1989).

38. See Hunter and Dooley, *Claudius Crozet.*

39. Claudius Crozet quoted in William Couper, *Claudius Crozet: Soldier, Scholar, Educator, Engineer,* Southern Sketches, no. 8, 1st series (Charlottesville, Va.: Historical Publishing Company, 1935), 58; Lyons, *Virginia Blue Ridge Railroad,* 17-21.

40. See Mary Lee Dunn, *Ballykilcline Rising: From Famine Ireland to Immigrant America* (Amherst: University of Massachusetts Press, 2008); Edward Laxton, *Famine Ships: The Irish Exodus to America* (New York: Henry Holt, 1996); Robert James Scally, *End of Hidden Ireland: Rebellion, Famine, and Emigration* (New York: Oxford University Press, 1995); Jay Martin Perry, "Shillelaghs, Shovels, and Secrets: Irish Immigrant Secret Societies and the Building of Indiana Internal Improvements, 1835-1837," M.A. thesis, Indiana University, 2009.

41. See Henry Sturgis Drinker, *Tunneling, Explosives, and Rock Drills* (New York: Wiley, 1882). On slave insurance, see Daina Ramey Berry, *The Price for Their Pound of Flesh: The Value of the Enslaved, from Womb to Grave, in the Building of a Nation* (Boston: Beacon, 2017); Sharon Ann Murphy, *Investing in Life: Insurance in Antebellum America* (Baltimore: Johns Hopkins University Press, 2010).

42. See Lyons, *Virginia Blue Ridge Railroad,* 143-44; Lyons, *Slave Labor on the Blue Ridge Railroad,* 127-38.

43. On slave hiring, see Schermerhorn, *Money over Mastery, Family over Freedom,* 16, 136; Jonathan D. Martin, *Divided Mastery: Slave Hiring in the American South* (Cambridge: Harvard University Press, 2004), 8; John J. Zaborney, *Slaves for Hire: Renting Enslaved Laborers in Antebellum Virginia* (Baton Rouge: Louisiana State University Press, 2012); Frederic Bancroft, *Slave Trading in the Old South* (1931; New York: Frederick Unger , 1959), 147; Eugene D. Genovese, *Roll, Jordan, Roll: The World the Slaves Made* (New York: Vintage, 1974), 390; Robert W. Fogel and Stanley L. Engerman, *Time on the Cross: The Economics of American Negro Slavery* (1974; New York: Norton, 1989), 53, 56; Sarah S. Hughes, "Slaves for Hire: The

Allocation of Black Labor in Elizabeth County, Virginia, 1782 to 1810," *William and Mary Quarterly* 35 (April 1978): 260–86; Randolph B. Campbell, "Research Note: Slave Hiring in Texas," *American Historical Review* 92 (February 1988): 107–14; William A. Byrne, "The Hiring of Woodson, Slave Carpenter of Savannah," *Georgia Historical Quarterly* 77 (Summer 1993): 245–63; Keith C. Barton, "'Good Cooks and Washers': Slave Hiring, Domestic Labor, and the Market in Bourbon County, Kentucky," *Journal of American History* 84 (September 1997): 436–60.

44. Frederick Law Olmsted, *A Journey in the Seaboard States* (New York: Mason Brothers, 1861), 30–31; Jennifer Oast, *Institutional Slaveholding: Slaveholding Churches, Schools, Colleges, and Businesses in Virginia, 1680–1860* (New York: Cambridge University Press, 2016), 203–31.

45. Claudius Crozet to Board of Public Works, August 2, 1853; Board of Public Works Journal, November 1853; Claudius Crozet to Board of Public Works, January 4, 1854, Blue Ridge Railroad Papers, Library of Virginia.

46. Lyons, *Virginia Blue Ridge Railroad*, 25–26; Solomon Northrup, *Twelve Years a Slave, Narrative of Solomon Northrup, A Citizen of New-York, Kidnapped in Washington City in 1841, and Rescued in 1853, from a Cotton Plantation Near the Red River, in Louisiana* (Auburn, N.Y.: Derby and Miller, 1853), 42–43.

47. Lyons, *Virginia Blue Ridge Railroad*, 25–26, 35, 61, 82, 117–19; David W. Coffey, "Into the Valley of Virginia: The 1852 Travel Account of Curran Swain," *Virginia Cavalcade* 39, no. 4 (Spring 1990): 14–27 (quotes on 14–15).

48. Claudius Crozet, Journal, 1838, Blue Ridge Railroad Papers, Library of Virginia.

49. List of Stockholders from 1836 to 1849, Virginia Central Railroad Papers, Library of Virginia; Woods, *Albemarle*, 98–99; Deyle, *Carry Me Back*, 280; Omohundro Slave Trade and Farm Accounts, 1857–1863, Special Collections, University of Virginia.

50. See List of Stockholders from 1836 to 1849, Virginia Central Railroad Papers, Library of Virginia; Oast, *Institutional Slaveholding*, 203–31.

51. See List of Stockholders from 1836 to 1849, Virginia Central Railroad Papers, Library of Virginia; Woods, *Albemarle*, 98–99.

52. See Omohundro Slave Trade and Farm Accounts, 1857–1863, MS 4122, Special Collections, University of Virginia; Schermerhorn, *Money over Mastery, Family over Freedom*, 110–76; Maurie D. McInnis, *Slaves Waiting for Sale: Abolitionist Art and the American Slave Trade* (Chicago: University of Chicago Press, 2011), 96–98.

53. Ellen Randolph to Nicholas Trist, April 17, 1848, Nicholas Philip Trist Papers, Southern Historical Collection, University of North Carolina.

54. See *Proceedings of the Stockholders of the Virginia Central Railroad Company, at Their Fifteenth Annual Meeting, Held at Louisa Courthouse, August 1, 1850* (Richmond: Colin, Baptist and Nowlan, 1850), 14, 24.

55. See Claudius Crozet, "Bidders for the Whole Line," Blue Ridge Railroad Papers, Library of Virginia.

56. Claudius Crozet, "Bidders for the Whole Line," Blue Ridge Railroad Papers, Library of Virginia.

57. Christopher Valentine to Thomas Jefferson Randolph, September 23, 1849, Octo-

ber 20, 1849, Randolph Family Papers, MS 8937-b, Special Collections, University of Virginia.

58. Christopher Valentine to Thomas Jefferson Randolph, January 6, 1850, Randolph Family Papers, MS 8937-b, Special Collections, University of Virginia.

59. Christopher Valentine to Thomas Jefferson Randolph, December 20, 1849, Randolph Family Papers, MS 8937-b, Special Collections, University of Virginia.

60. Blue Ridge Railroad payrolls do not list the names of enslaved people hired by Jeff Randolph. See Blue Ridge Tunnel Payrolls, contracts for slave labor, account books and miscellaneous records in Blue Ridge Railroad Papers, Library of Virginia. On enslaved individuals' resistance to being hired out to Virginia railroads, see Christopher Valentine to Thomas Jefferson Randolph, December 20, 1849, in Randolph Family Papers, MS 8937-b, Special Collections, University of Virginia.

61. 1840 U.S. Census, Albemarle County, Virginia, slave schedule, Thomas Jefferson Randolph, slave owner, National Archives and Records Administration, Washington, D.C.; 1850 U.S. Census, Albemarle County, Virginia, slave schedule, Thomas Jefferson Randolph, slave owner, National Archives and Records Administration, Washington, D.C.

62. Thomas Jefferson Randolph, Contract for Sections 7 & 8 with Blue Ridge Railroad, October 24, 1849, Blue Ridge Railroad Papers, Library of Virginia.

63. See Claudius Crozet to Board of Public Works, Annual Report, October 1850, Blue Ridge Railroad Papers, Library of Virginia; Christopher Valentine to Thomas Jefferson Randolph, May 14, 1851, Randolph Family Papers, MS 8937-b, Special Collections, University of Virginia.

64. Claudius Crozet to Board of Public Works, Annual Report, October 1850, Blue Ridge Railroad Papers, Library of Virginia; Christopher Valentine to Thomas Jefferson Randolph, May 14, 1851, Randolph Family Papers, MS 8937-b, Special Collections, University of Virginia.

65. Christopher Valentine to Thomas Jefferson Randolph, May 14, 1851, Randolph Family Papers, MS 8937-b, Special Collections, University of Virginia.

66. George Wythe Randolph to Mary B. Randolph, January 22, 1851, June 5, 1851, July 6, 1851, Edgehill-Randolph Papers, MS 1397, Special Collections, University of Virginia.

67. Christopher Valentine to Thomas Jefferson Randolph, May 14, 1851, Randolph Family Papers, MS 8937-b, Special Collections, University of Virginia.

68. See Thomas Jefferson Randolph, Contract for Sections 7 & 8 with Blue Ridge Railroad, October 24, 1849, Blue Ridge Railroad Papers, Library of Virginia.

69. Israel Gillette, "'Life Among the Lowly,' No. 3," *Pike County (Ohio) Republican* (December 25, 1873).

Chapter 4. Meriwether Lewis Randolph

1. *Arkansas Gazette* (May 19, 1835).

2. *The Times* Little Rock (April 4, 1836); *Arkansas Gazette* (November 10, 1835); *Arkansas Gazette* (October 22, 1835).

3. On capitalism as "creative destruction," see Calvin Schermerhorn, *The Business*

of Slavery and the Rise of American Capitalism, 1815–1860 (New Haven: Yale University Press, 2015), 1.

4. Michael A. Blaakman, *Speculation Nation: Land Mania in the Revolutionary American Republic* (Philadelphia: University of Pennsylvania Press, 2023), 321. On land speculation and state formation after the American Revolution, see also Gregory Ablavsky, *Federal Ground: Governing Property and Violence in the First U.S. Territories* (New York: Oxford University Press, 2023).

   On the Trans-Mississippi West, see Patrick Luck, *Replanting a Slave Society: The Sugar and Cotton Revolutions in the Lower Mississippi Valley* (Charlottesville: University of Virginia Press, 2022); Schermerhorn, *Business of Slavery;* John Craig Hammond, "Slavery, Sovereignty, and Empires: North American Borderlands and the American Civil War, 1660–1860," *Journal of the Civil War Era* 4 (June 2014): 264–98; Walter Johnson, *River of Dark Dreams: Slavery and Empire in the Mississippi Valley's Cotton Kingdom* (Cambridge: Harvard University Press, 2013); Joshua D. Rothman, *Flush Times and Fever Dreams: A Story of Capitalism and Slavery in the Age of Jackson* (Athens: University of Georgia Press, 2012); Adam Rothman, *Slave Country: American Expansion and the Origins of the Deep South* (Cambridge: Harvard University Press, 2005).

5. See *Catalogue of the Officers and Students of the University of Virginia, Second Session, Commencing February 1st, 1826* (Charlottesville: Chronicle Steam Book Printing House, 1880), 8.

6. Martha Jefferson Randolph to Ellen Wayles Randolph Coolidge, [ca. August 15, 1831], Ellen Wayles Randolph Coolidge Correspondence, MS 9090, Special Collections, University of Virginia.

7. See Cynthia A. Kierner, *Martha Jefferson Randolph, Daughter of Monticello: Her Life and Times* (Chapel Hill: University of North Carolina Press, 2012), 255; Lewis Randolph to Nicholas P. Trist, September 28, 1831, Nicholas Philip Trist Papers, Southern Historical Collection, University of North Carolina.

8. Meriwether Lewis Randolph to Septimia Anne Randolph, July 31, 1832, Septimia Anne Randolph Meikleham Papers, MS 4726-a, Special Collections, University of Virginia.

9. Meriwether Lewis Randolph to Septimia Anne Randolph, July 31, 1832, Septimia Anne Randolph Meikleham Papers, MS 4726-a, Special Collections, University of Virginia.

10. Francis Eppes to Nicholas P. Trist, November 7, 1826, Trist Papers, Southern Historical Collection, University of North Carolina.

11. Mary E. Randolph Eppes to Thomas Jefferson Randolph, April 1, 1827, Folder 3, Randolph Family Papers, MS 80-5, Florida State University Archives; Edward E. Baptist, *Creating an Old South: Middle Florida's Plantation Frontier Before the Civil War* (Chapel Hill: University of North Carolina Press, 2002), 26, 31, 33; Francis Eppes to Nicholas P. Trist, November 7, 1826, Trist Papers, Southern Historical Collection, University of North Carolina. "Cuffee" is a derogatory term for an enslaved man.

12. Meriwether Lewis Randolph to Septimia Anne Randolph, October 1, 1833, March 24, 1834, Septimia Anne Randolph Meikleham Papers, Special Collections, University of Virginia.

13. Meriwether Lewis Randolph to Septimia Anne Randolph, June 27, 1834, Septimia Anne Randolph Meikleham Papers, MS 4726-a, Special Collections, University of Virginia.

14. Martha Jefferson Randolph to Ann Cary Morris, March 22, 1835, Smith-Houston-Morris-Ogden Family Papers, American Philosophical Society, Philadelphia; C. E. Carter, ed., *The Territorial Papers of the United States,* 27 vols. (Washington, D.C.: Government Printing Office, 1934–1969), 22:1255–56.

15. See Malcolm J. Rohrborough, *The Land Office Business: The Settlement and Administration of American Public Lands, 1789–1837* (New York: Oxford University Press, 1968); "On the Expediency of Dividing the District of the Surveyor General for Missouri, Illinois and Arkansas," 2 March 1832, *American State Papers: Public Lands,* 8:402–3.

16. See Robert R. Logan, "Notes on the First Surveys in Arkansas," *Arkansas Quarterly* 19 (Autumn 1960): 260–70; David A. Smith, "Preparing the Arkansas Wilderness for Settlement: Public Land Survey Administration, 1803–1836," *Arkansas Historical Quarterly* 71 (Winter 2012): 381–406.

17. *Arkansas Gazette* (May 31, 1836); Lowell O. Stewart, *Public Land Surveys: History, Instructions, Methods* (Ames, Iowa: Collegiate Press, 1935), 140–98.

18. Caleb Langtree, Arkansas General Land Office Survey, 1855, Book 2289, p. 6, Government Land Office Survey Notebooks, Arkansas Commissioner of State Lands, Little Rock, Arkansas; Don C. Bragg, "General Office Surveys as a Source for Arkansas History: The Example of Ashley County," *Arkansas Historical Quarterly* 63, no. 2 (Summer 2004): 166–84. A native of Ireland, Langtree was a civil engineer, working as a draftsman and clerk for the surveyor-general of Arkansas.

19. See "From Thomas Jefferson to Cherokee Deputation, 9 January 1809," *Founders Online,* National Archives, https://founders.archives.gov/documents/Jefferson/99 -01-02-9498; Morris S. Arnold, *The Rumble of a Distant Drum: The Quapaws and Old World Newcomers, 1673–1804* (Fayetteville: University of Arkansas Press, 2000); Kathleen DuVal, *The Native Ground: Indians and Colonists in the Heart of the Continent* (Philadelphia: University of Pennsylvania Press, 2006); Cane W. West, "Learning the Land: Indians, Settlers, and Slaves in the Southern Borderlands, 1500–1850." Ph.D. diss., University of South Carolina, 2019.

20. Lewis Randolph and William McKim (Lafayette County, Arkansas), land patent no. 3443; Lewis Randolph and William McKim (Nevada County, Arkansas), land patent nos. 3445, 3446, 3447, 3451, 3452 ; Lewis Randolph and John T. Jones (Lafayette County, Arkansas), land patent nos. 3392, 3396, 3473; Lewis Randolph and John T. Jones (Columbia County, Arkansas), land patent nos. 3473, 3311, 3312, 3442, General Land Office Records, Bureau of Land Management, U.S. Department of the Interior.

21. Lewis Randolph to Septimia Anne Randolph, March 20, 1836, Septimia Anne Randolph Meikleham Papers, MS 4726-a, Special Collections, University of Virginia.

22. Memoranda Book of Lewis Randolph, n.d., Andrew Jackson Donelson Papers, reel 11, Library of Congress.

23. Memoranda Book of Lewis Randolph, n.d., Andrew Jackson Donelson Papers, reel 11, Library of Congress; "Randolph's Description of the Lands," July 20, 1836, Woodruff Papers, Arkansas History Commission.

24. Meriwether Lewis Randolph to Septimia Anne Randolph, March 20, 1836, Septimia Anne Randolph Meikleham Papers, MS 4726-a, Special Collections, University of Virginia.

25. Meriwether Lewis Randolph to Septimia Anne Randolph, July 30, 1836, Septimia Anne Randolph Meikleham Papers, MS 4726-a, Special Collections, University of Virginia; Will of Martha Jefferson Randolph, January 6, 1836, Albemarle County Will Book, 12:270–71, Library of Virginia; Meriwether Lewis Randolph to Septimia Anne Randolph, March 20, 1836, Septimia Anne Randolph Meikleham Papers, MS 4726-a, Special Collections, University of Virginia.

26. Lewis Randolph to Septimia Randolph, March 20, 1836, Septimia Anne Randolph Meikleham Papers, MS 4726-a, Special Collections, University of Virginia; Grace Benton Nelson, *The Life and Times of Meriwether Lewis Randolph: Grandson of Thomas Jefferson and Arkansas's Last Territorial Secretary* (Arkadelphia, Ark.: Clark County Historical Association, 2014).

27. Elizabeth Martin Randolph to Emily Donelson, November 8, 1835, Randolph Family Letters, Library of Virginia.

28. Andrew Jackson to Meriwether Lewis Randolph, July 6, 1836, Andrew Jackson Papers, Library of Congress.

29. Joseph Coolidge to Meriwether Lewis Randolph, October 8, 1836, Randolph Family Letters, Library of Virginia; Jacques M. Downs, *The Golden Ghetto: The American Commercial Community at Canton and the Shaping of American China Policy, 1784–1844* (1997; repr. Hong Kong: Hong Kong University Press, 2014); Stephen Lockwood, *Augustine Heard and Company, 1858–1862: American Merchants in China* (Cambridge, Mass.: East Asian Research Center, Harvard University, 1971).

30. See Augustine Heard to Meriwether Lewis Randolph, February 29, 1836, Russell and Company Records, series 2, box 6, Library of Congress.

31. Augustine Heard to Samuel Russell, January 1, 1838, Russell and Company Records, series 2, box 7, Library of Congress.

32. "From Thomas Jefferson to Bernard Peyton, 13 May 1824," *Founders Online,* National Archives, https://founders.archives.gov/documents/Jefferson/98-01-02-4266; *Richmond Enquirer* (February 27, 1819, and July 14, 1840); "Thomas Jefferson to Joseph Marx, 24 August 1819," *Founders Online,* National Archives, https://founders.archives.gov/documents/Jefferson/03-14-02-0593; *Richmond Whig and Public Advertiser* (July 17, 1840).

33. Agreement between Lewis Randolph, Wyndham Robertson, George E. Harrison, and Joseph Marx, November 4, 1836, Randolph Family Letters, Library of Virginia.

34. Agreement between Lewis Randolph, Wyndham Robertson, George E. Harrison, and Joseph Marx, November 4, 1836, Randolph Family Letters, Library of Virginia.

35. See Duc de La Rochefoucauld-Liancourt, *Travels through the United States of North America,* 8 vols. (London: B. Phillips, 1799) 3:122–25; Ronald Lewis, "'Darkest Abode of Man': Black Miners in the First Southern Coalfield, 1780–1865," *Virginia Magazine of History and Biography* 87 (1979): 190–202; Frederick Law Olmsted, *Journey in Seaboard States* (New York: Dix & Edwards, 1856), 47;

Joseph Martin, ed., *A New and Comprehensive Gazetteer of Virginia, and the District of Columbia* (Charlottesville: J. Martin, 1835), 151–52; *Richmond Enquirer* (March 3, 1832); Beverly Randolph to Harry Heth, August 25, 1819, John Heth Papers, Special Collections, University of Virginia; *Richmond Enquirer* (March 23, 1839).

36. See "Thomas Jefferson to John S. Skinner, 24 February 1820," *Founders Online*, National Archives, https://founders.archives.gov/documents/Jefferson/03-15-02 -0387; "Thomas Jefferson to John S. Skinner, 16 May 1820," *Founders Online*, National Archives, https://founders.archives.gov/documents/Jefferson/03-15-02 -0561; "Thomas Jefferson to John S. Skinner, 4 October 1820," *Founders Online*, National Archives, https://founders.archives.gov/documents/Jefferson/03-16-02 -0251.

37. J. S. Skinner to John Heth, October 31, 1836, John Heth Papers, MS 38-114, Special Collections, University of Virginia.

38. Memorandum of Agreement: Lewis Randolph, John S. Nicholas, John Heth, and James Lyons, January 1, 1837, Andrew Donelson Papers, reel 11, Library of Congress.

39. See Memorandum of Agreement: Lewis Randolph, John S. Nicholas, John Heth, and James Lyons, January 1, 1837, Andrew Donelson Papers, reel 11, Library of Congress.

40. See Maurie D. McInnis, *Slaves Waiting for Sale: Abolitionist Art and the American Slave Trade* (Chicago: University of Chicago Press, 2011); Eyre Crowe, *With Thackeray in America* (New York: Scribner's, 1893), 131–36.

41. Crowe, *With Thackeray in America,* 131–36; *New York Daily Tribune* (March 10, 1853).

42. Martha Jefferson Randolph to Meriwether Lewis Randolph, February 6, 1836, Randolph Family Letters, Library of Virginia.

43. Martha Jefferson Randolph to Lewis Randolph, February 6, 1836, Randolph Family Letters, Library of Virginia; Kierner, *Martha Jefferson Randolph,* 252–53.

44. Elizabeth Randolph to ?, November 25, 1838, Andrew Jackson Donelson Papers, reel 11, Library of Congress.

45. Elizabeth Randolph to ?, November 25, 1838, Andrew Jackson Donelson Papers, reel 11, Library of Congress.

46. Elizabeth Randolph to ?, November 25, 1838, Andrew Jackson Donelson Papers, reel 11, Library of Congress.

47. Elizabeth Randolph to ?, November 25, 1838, Andrew Jackson Donelson Papers, reel 11, Library of Congress; Elizabeth Randolph to James Martin, October 1, 1837, Randolph Family Letters, Library of Virginia.

48. Elizabeth Randolph to ?, November 25, 1838, Andrew Jackson Donelson Papers, reel 11, Library of Congress.

49. Elizabeth Randolph to ?, November 25, 1838, Andrew Jackson Donelson Papers, reel 11, Library of Congress.

50. John S. Nicholas to Elizabeth Randolph, April 12, 1838, Andrew Jackson Donelson Papers, reel 11, Library of Congress.

51. John S. Nicholas to Elizabeth Randolph, April 12, 1838; Elizabeth Randolph to ?, November 25, 1838, Andrew Jackson Donelson Papers, reel 11.

52. Augustine Heard to Samuel Russell, January 8, 1838, Russell and Company Papers, series 2, box 7, Library of Congress.

53. Augustine Heard to Samuel Russell, September 23, 1838, Russell and Company Papers, reel 5, Library of Congress; Augustine Heard to Samuel Russell, July 12, 1843, Russell and Company Papers, reel 6, Library of Congress.

54. See Donald P. McNeilly, *The Old South Frontier: Cotton Plantations and the Formation of Arkansas Society, 1819–1861* (Fayetteville: University of Arkansas Press, 2000); Jeannie M. Whayne, "Cotton's Metropolis: Memphis and Plantation Development in the Trans-Mississippi West, 1840–1920," in *Comparing Apples, Oranges, and Cotton: Environmental Histories of the Global Plantation*, ed. Frank Uekötter (Frankfurt: Campus Verlag, 2014).

55. Charles S. Bolton, "Slavery and the Defining of Arkansas," *Arkansas Historical Quarterly* 58, no. 1 (1999): 45–60; Carl H. Moneyhon, *The Impact of Civil War and Reconstruction on Arkansas: Persistence in the Midst of Ruin* (Fayetteville: University of Arkansas Press, 1994).

56. See Martha Jefferson Randolph to Ellen Wayles Coolidge, [ca. August 15, 1831], Correspondence of Ellen Wayles Randolph Coolidge, Special Collections, University of Virginia.

57. See George Shackleford, *Collected Papers to Commemorate Fifty Years of the Monticello Association of the Descendants of Thomas Jefferson* (Princeton: Princeton University Press, 1965).

Chapter 5. Madison Hemings

1. Thomas Jefferson, *Farm Book,* Electronic Edition, Massachusetts Historical Society, 128, 130, 134, 136, 137, 139, 142, 145, 147, 148, 153, 154, 157, 158, 160, 162, 163, 168, 170, 171, 173, 174; "Thomas Jefferson: Will and Codicil, 16–17 Mar. 1826, 16 March 1826," *Founders Online,* National Archives, https://founders.archives.gov/documents /Jefferson/98-01-02-5963.

2. Madison Hemings, "'Life among the Lowly,' No. 1," *Pike County (Ohio) Republican* (March 13, 1873); Annette Gordon-Reed, *The Hemingses of Monticello: An American Family* (New York: Norton, 2008), 596.

3. Hemings, "'Life among the Lowly,' No. 1"; "Thomas Jefferson: Will and Codicil."

4. Albemarle County Minute Book, September 6, 1831, p. 123, Albemarle County Courthouse, Charlottesville, Virginia.

5. See Samuel Shepherd, ed., *The Statutes at Large of Virginia, from October Session 1792, to December Session 1806* (Richmond: Samuel Shepherd, 1836), 3:251–53; "Thomas Jefferson: Will and Codicil"; Kirt von Daacke, *Freedom Has A Face: Race, Identity, and Community in Jefferson's Virginia* (Charlottesville: University of Virginia Press, 2012).

6. See Samantha Seeley, *Race, Removal, and the Right to Remain: Migration and the Making of the United States* (Chapel Hill: University of North Carolina Press for the Omohundro Institute, 2021), 223–51; Eva Sheppard Wolf, *Race and Liberty in the New Nation: Emancipation in Virginia from the Revolution to Nat Turner's Rebellion* (Baton Rouge: Louisiana State University Press, 2006), 117–43; Martha S.

Jones, *Birthright Citizens: A History of Race and Rights in Antebellum America* (New York: Cambridge University Press, 2018), 10.

7. See John Craig Hammond, "'The Most Free of the Free States': Politics, Slavery, Race, and Regional Identity in Early Ohio," *Ohio History* 121 (2014): 35–57; Stephen Middleton, T*he Black Laws: Race and the Legal Process in Early Ohio* (Athens: Ohio University Press, 2005); Eugene H. Berwanger, *The Frontier Against Slavery: Western Anti-Negro Prejudice and the Slavery Extension Controversy* (Champaign: University of Illinois Press, 1967), 22–23; Nikki Marie Taylor, *Frontiers of Freedom: Cincinnati's Black Community, 1802–1868* (Athens: Ohio University Press, 2005): 34; Michael John Witgen, *Seeing Red: Indigenous Land, American Expansion, and the Political Economy of Plunder* (Chapel Hill: University of North Carolina Press for the Omohundro Institute, 2021), 279–80.

8. Gordon-Reed, *The Hemingses of Monticello;* Lucia Stanton, "*Those Who Labor for My Happiness*": *Slavery at Thomas Jefferson's Monticello* (Charlottesville: University of Virginia Press, 2012).

9. See Kunal M. Parker, *Making Foreigners: Immigration and Citizenship Law in America, 1600–2000* (New York: Cambridge University Press, 2015); Gerald L. Neuman, *Strangers to the Constitution: Immigrants, Borders, and Fundamental Law* (Princeton: Princeton University Press, 1996); Kevin Kenny, *The Problem of Immigration in a Slaveholding Republic: Policing Mobility in the 19th-century United States* (New York: Oxford University Press, 2023); Kate Masur, "State Sovereignty and Migration Before Reconstruction," *Journal of the Civil War Era* 9, no. 4 (2019): 588–611; Masur, "The People's Welfare, Police Powers, and the Rights of Free People of African Descent," *American Journal of Legal History* 57, no. 2 (2017): 238–42; Allison Brownwell Tirres, "Ownership Without Citizenship: The Creation of Non-Citizen Property Rights," *Michigan Journal of Race and Law* 19, no. 1 (Fall 2013): 1–52.

10. John Malvin, *Autobiography of John Malvin: A Narrative, Containing an Authentic Account of His Fifty Years' Struggle in the State of Ohio in Behalf of the American Slave, and the Equal Rights of All Men Before the Law Without Reference to Race or Color; Forty-Seven Years of Said Time Being Expended in the City of Cleveland* (Cleveland: Leader Printing, 1879), 11–12.

11. Madison Hemings's life and family have been extensively studied and documented by Annette Gordon-Reed and Lucia Stanton. See Stanton, *"Those Who Labor for My Happiness"*; Gordon-Reed, *The Hemingses of Monticello;* Gordon-Reed, *Thomas Jefferson and Sally Hemings: An American Controversy* (Charlottesville: University of Virginia Press, 1997), 7–58. Madison Hemings's history and descendants in Ohio have been documented by Beverly Gray, Lucia Stanton, and Dianne Swann-Wright through the Getting Word: African American Oral History Project at Monticello: https://gettingword.monticello.org/families/hemings-madison/. On the concept of "homemade citizenship," see Koritha Mitchell, *From Slave Cabins to the White House: Homemade Citizenship in African American Culture* (Champaign: University of Illinois Press, 2021).

12. Beginning in 1793 the Virginia General Assembly mandated that free Black people register with the local court every three years. Those who did not do so—or who

failed to produce the "free papers" reissued at every registration—could be imprisoned or fined. Albemarle County Court Book, August 6, 1827, p. 223, Albemarle County Courthouse, Charlottesville, Virginia.

13. Albemarle County Court Book, August 6, 1827, p. 223, September 6, 1831, p. 123, Albemarle County Courthouse, Charlottesville, Virginia; Ervin L. Jordan, Jr., "'A Just and True Account': Two 1833 Parish Censuses of Albemarle County Free Blacks," *Magazine of Albemarle County History* 53 (1995): 114–39.

14. See James Sidbury, *Ploughshares into Swords: Race, Rebellion, and Identity in Gabriel's Virginia* (New York: Cambridge University Press, 1997); Douglas R. Egerton, *Gabriel's Rebellion: The Virginia Slave Conspiracies of 1800 and 1802* (Chapel Hill: University of North Carolina Press, 1993); Julius S. Scott, *The Common Wind: Afro-American Currents in the Age of the Haitian Revolution* (New York: Verso, 2018); John Craig Hammond, "Slavery, Sovereignty, and Empires: North American Borderlands and the American Civil War, 1660–1860," *Journal of the Civil War Era* 4 (June 2014): 264–98.

15. As the historian Lucia Stanton has suggested, free Black people "lived in a kind of littoral zone," in an "unsettled environment" in Charlottesville; their contracts and purchases helped provide security for a group of legally insecure people. See Stanton, *"Those Who Labor for My Happiness,"* 223, 343n32.

16. See Kate Masur, "The Second Missouri Compromise, State Citizenship, and African Americans' Rights in the Antebellum United States," in *A Fire Bell in the Past: The Missouri Crisis at 200*, vol. 2: *"The Missouri Question" and Its Answers*, ed. Jeffrey L. Pasley and John Craig Hammond, 129–62 (Columbia: University of Missouri Press, 2021); Tirres, "Ownership Without Citizenship."

17. Albemarle County Deed Book, February 6, 1832, p. 12, August 6, 1831, pp. 267–77, Albemarle County Courthouse, Charlottesville, Virginia; James Alexander, "Early Charlottesville: Recollections of James Alexander, 1828–1874. Reprinted from the Jeffersonian Republican," *The Haskell Monroe Collection: Life in the Confederacy*, https://library.missouri.edu/confederate/items/show/1681.

18. See Stanton, *"Those Who Labor for My Happiness,"* 217–23; Joshua D. Rothman, *Notorious in the Neighborhood: Sex and Families Across the Color Line in Virginia, 1787–1861* (Chapel Hill: University of North Carolina Press, 2003), 39–90.

19. See Edgar Woods, *Albemarle County in Virginia. Giving Some Account of What It Was by Nature, of What It Was Made by Man, and of Some of the Men Who Made It* (Charlottesville: Michie Company, 1901), 294–95; K. Edward Lay, *The Architecture of Jefferson Country: Charlottesville and Albemarle County, Virginia* (Charlottesville: University of Virginia Press, 2000), 99–101, 160–61; "Thomas Jefferson to John M. Perry, 3 June 1817," *Founders Online*, National Archives, https://founders .archives.gov/documents/Jefferson/03-11-02-0335; Admission of Thomas Jefferson's Will to Probate and Appointment of Appraisers, Albemarle County Order Book [1826], 247, Albemarle County Courthouse, Charlottesville, Virginia; John M. Perry, Bill for Monticello Estate Sale, 1827, Jefferson-Kean Papers, Special Collections Library, University of Virginia.

20. Hemings, "'Life Among the Lowly,' No. 1"; Gordon-Reed, *Hemingses of Monticello,* 701.

21. Hemings, "'Life Among the Lowly,' No. 1"; Stanton, *Those Who Labor for My Happiness,"* 219.

22. Albemarle County Marriage Bonds, November 21, 1831, Albemarle County Courthouse, Charlottesville, Virginia; Sidbury, *Ploughshares into Swords,* 61–84.

23. Hemings, "'Life Among the Lowly,' No. 1"; Gordon-Reed, *Hemingses of Monticello,* 404–6.

24. Albemarle County Marriage Bonds, November 21, 1831, Albemarle County Courthouse, Charlottesville, Virginia; Hemings, "'Life Among the Lowly,' No. 1."

25. See Christopher Tomlins, *In the Matter of Nat Turner: A Speculative History* (Princeton: Princeton University Press, 2020); Patrick Breen, *The Land Shall Be Deluged in Blood: A New History of the Nat Turner Rebellion* (New York: Oxford University Press, 2015); Martha Jefferson Randolph to Joseph Coolidge, September 5 and October 27, 1831, Edgehill-Randolph Papers, MS 1397, Special Collections, University of Virginia; Stanton, *Those Who Labor for My Happiness,"* 200.

26. See Ervin L. Jordan, "'A Just and True Account': Two 1833 Parish Censuses of Albemarle County Free Blacks," *Magazine of Albemarle County History* 53 (1995): 114–39; Stanton, *Those Who Labor for My Happiness,"* 225, 288–89.

27. Benjamin G. Freeman, *Careysburg: Freed Negro American Settlers' Quest for Freedom and the Impact on the Social and Cultural Relationship with Indigenous Africans in the St. Paul River Settlement of Liberia, West Africa* (Parker, Colo.: Outskirts Press, 2014); Bill Webb, July 15, 2007, Oral History Interview, Getting Word: African American Oral History Project, Monticello, https://www.youtube.com/watch?v=zBEj1NbJpGs&t=14s.

28. See Jordan, "'A Just and True Account'"; Stanton, *Those Who Labor for My Happiness,"* 222–26.

29. Hemings, "'Life Among the Lowly,' No. 1."

30. *Jefferson at Monticello: "Memoirs of a Monticello Slave" and "Jefferson at Monticello: The Private Life of Thomas Jefferson,"* ed. James A. Bear (Charlottesville: University of Virginia Press, 1967); Ellen Wayles Coolidge to Joseph Coolidge, October 24, 1858, Ellen Wayles Randolph Coolidge Correspondence, MS 9090, Special Collections, University of Virginia; Stanton, *Those Who Labor for My Happiness,"* 8, 178–79, 248; Hemings, "'Life Among the Lowly,' No. 1."

31. Hemings, "'Life Among the Lowly,' No. 1" 3; Catherine Kerrison, "Harriet Hemings: Daughter of the President's Slave," in *Virginia Women: Their Lives and Times,* ed. Cynthia Kierner and Sandra Treadway (Athens: University of Georgia Press, 2015), 222–43, Allyson Hobbs, *A Chosen Exile: A History of Racial Passing in American Life* (Cambridge: Harvard University Press), 1–27.

32. See Hemings, "'Life Among the Lowly,' No. 1."

33. See Hemings, "'Life Among the Lowly,' No. 1"; Stanton, *Those Who Labor for My Happiness,"* 224, 234; Kate Masur, *Until Justice Be Done: America's First Civil Rights Movement, from the Revolution to Reconstruction* (New York: Norton, 2021), 14–18.

34. Bartholomew Cardiveau to Arthur St. Clair, June 30, 1789, in *The St. Clair Papers,* 2 vols., ed. B. Smith, 2:117–19 (Cincinnati: R. Clarke, 1882); Gregory Ablavsky, *Federal Ground: Governing Property and Violence in the First U.S. Territories* (New

York: Oxford University Press, 2021); Paul Finkelman, "The Strange Career of Race Discrimination in Antebellum Ohio," *Case Western Reserve Law Review* 55, no. 2 (2004), https://scholarlycommons.law.case.edu/caselrev/vol55/iss2/5.

35. See Masur, "State Sovereignty and Migration Before Reconstruction"; Mae M. Ngai, "Birthright Citizenship and the Alien Citizen," *Fordham Law Review* 75, no. 5 (2007): 2521–30.

36. See Leslie M. Harris, *In the Shadow of Slavery: African Americans in New York City, 1626–1863* (Chicago: University of Chicago Press, 2003); Richard S. Newman, *The Transformation of American Abolitionism: Fighting Slavery in the Early Republic* (Chapel Hill: University of North Carolina Press, 2003); Gary B. Nash, *Forging Freedom: The Formation of Philadelphia's Black Community, 1729–1840* (Cambridge: Harvard University Press, 1988); Patrick Rael, *Eighty-Eight Years: The Long Death of Slavery in the United States, 1777–1865* (Athens: University of Georgia Press, 2015); Joanne Pope Melish, *Disowning Slavery: Gradual Emancipation and "Race" in New England, 1620–1776* (Ithaca: Cornell University Press, 2016).

37. Austin Steward, *Twenty-Two Years a Slave, and Forty Years a Freeman; Embracing a Correspondence of Several Years, While President of Wilberforce Colony, London, Canada West* (Rochester, N.Y.: William Alling, 1857), 175; Paul D. Frymer, *Building an American Empire: The Era of Territorial and Political Expansion* (Princeton: Princeton University Press, 2017), 236–37.

38. "An Act, to Regulate Black and Mulatto Persons," January 5, 1804, *Acts of the State of Ohio, Second Session of the General Assembly, 1804* (Norwalk, Ohio: Laning, 1901), 63–66; "An Act to Amend the Act, Entitled 'An Act Regulating Black and Mulatto Persons," January 25, 1807, *Acts of the State of Ohio, Fifth Session of the General Assembly, 1807* (Norwalk, Ohio: Laning, 1901), 53–55; Paul Finkleman, "Before the Fourteenth Amendment: Black Legal Rights in the Antebellum North," *Rutgers Law Journal* 17 (1985–1986): 435–36; Hammond, "'The Most Free of the Free States'"; Masur, *Until Justice Be Done*, 12–18.

39. *Daily Scioto Gazette* (June 16, 1819); *Cincinnati Daily Gazette* (June 30, 1829).

40. Robert Finley to Ralph Gurley, November 9, 1826, Records of the American Colonization Society, Manuscript Division, Library of Congress. My thanks to Craig Hammond for sharing this source.

41. Ohio General Assembly (House), Memorial of Israel Lewis and Thomas Crisup, Commissioners Representing the People of Color, Late Residents of Cincinnati, in the State of Ohio, 28th General Assembly, 1st session, December 13, 1829.

42. Ohio General Assembly (House), Memorial of Israel Lewis and Thomas Crisup,; Nikki Marie Taylor, *Frontiers of Freedom: Cincinnati's Free Black Community, 1802–1868* (Athens: Ohio University Press, 2005), 50–65.

43. See Keith P. Griffler, *Front Line of Freedom: African Americans and the Forging of the Underground Railroad in the Ohio Valley* (Lexington: University Press of Kentucky, 2004), 38–51; Taylor, *Frontiers of Freedom*, 111–13; Stephen Middleton, *Ohio and the Antislavery Activities of Attorney Salmon Portland Chase, 1830–1849* (New York: Garland, 1990), 54–57; Betty Fladeland, *James Gillespie Birney: Slaveholder to Abolitionist* (Ithaca: Cornell University Press, 1955), 80–89.

44. See Taylor, *Frontiers of Freedom*, 111–13; Fladeland, *James Gillespie Birney*, 80–89; Brent Morris, *Oberlin, Hotbed of Abolitionism: College, Community, and the Fight*

for Freedom and Equality in Antebellum America (Chapel Hill: University of North Carolina Press, 2014).

45. Israel Gillette Jefferson, "'Life Among the Lowly,' No. 3," *Pike County (Ohio) Republican,* December 25, 1873.

46. Peter Fossett, "Reminiscences of Jefferson, Lafayette, Madison, and Monroe," *New York World* (January 30, 1898).

47. "An Act to Support a Fund for the Support of Common Schools," March 10, 1831, and "An Act for the Relief of the Poor," March 14, 1831, in *Acts of the Twenty-Ninth General Assembly of the State of Ohio* (Columbus: Olmstead & Bailhache, 1831); *Journal of the House of Representatives of the State of Ohio, 30th General Assembly, 1831-2* (Columbus: David Smith, 1831), 10–11, 234–35; Wolf, *Race and Liberty in the New Nation,* 202–6, 229–33; Masur, *Until Justice Be Done,* 87–89.

48. "Free African American Population in the United States, 1790–1860," Geostat Historical Census Browser, University of Virginia, https://www.ncpedia.org/sites /default/files/census_stats_1790-1860.pdf.

49. See Ross County, Ohio, Deed Book, No. 68, pp. 562–63, Ross County Courthouse, Chillicothe, Ohio; Madison Hemings Estate, 1877, Ross County, Ohio, Probate Records, Ross County Courthouse, Chillicothe, Ohio; Jones, *Birthright Citizens,* 10; Mitchell, *From Slave Cabins to the White House,* 1-3; Hemings, "'Life Among the Lowly,' No. 1."

50. Hemings, "'Life Among the Lowly,' No. 1."

51. *History of Lower Scioto Valley* (Chicago: Interstate, 1884), 713–14 and 736–37; James Emmitt, *Life and Reminiscences* (Chillicothe, Ohio: Peerless, 1888), 287–92.

52. Andrew Feight, "'Black Friday': Enforcing Ohio's 'Black Laws' in Portsmouth, Ohio," *Scioto Historical,* https://sciotohistorical.org/items/show/164; Edward S. Abdy, *Journal of a Residence and Tour of the United States of North America, from April 1833 to October 1834* (London: John Murray, 1835), 3:38–39, 48–49; *Journal of the House of Representatives of the State of Ohio: Being the Second Session of the 30th General Assembly* (Columbus: David Smith, State Printer, 1831), 235, https:// llmc.com/docDisplay5.aspx?set=40756&volume=1831&part=120.

53. Emmitt, *Life and Reminiscences,* 287–92.

54. Emmitt, *Life and Reminiscences,* 287–92.

55. "Free African American Population in the United States, 1790–1860."

56. Ray Malone, October 28, 1999, Oral History Interview, Getting Word: African American Oral History Project at Monticello, https://gettingword.monticello.org /stories/; Shay Banks-Young, May 31, 1996, and July 19, 2000, Oral History Interview, Getting Word: African American Oral History Project at Monticello, https:// gettingword.monticello.org/stories/.

57. Ross County Deed Book, 59:389–90, 63:624, 68:562–63, Ross County Courthouse, Chillicothe, Ohio.

58. Madison Hemings Estate, 1877.

59. See Kevin Kenny, *The Problem of Immigration in a Slaveholding Republic: Policing Mobility in the Nineteenth-Century United States* (New York: Oxford University Press, 2023); Michael A. Schoeppner, "Black Migrants and Border Regulation in the Early United States," *Journal of the Civil War Era* 11, no. 3 (September 2021): 317–39.

60. "Population Schedule," Ross County, Huntington Township, Ohio, July 7, 1870; Hemings, "'Life Among the Lowly,' No. 1"; Gordon-Reed, *Thomas Jefferson and Sally Hemings,* 7–58.

61. Hemings, "'Life Among the Lowly,' No. 1"; Hannah Spahn, *Black Reason, White Feeling: The Jeffersonian Enlightenment in the African American Tradition* (Charlottesville: University of Virginia Press, 2024).

62. Hemings, "'Life Among the Lowly,' No. 1"; Gordon-Reed, *Hemingses of Monticello,* 106–7.

63. Hemings, "'Life Among the Lowly,' No. 1."

Chapter 6. J. W. Jefferson

1. John W. Jefferson to Benjamin Harrison, November 9, 1888, in John Wayles Jefferson Scrapbook, Jefferson Family Papers, MS 1218, University of California, Los Angeles (hereafter UCLA). On the election of 1888, see Richard White, *The Republic for Which It Stands: The United States During Reconstruction and the Gilded Age, 1865–1896* (New York: Oxford University Press, 2017), 602–27.

2. See Lucia Stanton, *"Those Who Labor for My Happiness": Slavery at Thomas Jefferson's Monticello* (Charlottesville: University of Virginia Press, 2012), 270–74; Fawn M. Brodie, "Jefferson's Unknown Grandchildren: A Study in Historical Silences," *American Heritage* 27, no. 6 (1976): 28–33, 94–99.

3. *Daily Scioto Gazette* (August 1, 1902).

4. *Daily* Scioto *Gazette* (August 1, 1902). For recent scholarship on racial passing, see Allyson Hobbs, *A Chosen Exile: A History of Racial Passing in American Life* (Cambridge: Harvard University Press, 2014); Daniel J. Sharfstein, *The Invisible Line: Three American Families and the Secret Journey from Black to White* (New York: Penguin, 2011); Martha Sandweiss, *Passing Strange: A Gilded Age Tale of Love and Deception Across the Color Line* (New York: Penguin, 2009); Elizabeth Smith-Pryor, *Property Rites: The Rhinelander Trial, Passing, and the Protection of Whiteness* (Chapel Hill: University of North Carolina Press, 2009); Ariela Gross, *What Blood Won't Tell: A History of Race on Trial in America* (Cambridge: Harvard University Press, 2008); Kathleen Pfieffer, *Race Passing and American Individualism* (Amherst: University of Massachusetts Press, 2003).

5. On Jefferson's Civil War experience, see Stanton, *"Those Who Labor For My Happiness,"* 270–74; Brodie, "Jefferson's Unknown Grandchildren." Historians have not yet considered racial passing during the Civil War. For studies detailing the role of African Americans in the Civil War, see Holly A. Pinheiro, Jr., *The Families' Civil War: Black Soldiers and the Fight for Racial Justice* (Athens: University of Georgia Press, 2022), and Douglas R. Egerton, *Thunder at the Gates: The Black Civil War Regiments That Redeemed America* (New York: Basic, 2016). Pinheiro's emphasis on the baneful effects of Civil War service on the lives of African Americans in the postbellum period helps explain why Jefferson chose to enlist as a white person.

6. Albemarle County Minute Book, 1832–1843, p. 12, Albemarle County Courthouse, Charlottesville, Virginia. Hemings registered as a free person along with Ludwell Coles, Burwell Colbert, and Robert Scott.

7. Albemarle County Deed Book, No. 22, p. 177, No. 35, pp. 264–66, 340, Albemarle County Courthouse, Charlottesville, Virginia; Mutual Assurance Declaration No. 8597 (1837), Albemarle County Courthouse, Charlottesville, Virginia; Albemarle County Land Tax Books, 1828–1838, Albemarle County Courthouse, Charlottesville, Virginia; Estate of Critty Bowles, Albemarle County Minute Book, 1834–36, p. 276, Albemarle County Courthouse, Charlottesville, Virginia; Albemarle County Deed Book, No. 35, pp. 265–66, Albemarle County Courthouse, Charlottesville, Virginia; Stanton, *"Those Who Labor for My Happiness,"* 220–24; Joshua D. Rothman, *Notorious in the Neighborhood: Sex and Families Across the Color Line in Virginia, 1787–1861* (Chapel Hill: University of North Carolina Press, 2003), 39–90.

8. *Chillicothe Leader* (January 26, 1887); *Daily Scioto Gazette* (August 1, 1902).

9. "Population Schedule," Ross County, Scioto Township, Ohio, July 29, 1850; *Daily Scioto Gazette* (August 1, 1902); Julia Westerinen, Oral History Interview, July 19, 2000, Getting Word: African American Oral History Project at Monticello, https:// gettingword.monticello.org/stories/.

10. On the Fugitive Slave Law, see Stanley Harrold, *Border War: Fighting over Slavery Before the Civil War* (Chapel Hill: University of North Carolina Press, 2010); James Oakes, *Freedom National: The Destruction of Slavery in the United States, 1861– 1865* (New York: Norton, 2012); John Craig Hammond, "Slavery, Sovereignty, and Empires," *Journal of the Civil War Era* 4, no. 2 (June 2014): 264–98; Steven Lubet, *Fugitive Justice: Runaways, Rescuers, and Slavery on Trial* (Cambridge: Harvard University Press, 2010); R. J. M. Blackett, *The Captive's Quest for Freedom: Fugitive Slaves, the 1850 Fugitive Slave Law, and the Politics of Slavery* (New York: Cambridge University Press, 2017).

11. Madison Hemings, "'Life Among the Lowly,' No. 1"; Ross County Deed Book, No. 50, pp. 574–75, Ross County Courthouse, Chillicothe, Ohio; Hobbs, *A Chosen Exile*; Sharfstein, *The Invisible Line*.

12. Julia Westerinen, Oral History Interview, July 19, 2000; Mary Jefferson and Colby Boggs, Oral History Interview, December 5, 1998, Getting Word: African American Oral History Project at Monticello, https://gettingword.monticello.org/stories/; Stanton, *"Those Who Labor For My Happiness,"* 236.

13. See Reuben Gold Thwaites, "Notes on Early Lead Mining in the Fever (or Galena) River Region," *Collections of the State Historical Society of Wisconsin,* vol. 13 (Madison: State Historical Society of Wisconsin, 1895); John Nelson Davidson, *Negro Slavery in Wisconsin and the Underground Railroad* (Milwaukee: Parkman Club, 1897), 33; *Unconstitutionality of the Fugitive Slave Act. Decisions of the Supreme Court of Wisconsin in the Cases of Booth and Rycraft* (Milwaukee: Rufus King, 1854), 6.

14. *William N. Seymour's Madison Directory, 1855, and Business Advertiser* (Madison: Atwood & Rublee, 1855); Record of John Wayles [Hemings] Jefferson, Beverly [Hemings] Jefferson, and Julia Ann [Hemings] Jefferson, and Hotel Staff, United States Federal Census for 1860, https://tjrs.monticello.org/letter/1771.

15. *Wisconsin Patriot* (December 29, 1860).

16. *Wisconsin State Journal* (October 10, 1861).

17. Beverly Jefferson, Military Service Records, National Archives and Records Administration, Washington, D.C. (hereafter NARA); William B. Hemings, Military

Service Records, NARA; Thomas E. Hemings, Military Service Records, NARA; Madison Hemings, "'Life Among the Lowly,' No. 1," *Pike County (Ohio) Republican* (March 13, 1873); The Civil War in Southern Ohio, Overview, http://www.angelfire.com/oh/chillicothe/CivilWar.html; William Cheek and Aimee Lee Cheek, *John Mercer Langston and the Fight for Black Freedom, 1829–65* (Champaign: University of Illinois Press, 1996), 250–51, 409–10; Stanton, *"Those Who Labor for My Happiness,"* 270–74.

18. See Elizabeth R. Varon, "From Carter's Mountain to Morganza Bend: A U.S.C.T. Odyssey (Part 1)," January 11, 2017, https://naucenter.as.virginia.edu/usct_odyssey_part_1; Stanton, *"Those Who Labor for My Happiness,"* 270–74.

19. See George W. Driggs, *Opening of the Mississippi; or, Two Years' Campaigning in the South-west. A Record of the Campaigns, Sieges, Actions and Marches in Which the 8th Wisconsin Volunteers Have Participated* (Madison: William J. Park & Co., 1864), 11–13; E. B. Quiner, *The Military History of Wisconsin: A Record of the Civil and Military Patriotism of the State, in The War for the Union, with a History of the Campaigns in Which Wisconsin Soldiers Have Been Conspicuous, Regimental Histories, Sketches of Distinguished Officers, the Roll of the Illustrious Dead, Movements of the Legislature and State Officers, etc.* (Chicago: Clarke & Co., 1866), 527.

20. John W. Jefferson, "An Interesting Account of the Battle of Fredericktown, October 21, 1861," clipping from unidentified newspaper, Quiner Scrapbooks, Wisconsin Historical Society.

21. John Wayles Jefferson Scrapbook, 1874, Jefferson Family Papers, MS 1218, UCLA.

22. John Wayles Jefferson Scrapbook, 1874.

23. John W. Jefferson to Beverly Jefferson, [1862], published in *Wisconsin Patriot* (March 9, 1862).

24. See Driggs, *Opening of the Mississippi,* 15–17; Quiner, *Military History of Wisconsin,* 527; John W. Jefferson to Beverly Jefferson, in *Wisconsin Patriot.* On the Battle for Island No. 10, see Larry J. Daniel and Lynn N Bock, *Island No. 10: Struggle for the Mississippi Valley* (Tuscaloosa: University of Alabama Press, 1996); Benton Rain Patterson, *The Mississippi River Campaign, 1861–1863: The Struggle for Control of the Western Waters* (Jefferson, N.C.: Macfarland, 2010).

25. See Benjamin Franklin Cooling, *Forts Henry and Donelson: The Key to the Confederate Heartland* (Knoxville: University of Tennessee Press, 1987).

26. Driggs, *Opening of the Mississippi,* 17 (quotations); Quiner, *Military History of Wisconsin,* 527–28.

27. Lt. John Woodworth to Editors, Milwaukee *Daily Sentinel* (August 21, 1862).

28. See Driggs, *Opening of the Mississippi,* 18–19; Stanton, *"Those Who Labor for My Happiness,"* 103, 325n29; *Moulton Advertiser* (November 24, 1898).

29. Driggs, *Opening of the Mississippi,* 19–21.

30. Clippings in Quiner scrapbooks, October 1862, Wisconsin Historical Society; *Milwaukee Daily Sentinel* (October 18, 1862).

31. See Driggs, *Opening of the Mississippi,* 19–20.

32. John W. Jefferson to Beverly Jefferson, May 21, 1863, published in *Wisconsin Patriot* (June 13, 1863); Stanton, *"Those Who Labor for My Happiness,"* 276–77.

33. John W. Jefferson to Beverly Jefferson, May 21, 1863, published in *Weekly Wisconsin Patriot;* Stanton, *"Those Who Labor for My Happiness,"* 276–77.

34. Ulysses S Grant to Stephen A. Hurlbut, May 31, 1863, #GLC07055, Gilder Lehrman Collection, New York.

35. Driggs, *Opening of the Mississippi*, 25, 134; John W. Jefferson to Beverly Jefferson, May 21, 1863.

36. Quiner, *Military History of Wisconsin*, 532; John Wayles Jefferson to Editor, July 4, 1863, *Wisconsin State Journal* (July 14, 1863).

37. Driggs, *Opening of the Mississippi*, 116, 128.

38. Driggs, *Opening of the Mississippi*, 116, 128; excerpt from *Madison Journal* in *Milwaukee Daily Sentinel* (April 14, 1864).

39. Driggs, *Opening of the Mississippi*, 19, 107, 99, 107; Stanton, *"Those Who Labor for My Happiness,"* 278.

40. John Wayles Jefferson Scrapbook, 1874, UCLA.

41. See Michael Thomas Smith, "'For the Love of Cotton': Nathanial P. Banks, Union Strategy, and the Red River Campaign," *Louisiana History* 51 (Winter 2010): 5-26; *Milwaukee Daily Sentinel* (June 16, 1864).

42. J. W. Jefferson to Lt Col WG [?], Asst. Adjutant General, Department of the Tennessee, June 15, 1864, John Wayles Jefferson Compiled Military Service Records, NARA.

43. J. S. C. Mower to Headquarters, Memphis, June 16, 1864, NARA; J. W. Jefferson to Lt. Charles A. Townshend, August 6, 1864, NARA; J. S. C. Mower to Captain J. Hough, Assistant Adj. Gen., June 20, 1864, NARA; J. P. Sample to J. W. Jefferson, Special Orders, August 4, 1864, NARA; Special Orders No. 161, Brigadier General Morgan L. Smith, October 6, 1864, John Wayles Jefferson Compiled Military Service Records, NARA.

44. Hannah Heidi Levy, *Famous Wisconsin Artists and Architects* (Oregon, Wis.: Badger Books, 2004), 31-32.

45. Portrait of John W. Jefferson, 1874, Museum of Wisconsin Art; Porter Butts, *Art in Wisconsin* (Madison: Democrat Printing Company, 1936), 81, 129.

46. See *Biographical and Historical Memoirs of Eastern Arkansas: Comprising a Condensed History of the State, a Number of Biographies of Distinguished Citizens of the Same, a Brief Descriptive History of Each of the Counties* (Chicago: Goodspeed, 1890); John McLeod Keating and O. F. Vedder, *History of the City of Memphis and Shelby County, Tennessee* (Memphis: D. Mason and Company, 1888), 1:897-900; *History of Dane County: Biographical and Genealogical* (Madison: Western Historical Association, 1906), 455-56.

Epilogue

1. Ellen Wayles Hemings Roberts Photograph, ca. 19[?], Getting Word: African American Oral History Project at Monticello, https://gettingword.monticello.org/people/ellen-hemings-roberts/#:~:text=Ellen%20Wayles%20Hemings%2C%20the%20youngest,its%20population%20was%20African%20American.

2. See Lucia Stanton, *"Those Who Labor for My Happiness": Slavery at Thomas Jefferson's Monticello* (Charlottesville: University of Virginia Press, 2012), 282-87.

3. See Patricia Roberts, Oral History Interview, December 5, 1998, https://getting word.monticello.org/stories/; Lucille Balthazaar, Oral History Interview, October

23, 1995, Getting Word: African American Oral History Project at Monticello, https://gettingword.monticello.org/stories/; John Craig Hammond, "'The Most Free of the Free States': Politics, Slavery, Race, and Regional Identity in Early Ohio," *Ohio History* 121 (2014): 35–57; Stephen Middleton, *The Black Laws: Race and Legal Process in Early Ohio* (Athens: Ohio University Press, 2005); 247–64; Robert D. Sawrey, *Dubious Victory: The Reconstruction Debate in Ohio* (Lexington: University of Kentucky Press, 1992); Marilyn K. Howard, "Black Lynching in the Promised Land: Mob Violence in Ohio, 1876–1916," Ph.D. diss., Ohio State University, 1999.

4. See Lucia Stanton, *"Those Who Labor for My Happiness,"* 282–87; Lucille Balthazaar, Oral History Interview, October 23, 1995; Patricia Roberts, Oral History Interview, December 5, 1998.

5. Lucia Stanton, *"Those Who Labor for My Happiness,"* 286–87; Frederick Roberts, editorial, *New Age* (March 25, 1915).

6. A. J. Davis to Hon. Myer [*sic*] Lissner, August 4, 1912, quoted in Douglass Flamming, *Bound for Freedom: Black Los Angeles in Jim Crow America* (Berkeley: University of California Press, 2005), 81–82; Louise McDonald, *Crisis* (July 1912).

7. Frederick Roberts, editorial, *New Age* (October 24, 1913); Frederick Roberts, editorial, *New Age* (February 5, 1915); Flamming, *Bound for Freedom,* 81–91.

8. Frederick Roberts, editorial, *New Age* (September 11, 1914); Flamming, *Bound for Freedom,* 170–71.

9. Pearl Hinds Roberts, Recollections, African American Museum and Library, Oakland, California; *Los Angeles Times* (November 8, 1918); *California Eagle* (February 15, 1919); Flamming, *Bound for Freedom,* 168–87.

10. Frederick Roberts, editorial, *New Age* (June 17, 1921); Flamming, *Bound for Freedom,* 196–202; Stanton, *"Those Who Labor for My Happiness,"* 187.

11. See Madison Hemings, "'Life Among the Lowly,' No. 1," *Pike County (Ohio) Republican* (March 13, 1873).

12. See Lucia Stanton, *"Those Who Labor for My Happiness,"* 282–87.

13. Patricia Roberts, Oral History Interview, December 5, 1998.

14. See Hannah Spahn, *Black Reason, White Feeling: The Jeffersonian Enlightenment in the African American Tradition* (Charlottesville: University of Virginia Press, 2024).

Acknowledgments

I FIRST HAD THE IDEA FOR THIS BOOK in a corner of the Monticello curatorial department in 2011. Rummaging through a few storage boxes, I came across several sketches drawn by Virginia Randolph Trist, Jefferson's granddaughter, in Cuba in the 1840s. What eventually emerged from that afternoon was a book project: a global history of Jefferson's family members on both sides of the color line.

This book is dedicated to two wonderful people who jumpstarted the professional career of a young scholar. Susan Stein, the Richard Gilder Senior Curator at Monticello, took a big chance on me when I was still a graduate student, but she always believed in and encouraged my ideas. I will always be grateful to her for setting the bar high, and for never giving up on me. Andrew O'Shaughnessy, professor of history at the University of Virginia and formerly director of the Robert H. Smith International Center for Jefferson Studies at Monticello, has been a close friend and staunch supporter, especially during my mother's long illness. It was Andrew who helped me secure a publisher for this book, and I'm indebted to him for his help and encouragement. Without support and love from Andrew and Susan, I would not be where I am today.

A number of wonderful colleagues have made this a better book. First on that list is Peter Onuf, who read more than a few drafts, patiently talking through them with me in countless Zoom sessions. Since I first met Peter twenty years ago, he has been relentless in his challenges to my scholarly work, but those challenges have always come from a place of real love and friendship, and his desire to see me be my best self. He is one of the finest human beings on the planet. Three dear friends, Frank Cogliano, Nick Guyatt, and Jay Sexton, read the entire manuscript and offered invaluable comments and suggestions. Several other colleagues read draft chapters and offered great insights and suggestions: Andrew Davenport, Lisa Francavilla, Eliga Gould, Paul Halliday, John Craig Hammond, Caroline Janney, and Dael Norwood. A number of scholars offered sound advice as I was working through this project, including Annette Gordon-

Reed, Niya Bates, Lucia Stanton, Hannah Spahn, Maurizio Valsania, Ann Lucas Birle, Nadine Zimmerli, Holly Pinheiro, Patrick Griffin, and David Konig. The late Jan Ellen Lewis was enthusiastic about this project, and I'm sorry she didn't get to see its completion.

Although I first had the idea for this book as a curator at Monticello, I did most of the writing and research as a faculty member, first at the University of Missouri, and then at the University of Virginia. My colleagues at the Kinder Institute on Constitutional Democracy and in the history department at Mizzou created a fun and warmly supportive environment in which to write. Jay Sexton moved mountains for me, and Jeff Pasley, Catherine Rymph, and Alec Zuercher Reichardt became close friends who cheered me on from the sidelines. At the University of Virginia, my Early Americanist colleagues Max Edelson and Alan Taylor supported this project, and I received wonderful advice and mentorship from several colleagues in the history department, especially Paul Halliday, Caroline Janney, and Claudrena Harold. I am also deeply indebted to the Jefferson Scholars Foundation for continued support.

I conducted research for this project on both sides of the Atlantic. In the United Kingdom, the archivists at the British Library, the National Archives at Kew, the University of Cambridge library, and ING offered able assistance on this project's British angle. In Boston, archivists at the Baker Library at Harvard Business School and at the Massachusetts Historical Society provided help researching the Coolidges' China connections. In Virginia, archivists at the Library of Virginia and at Special Collections at the University of Virginia always went the extra mile, sometimes scanning and emailing me material during the pandemic. Several repositories provided key information and archival records related to the Hemings family, including the Oakland Museum of California, the University of California, Los Angeles, library, the Wisconsin Historical Society, the Shelby County Archives in Memphis, and the Tennessee State Library and Archives. At Monticello, the family research on African American descendants conducted by Lucia Stanton, Dianne Swann-Wright, and Beverly Gray was central to this project.

A number of people shepherded this book to completion. Chris Rogers, first my editor at Yale University Press and now my agent, took a gamble on this book and its author, and I am forever grateful for his support. My editor at Yale, Adina Popescu, offered encouragement and showed incredible patience, even when it felt as if I would never cross the finish line. Susan Laity proved to be an invaluable copyeditor, injecting expertise and humor into the editing process. Jennifer Levin served as a top-notch research assistant, gathering all the necessary image permissions with aplomb. And my close friend Leah Stearns created a much-needed genealogy when I pled ignorance of Adobe Illustrator.

They say that the second book is the hardest to write. I would agree, and I have leaned heavily on several close friends as I inched toward this project's completion. In Charlottesville and beyond, a number of people fed me, talked through my anxieties, and tolerated my stressed-out self, especially Gabriele Rausse, Leah Stearns and Joey Toombs, Shawn and Mike Lipinski, and Catherine Dunn. My horses, Gus and Hope, and my dogs, Lampo Colombini and the late great Enie Nash, were an endless source of joy and fulfillment. I would not have made it to page proofs without them.

Index

Page numbers in italics refer to figures.